A WAVE BLUE WORLD
PRESENTS

THE COLOR OF

CO-CREATED AND EDITED BY
BRENT FISHER AND MICHELE ABOUNADER

ALWAYS

AN LGBTQIA+
LOVE ANTHOLOGY

CREATIVE ADVISORS AND EDITORS
FELL HOUND AND JUSTIN RICHARDS

COVER ARTIST
ELISA ROMBOLI

LOGO DESIGNER
LUCAS GATTONI

BOOK DESIGNER
PETE CARLSSON

THE COLOR OF ALWAYS. MAY 2023. PUBLISHED BY A WAVE BLUE WORLD, INC. COPYRIGHT © 2023. ALL RIGHTS RESERVED. "THE COLOR OF ALWAYS" CONCEPT AND LOGO ARE TRADEMARKS™ OF BRENT FISHER AND MICHELE ABOUNADER. ALL STORIES ARE © 2023 THEIR RESPECTIVE CREATORS. A WAVE BLUE WORLD AND ITS LOGOS ARE REGISTERED TRADEMARKS ® OF A WAVE BLUE WORLD, INC. NO PART OF THIS PUBLICATION MAY BE REPRODUCED OR TRANSMITTED IN ANY FORM (EXCEPT SHORT EXCEPTS FOR REVIEW PURPOSES) WITHOUT THE EXPRESS WRITTEN PERMISSION OF A WAVE BLUE WORLD, INC. ALL NAMES, CHARACTERS, EVENTS, AND LOCALES IN THIS PUBLICATION ARE ENTIRELY FICTIONAL. ANY RESEMBLANCE TO ACTUAL PERSONS (LIVING OR DEAD), EVENTS, OR PLACES WITHOUT SATIRICAL INTENT, IS COINCIDENCE.

ISBN 978-1-949518-24-5   PRINTED IN CANADA   AWBW.COM

Publisher's Cataloging-in-Publication
(Provided by Cassidy Cataloguing Services, Inc.).

Names: Fisher, Brent, creator, editor. | Abounader, Michele, creator, editor. | Hound, Fell, editor. | Richards, Justin (Comics author), editor. | Carlsson, Pete, designer. | Chin-Tanner, Tyler, publisher. | Chin-Tanner, Wendy, publisher

Title: The color of always : an LGBTQIA+ love anthology / co-created and edited by Brent Fisher and Michele Abounader ; creative advisors and editors, Fell Hound and Justin Richards ; cover artist, Elisa Romboli ; logo designer, Lucas Gattoni ; book designer, Pete Carlsson ; co-publisher, Tyler Chin-Tanner ; co-publisher, Wendy Chin-Tanner.

Description: [Rhinebeck, New York] : A Wave Blue World, 2023. | "A Wave Blue World presents"-- Half-title page.

Identifiers: ISBN: 9781949518245

Subjects: LCSH: Sexual minorities--Comic books, strips, etc. | Love--Comic books, strips, etc. | LCGFT: Graphic novels. | Queer comics. | Romance comics. | BISAC: COMICS & GRAPHIC NOVELS / Anthologies. | COMICS & GRAPHIC NOVELS / LGBTQ+. | COMICS & GRAPHIC NOVELS / Romance.

Classification: LCC: PN6727 .C656 2023 | DDC: 741.5/973--dc23

A WAVE BLUE WORLD
EST. 2005
GRAPHIC NOVELS • ANTHOLOGIES • ART BOOKS
AWBW

CO-PUBLISHER
TYLER CHIN-TANNER

CO-PUBLISHER
WENDY CHIN-TANNER

PRODUCTION DESIGNER
PETE CARLSSON

DIRECTOR OF MARKETING
DIANA KOU

BOOK PUBLICIST
JESSE POST

SOCIAL MEDIA COORDINATOR
HAZEL NEWLEVANT

SALES DEVELOPMENT MANAGER
MEGAN MARSDEN

TABLE OF CONTENTS

PRIDE

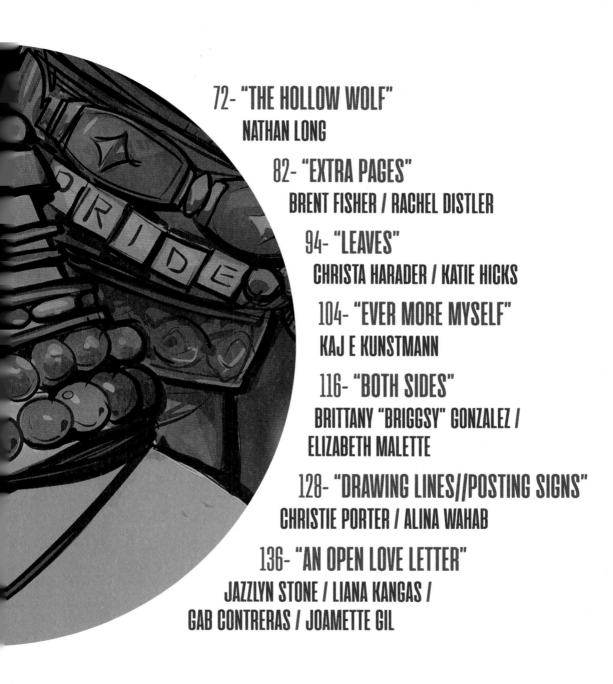

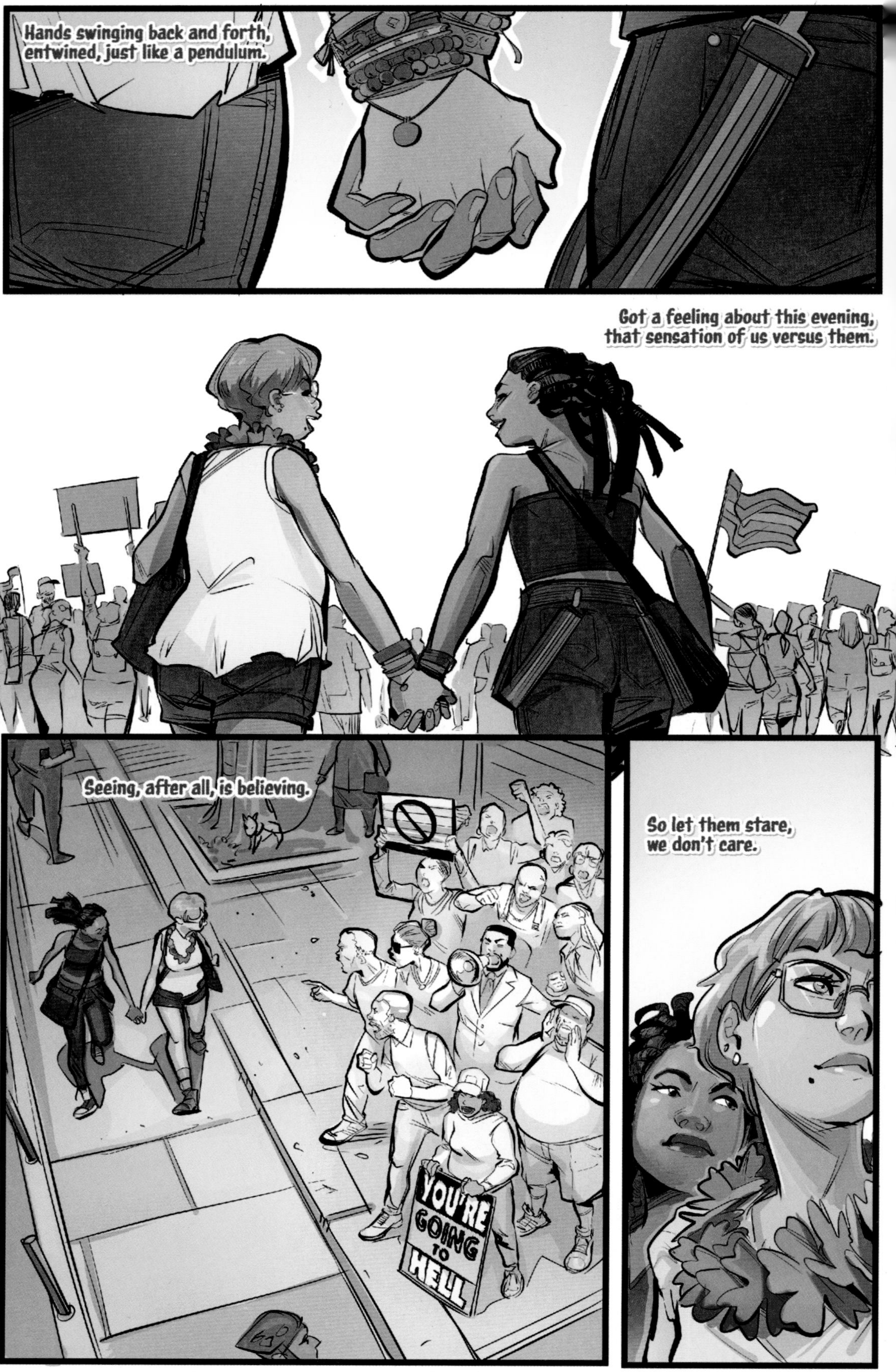
Hands swinging back and forth, entwined, just like a pendulum.
Got a feeling about this evening, that sensation of us versus them.
Seeing, after all, is believing.
YOU'RE GOING TO HELL
So let them stare, we don't care.

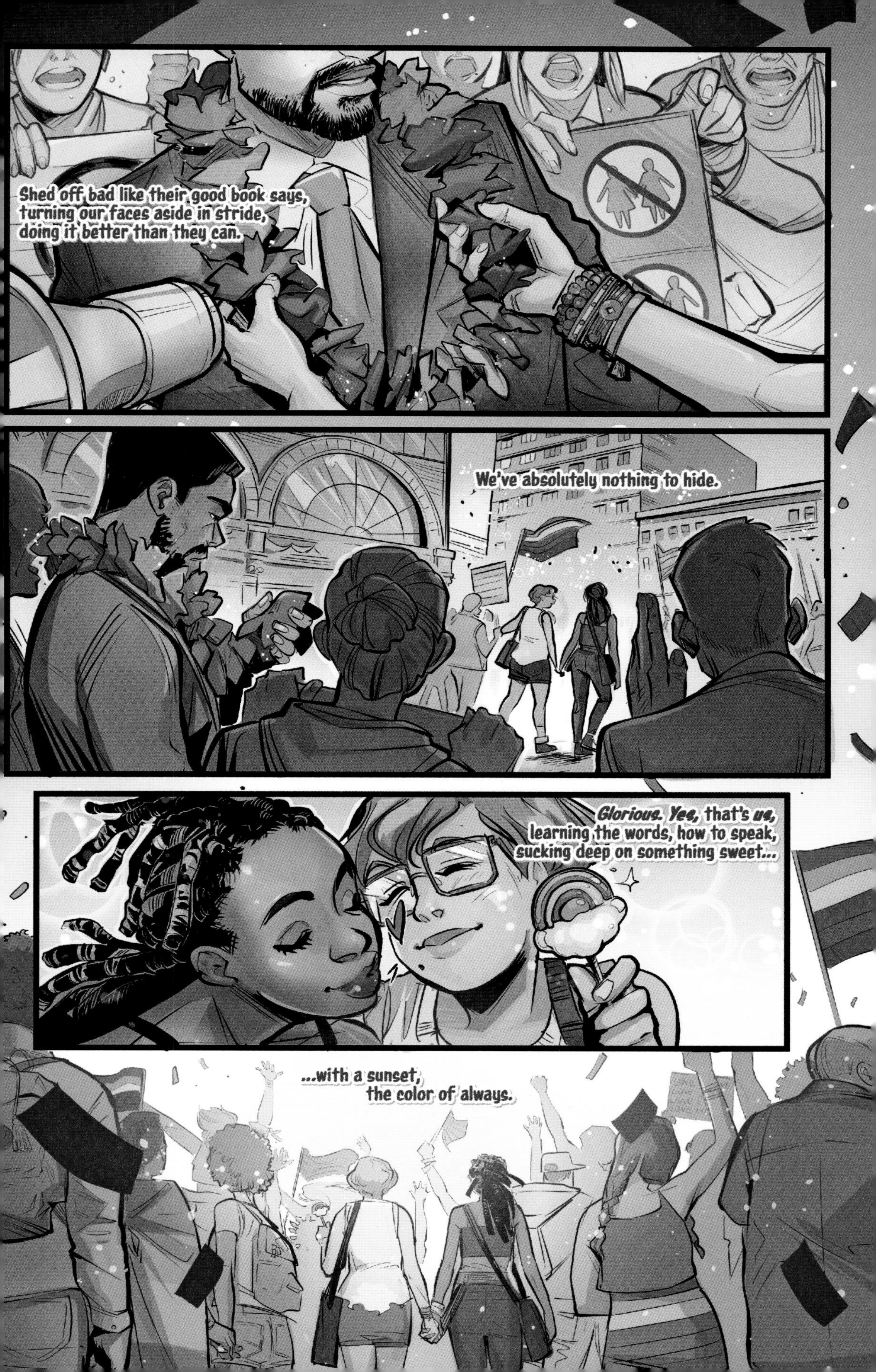
Shed off bad like their good book says,
turning our faces aside in stride,
doing it better than they can.
We've absolutely nothing to hide.
Glorious. Yes, that's us,
learning the words, how to speak,
sucking deep on something sweet...
...with a sunset,
the color of always.

"CLADDAGH"

WRITER-Julia Paiewonsky • Artist-Alex Putprush

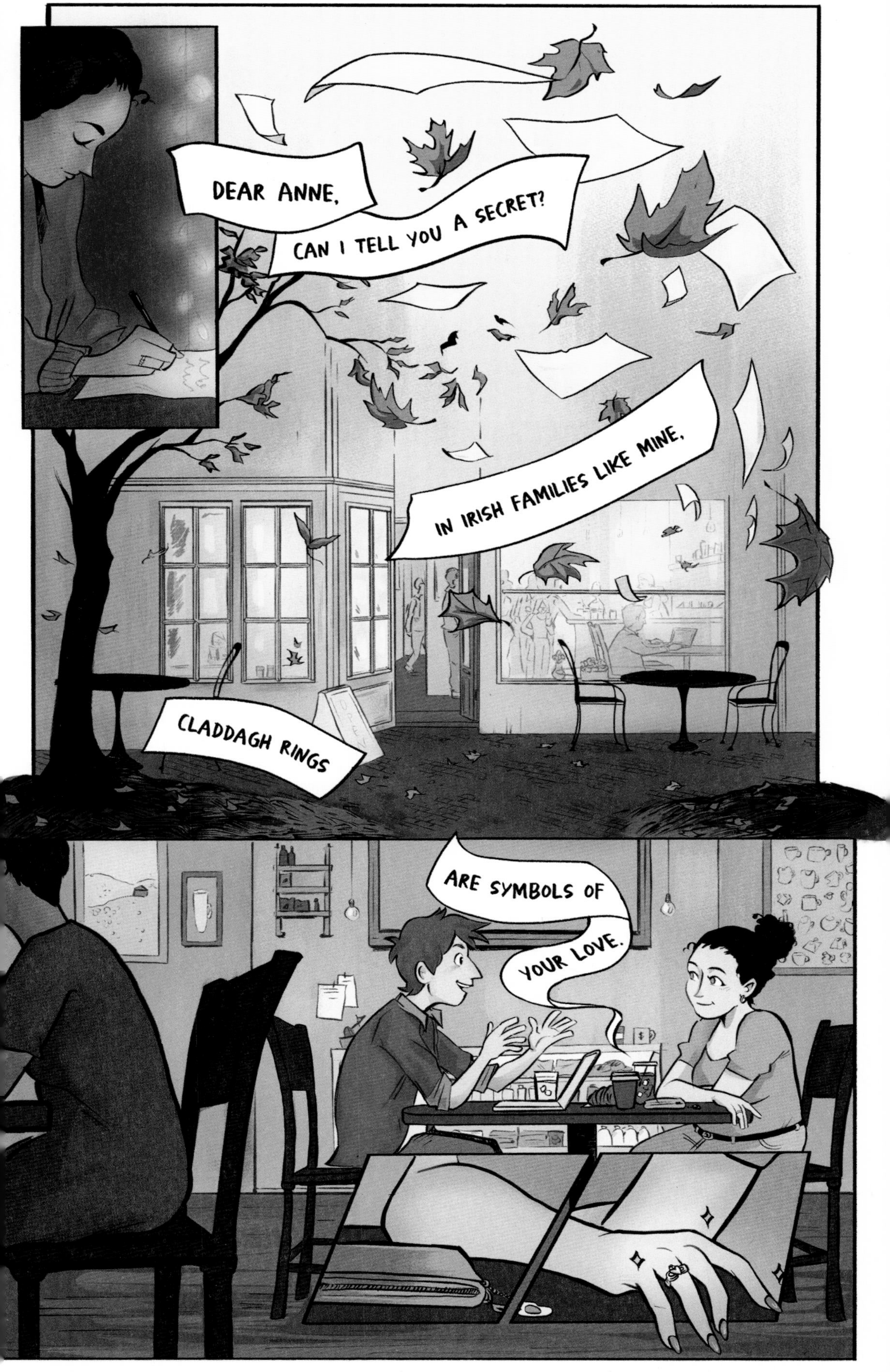
DEAR ANNE,
CAN I TELL YOU A SECRET?
IN IRISH FAMILIES LIKE MINE,
CLADDAGH RINGS
ARE SYMBOLS OF
YOUR LOVE.

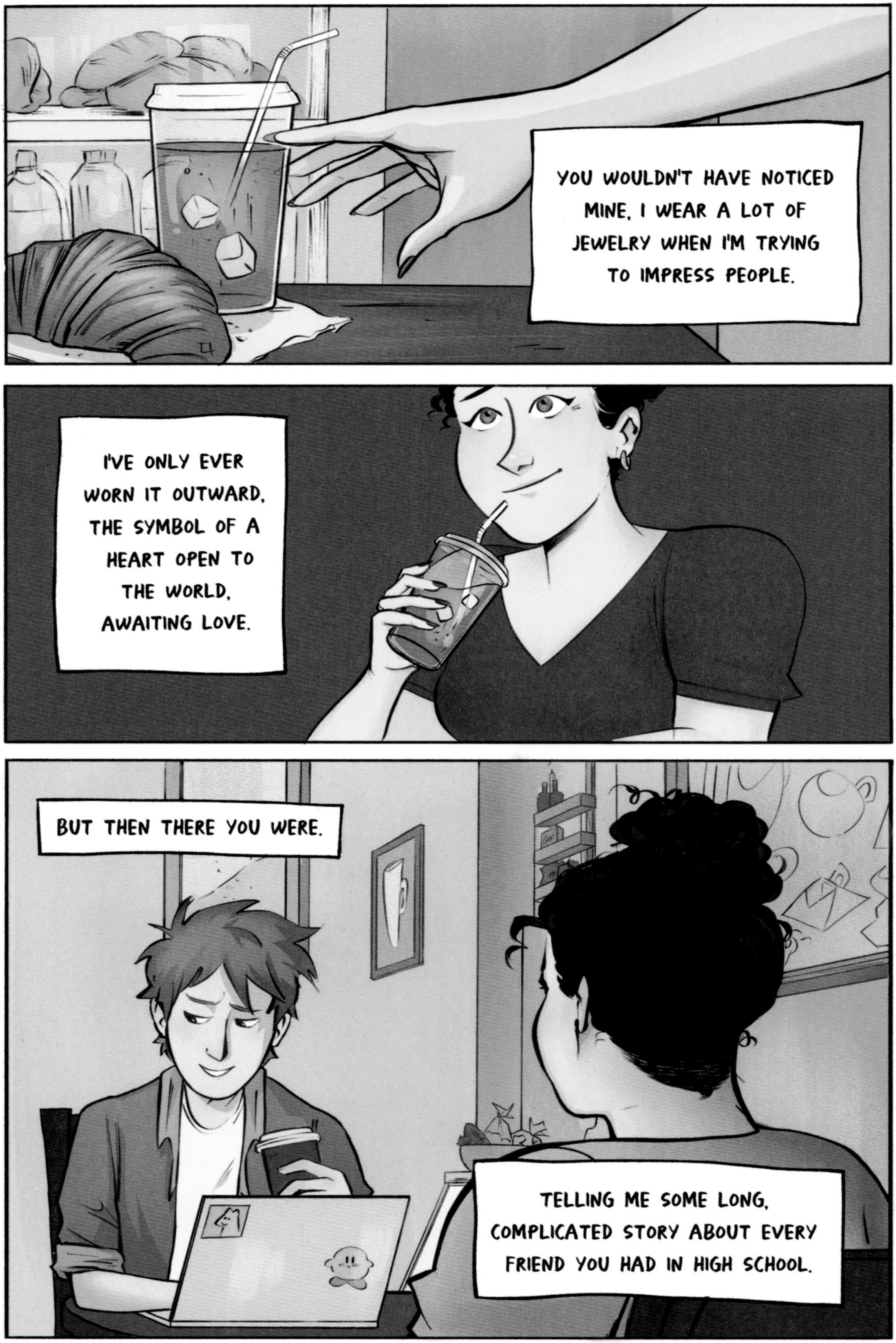
YOU WOULDN'T HAVE NOTICED MINE, I WEAR A LOT OF JEWELRY WHEN I'M TRYING TO IMPRESS PEOPLE.
I'VE ONLY EVER WORN IT OUTWARD, THE SYMBOL OF A HEART OPEN TO THE WORLD, AWAITING LOVE.
BUT THEN THERE YOU WERE.
TELLING ME SOME LONG, COMPLICATED STORY ABOUT EVERY FRIEND YOU HAD IN HIGH SCHOOL.

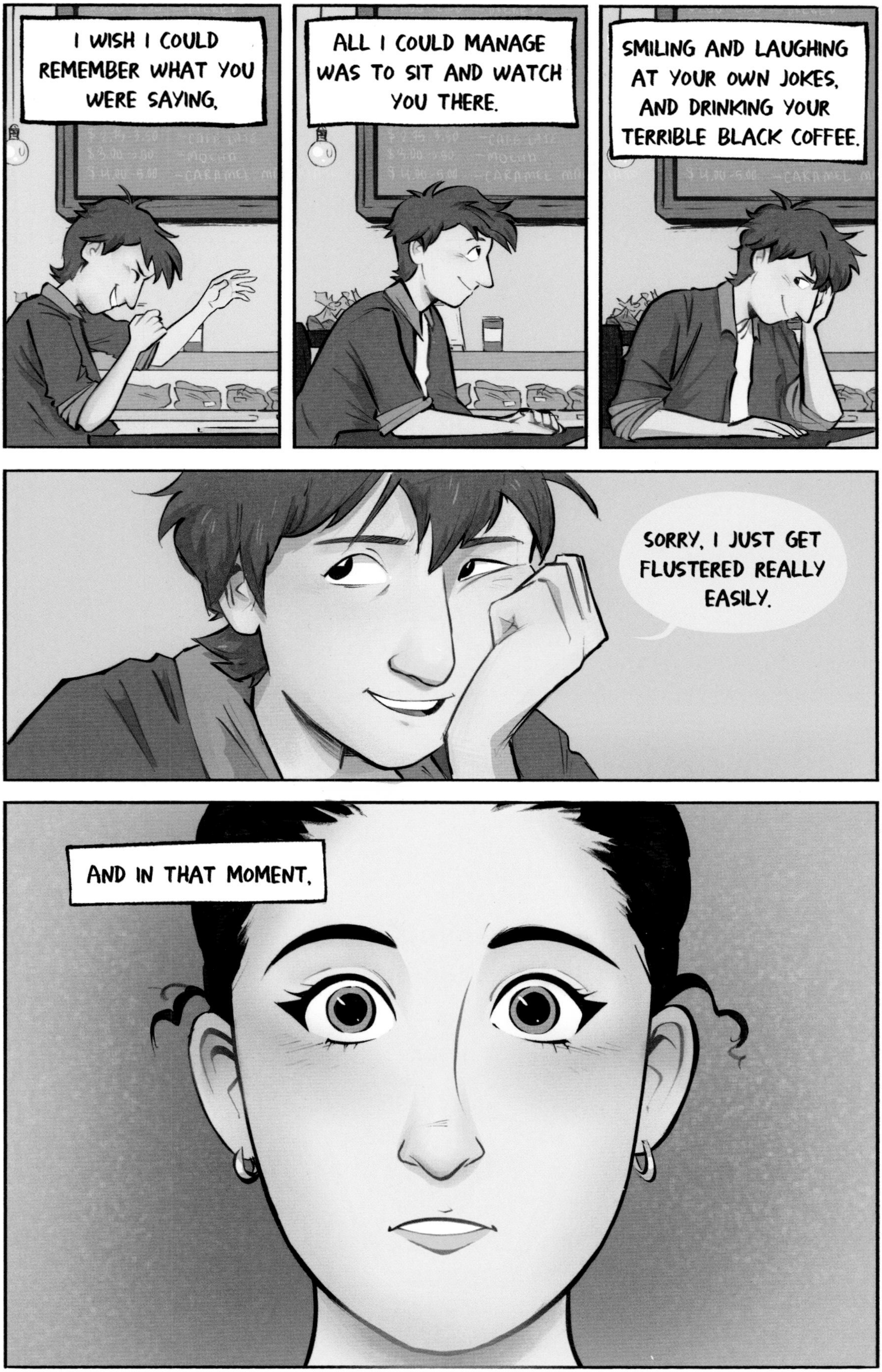
I WISH I COULD REMEMBER WHAT YOU WERE SAYING,
ALL I COULD MANAGE WAS TO SIT AND WATCH YOU THERE.
SMILING AND LAUGHING AT YOUR OWN JOKES, AND DRINKING YOUR TERRIBLE BLACK COFFEE.
SORRY, I JUST GET FLUSTERED REALLY EASILY.
AND IN THAT MOMENT,

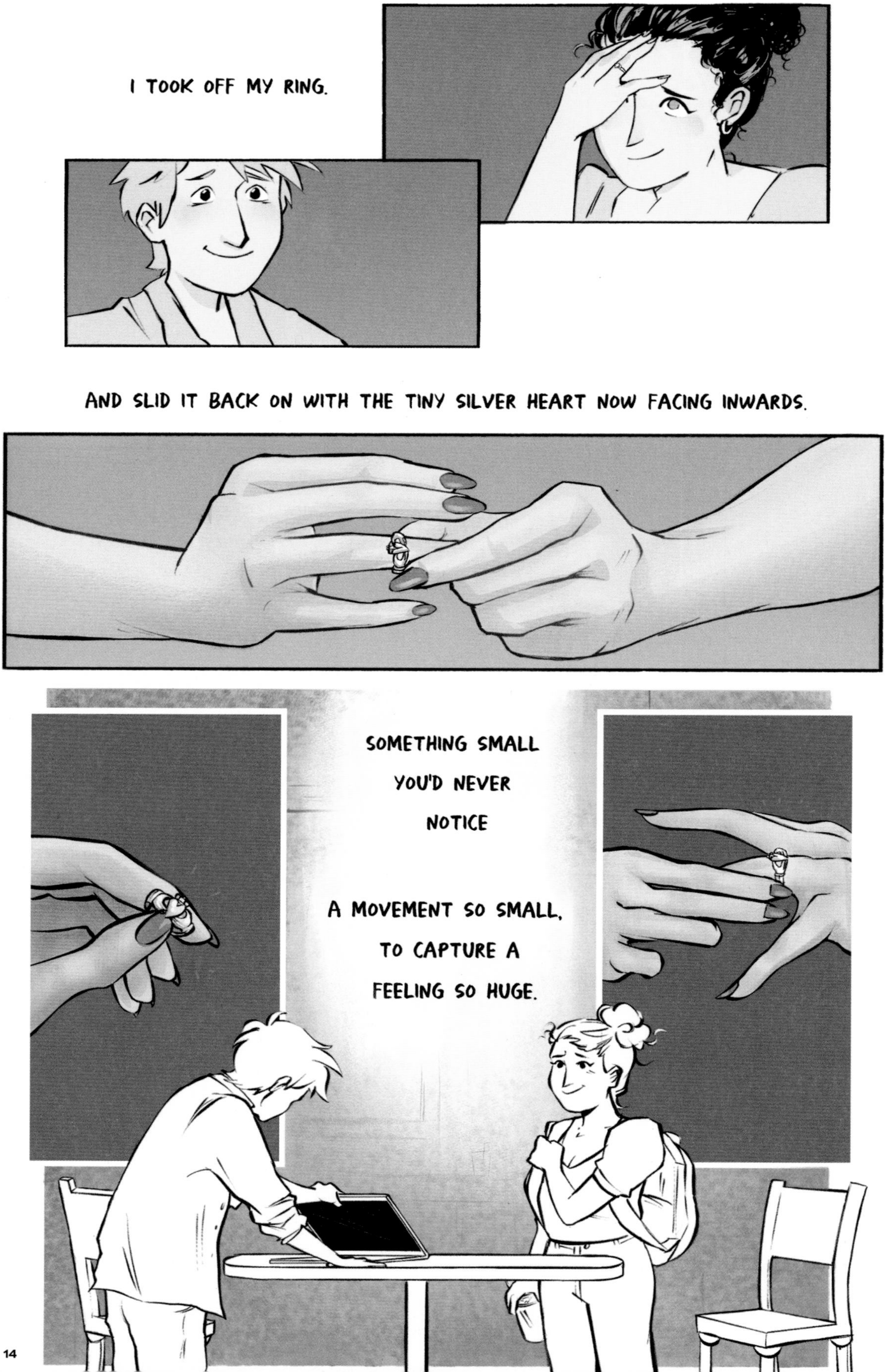
I TOOK OFF MY RING.
AND SLID IT BACK ON WITH THE TINY SILVER HEART NOW FACING INWARDS.
SOMETHING SMALL YOU'D NEVER NOTICE
A MOVEMENT SO SMALL, TO CAPTURE A FEELING SO HUGE.

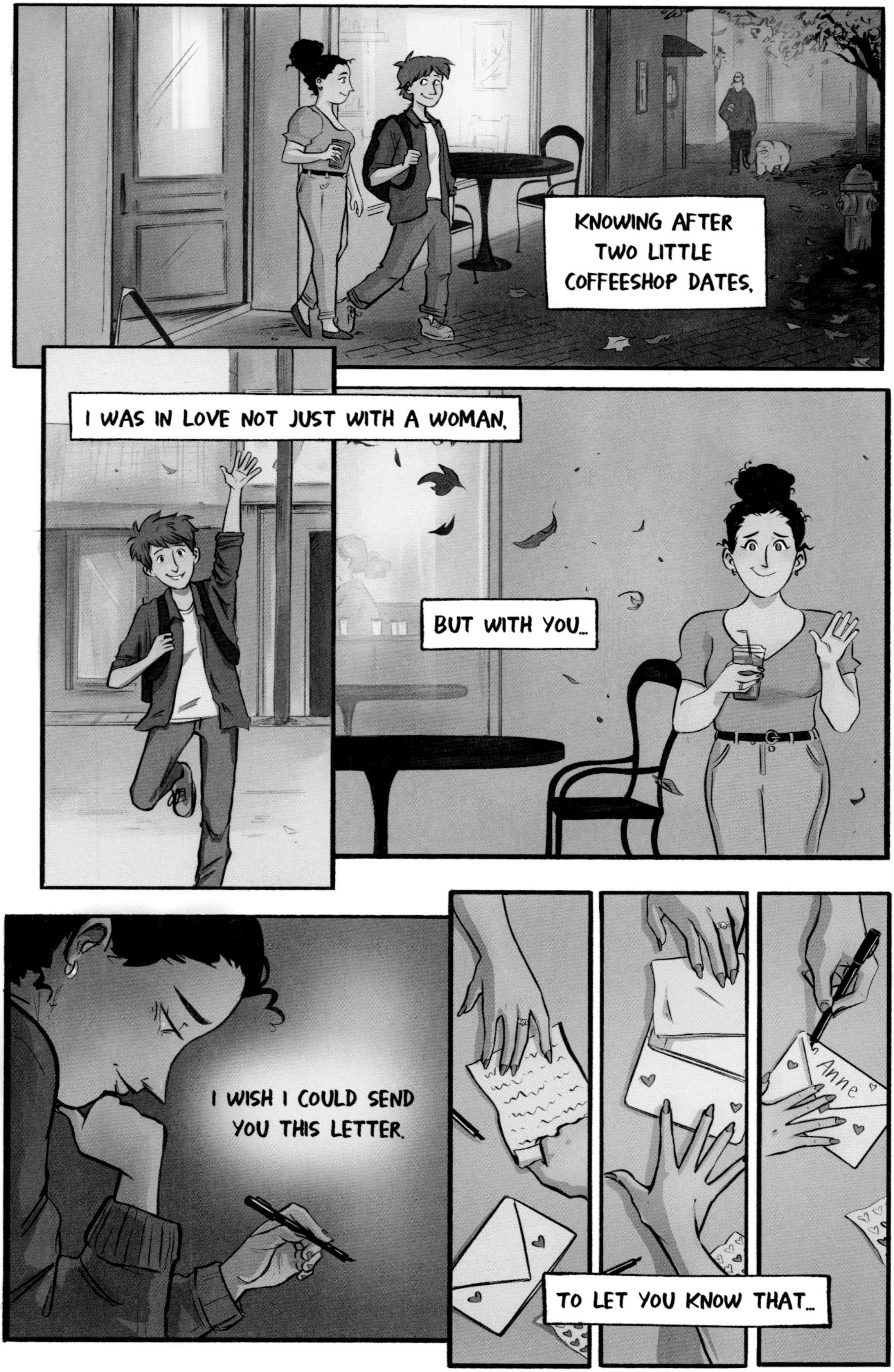
KNOWING AFTER TWO LITTLE COFFEESHOP DATES,
I WAS IN LOVE NOT JUST WITH A WOMAN,
BUT WITH YOU...
I WISH I COULD SEND YOU THIS LETTER.
Anne
TO LET YOU KNOW THAT...

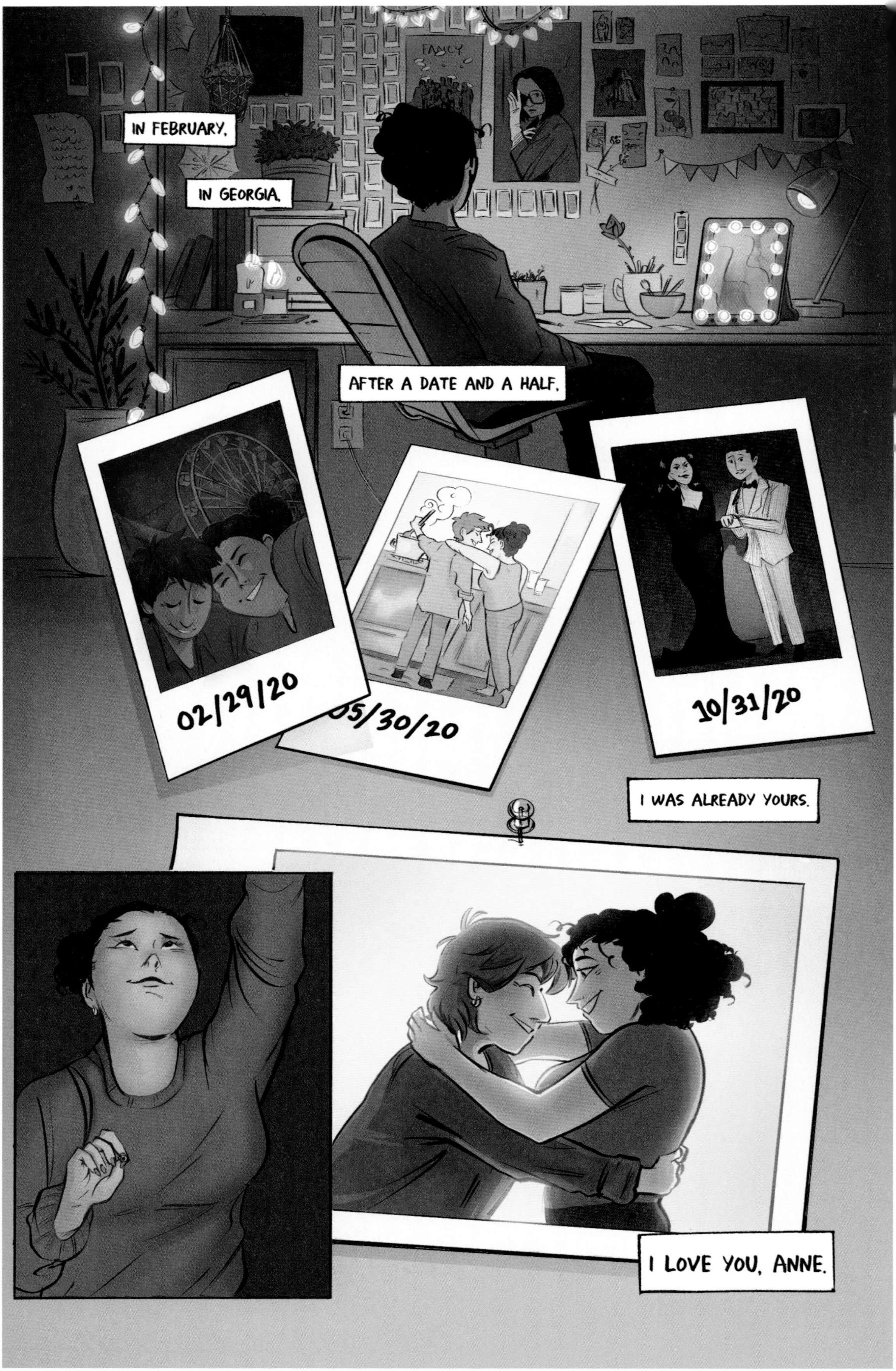
IN FEBRUARY,
IN GEORGIA,
AFTER A DATE AND A HALF,
02/29/20
05/30/20
10/31/20
I WAS ALREADY YOURS.
I LOVE YOU, ANNE.

ALWAYS

"TETHERED"

WRITER-MARIO CANDELARIA WITH LAURA HELSBY • ARTIST-LAURA HELSBY • COLORIST-JÃO CANOLA • LETTERER-SCOTT EWEN

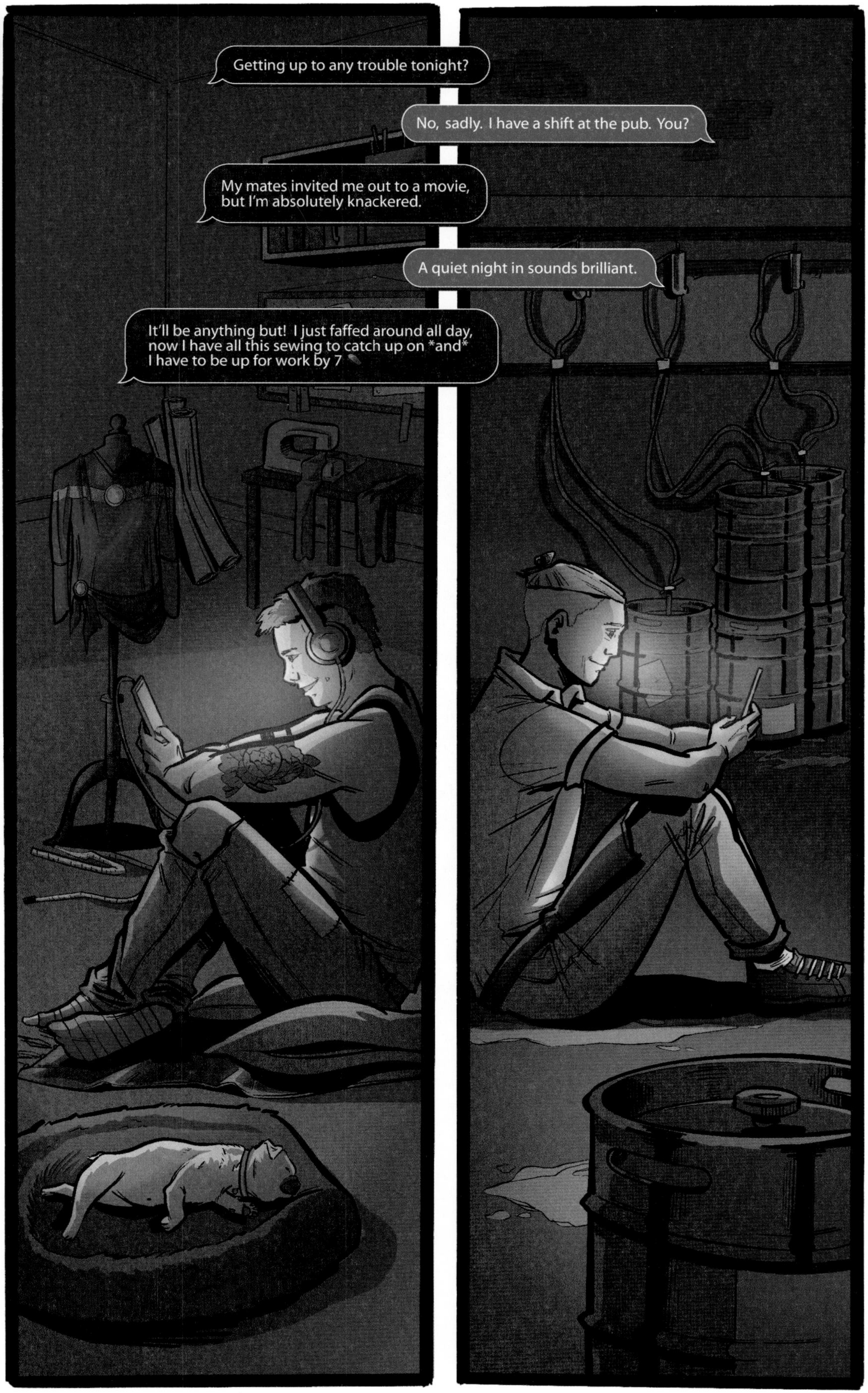

Getting up to any trouble tonight?
No, sadly. I have a shift at the pub. You?
My mates invited me out to a movie, but I'm absolutely knackered.
A quiet night in sounds brilliant.
It'll be anything but! I just faffed around all day, now I have all this sewing to catch up on *and* I have to be up for work by 7

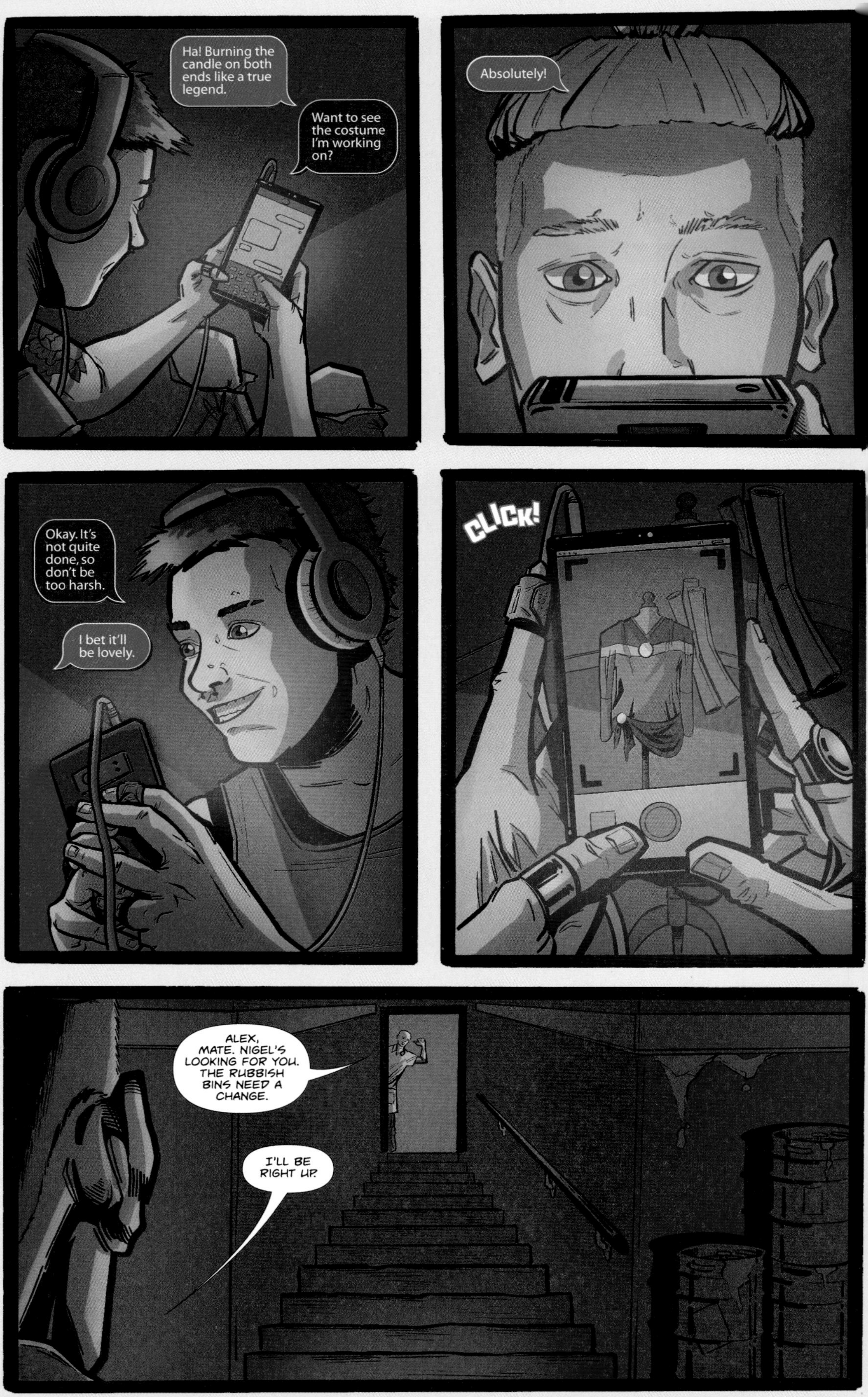
Ha! Burning the candle on both ends like a true legend.
Want to see the costume I'm working on?
Absolutely!
Okay. It's not quite done, so don't be too harsh.
I bet it'll be lovely.
CLICK!
ALEX, MATE. NIGEL'S LOOKING FOR YOU. THE RUBBISH BINS NEED A CHANGE.
I'LL BE RIGHT UP.

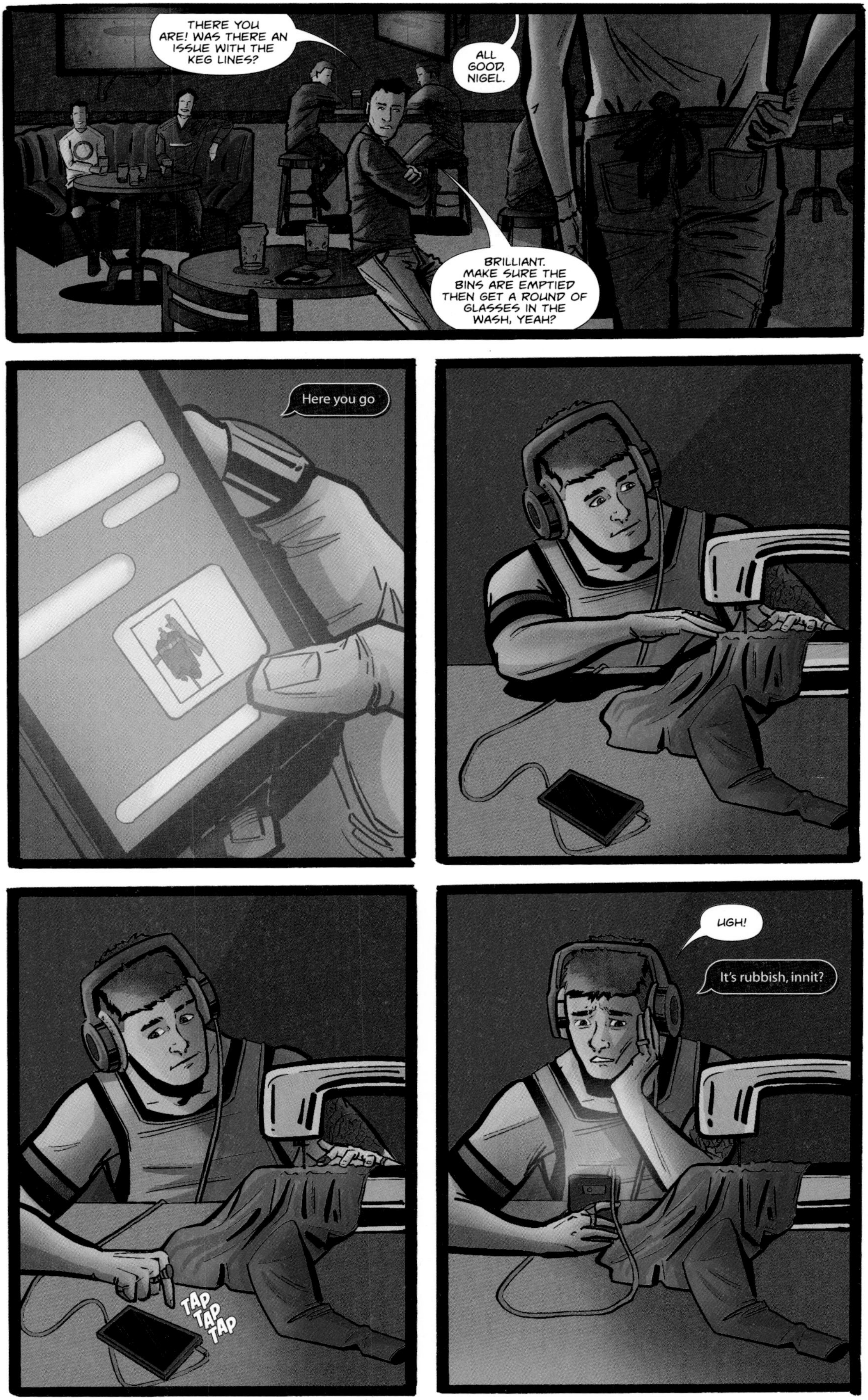
THERE YOU ARE! WAS THERE AN ISSUE WITH THE KEG LINES?
ALL GOOD, NIGEL.
BRILLIANT. MAKE SURE THE BINS ARE EMPTIED THEN GET A ROUND OF GLASSES IN THE WASH, YEAH?
Here you go
TAP TAP TAP
UGH!
It's rubbish, innit?

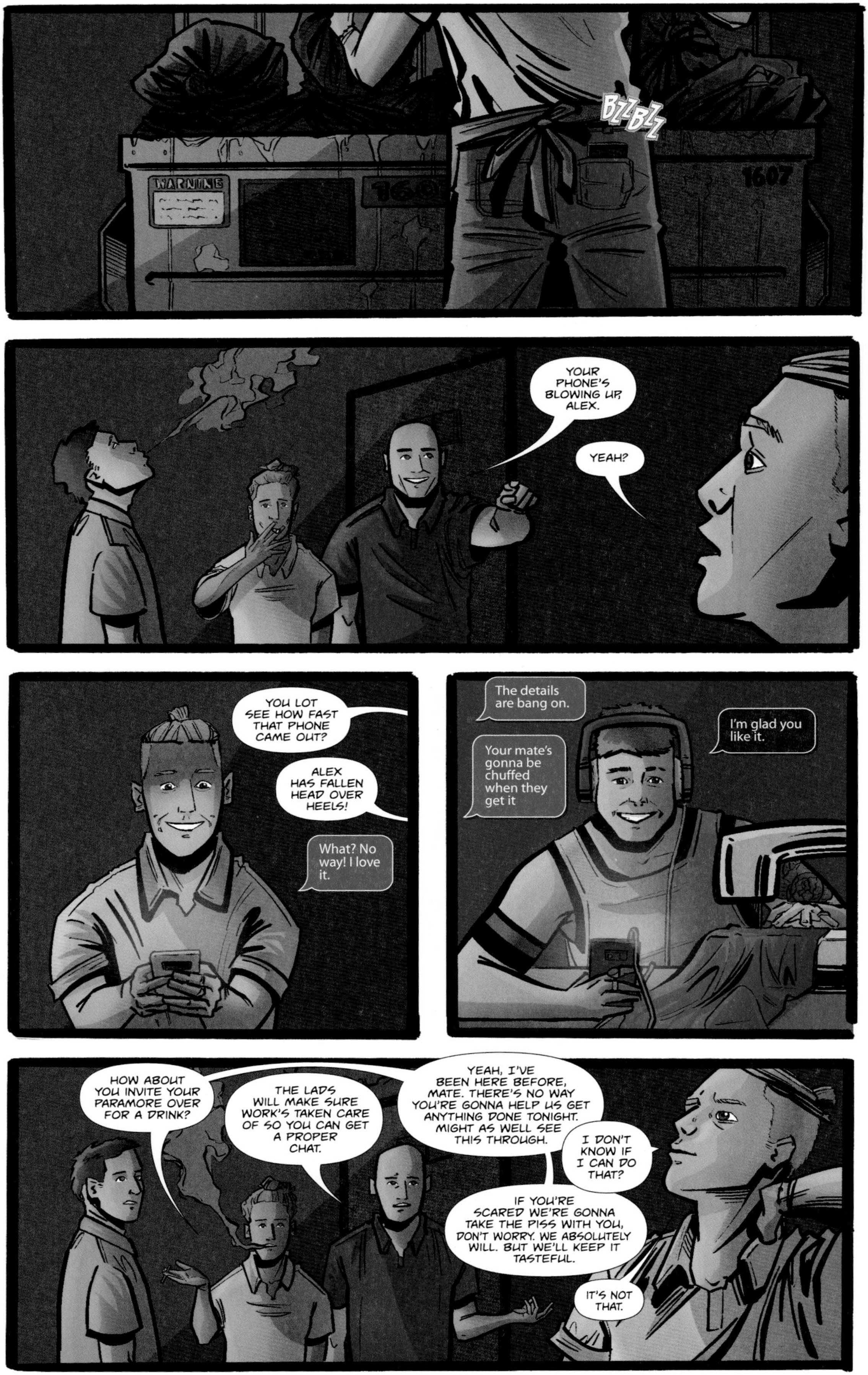
BZZBZZ
WARNING
1607
YOUR PHONE'S BLOWING UP, ALEX.
YEAH?
YOU LOT SEE HOW FAST THAT PHONE CAME OUT?
ALEX HAS FALLEN HEAD OVER HEELS!
What? No way! I love it.
The details are bang on.
Your mate's gonna be chuffed when they get it
I'm glad you like it.
HOW ABOUT YOU INVITE YOUR PARAMORE OVER FOR A DRINK?
THE LADS WILL MAKE SURE WORK'S TAKEN CARE OF SO YOU CAN GET A PROPER CHAT.
YEAH, I'VE BEEN HERE BEFORE, MATE. THERE'S NO WAY YOU'RE GONNA HELP US GET ANYTHING DONE TONIGHT. MIGHT AS WELL SEE THIS THROUGH.
I DON'T KNOW IF I CAN DO THAT?
IF YOU'RE SCARED WE'RE GONNA TAKE THE PISS WITH YOU, DON'T WORRY. WE ABSOLUTELY WILL. BUT WE'LL KEEP IT TASTEFUL.
IT'S NOT THAT.

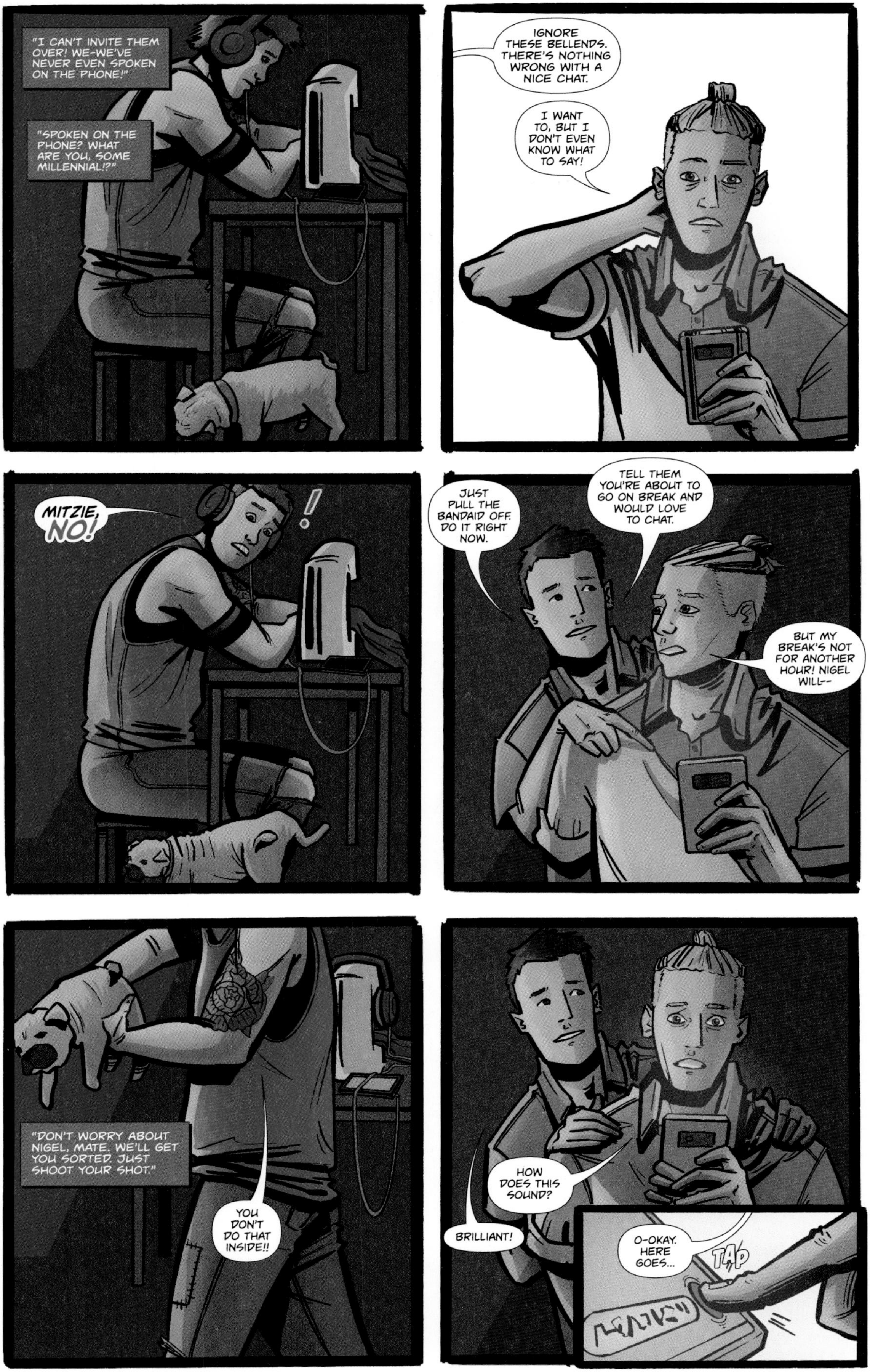
"I CAN'T INVITE THEM OVER! WE-WE'VE NEVER EVEN SPOKEN ON THE PHONE!"
"SPOKEN ON THE PHONE? WHAT ARE YOU, SOME MILLENNIAL!?"
IGNORE THESE BELLENDS. THERE'S NOTHING WRONG WITH A NICE CHAT.
I WANT TO, BUT I DON'T EVEN KNOW WHAT TO SAY!
MITZIE, NO!
!
JUST PULL THE BANDAID OFF. DO IT RIGHT NOW.
TELL THEM YOU'RE ABOUT TO GO ON BREAK AND WOULD LOVE TO CHAT.
BUT MY BREAK'S NOT FOR ANOTHER HOUR! NIGEL WILL--
"DON'T WORRY ABOUT NIGEL, MATE. WE'LL GET YOU SORTED. JUST SHOOT YOUR SHOT."
YOU DON'T DO THAT INSIDE!!
HOW DOES THIS SOUND?
BRILLIANT!
O-OKAY. HERE GOES...
TAP

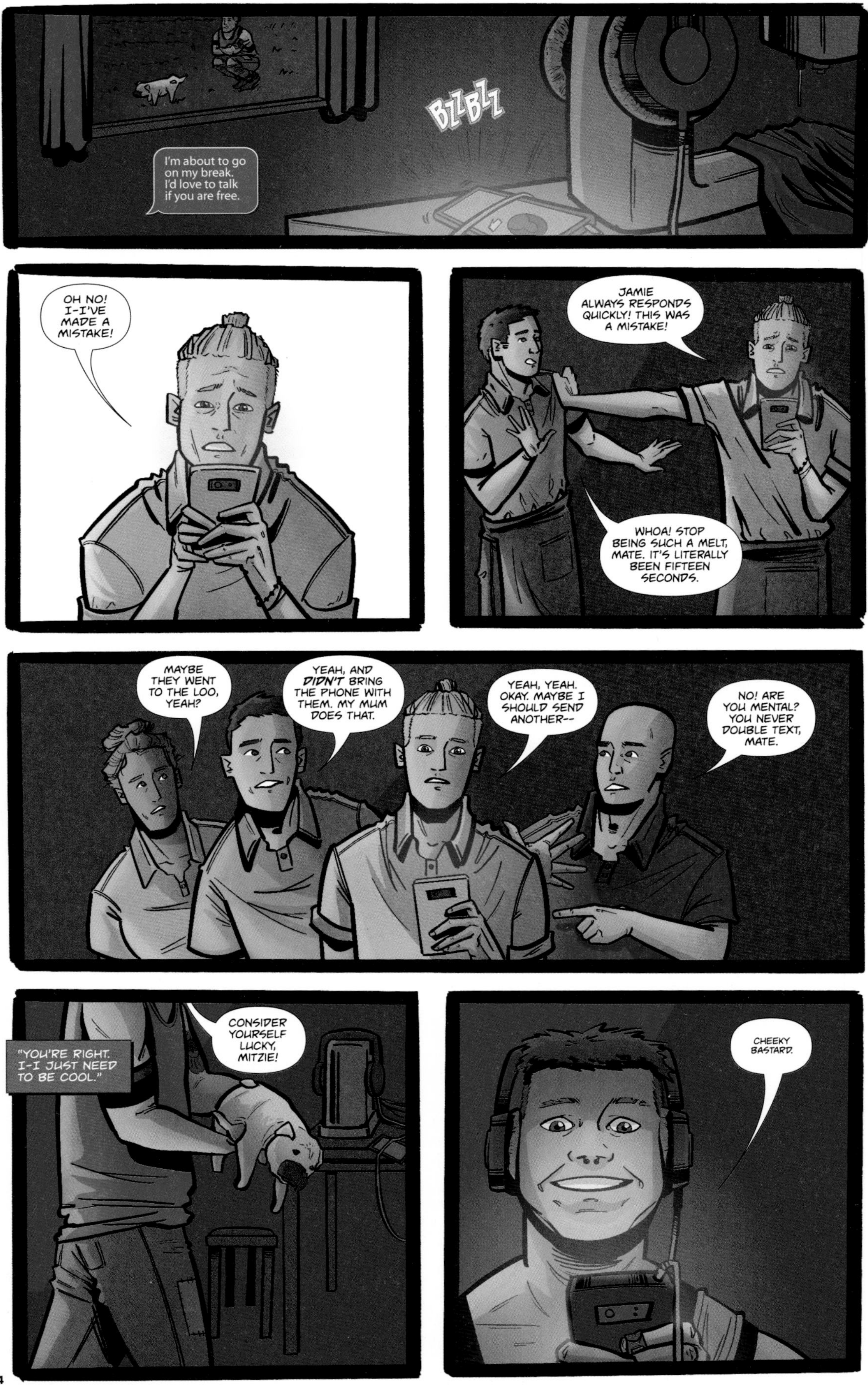
BZZBZZ
I'm about to go on my break. I'd love to talk if you are free.
OH NO! I-I'VE MADE A MISTAKE!
JAMIE ALWAYS RESPONDS QUICKLY! THIS WAS A MISTAKE!
WHOA! STOP BEING SUCH A MELT, MATE. IT'S LITERALLY BEEN FIFTEEN SECONDS.
MAYBE THEY WENT TO THE LOO, YEAH?
YEAH, AND DIDN'T BRING THE PHONE WITH THEM. MY MUM DOES THAT.
YEAH, YEAH. OKAY. MAYBE I SHOULD SEND ANOTHER--
NO! ARE YOU MENTAL? YOU NEVER DOUBLE TEXT, MATE.
"YOU'RE RIGHT. I-I JUST NEED TO BE COOL."
CONSIDER YOURSELF LUCKY, MITZIE!
CHEEKY BASTARD.

DOTS! I GOT THE THREE DOTS!

LEMME SEE!

YOU'RE BLOCKING MY VIEW!

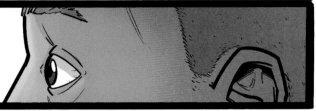

That would be lovely. Ring me when you're free.

JAMIE SAID YES! I— I AM GOING TO CALL!

BRILLIANT! YOU'LL BE SNOGGING IN NO TIME, WATCH.

QUIET DOWN—

—IT'S RINGING.

ALEX ☺

BZZ BZZ

ACCEPT

CLICK

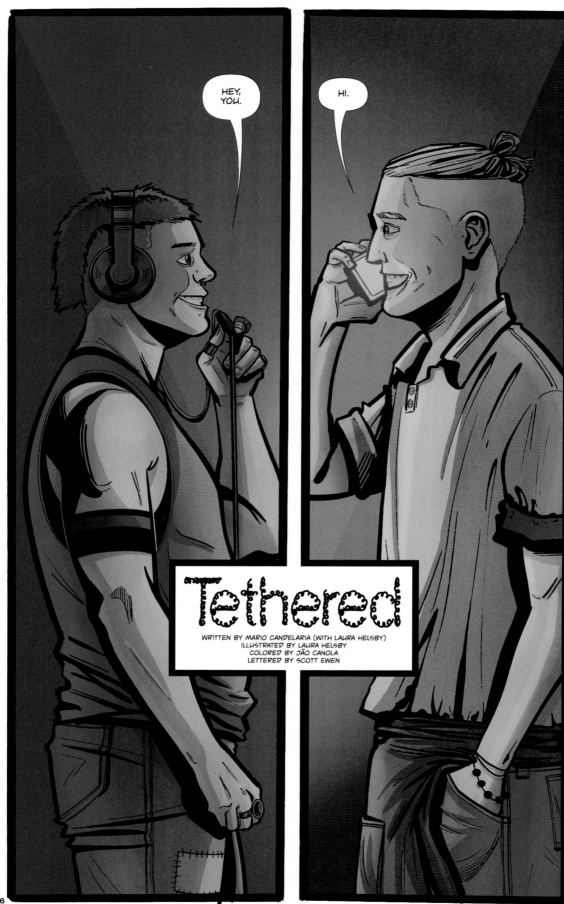

Tethered

WRITTEN BY MARIO CANDELARIA (WITH LAURA HELSBY)
ILLUSTRATED BY LAURA HELSBY
COLORED BY JÃO CANOLA
LETTERED BY SCOTT EWEN

ALWAYS

"SEA CHANGE"

WRITER–LILLIAN HOCHWENDER • ARTIST–GABE MARTINI

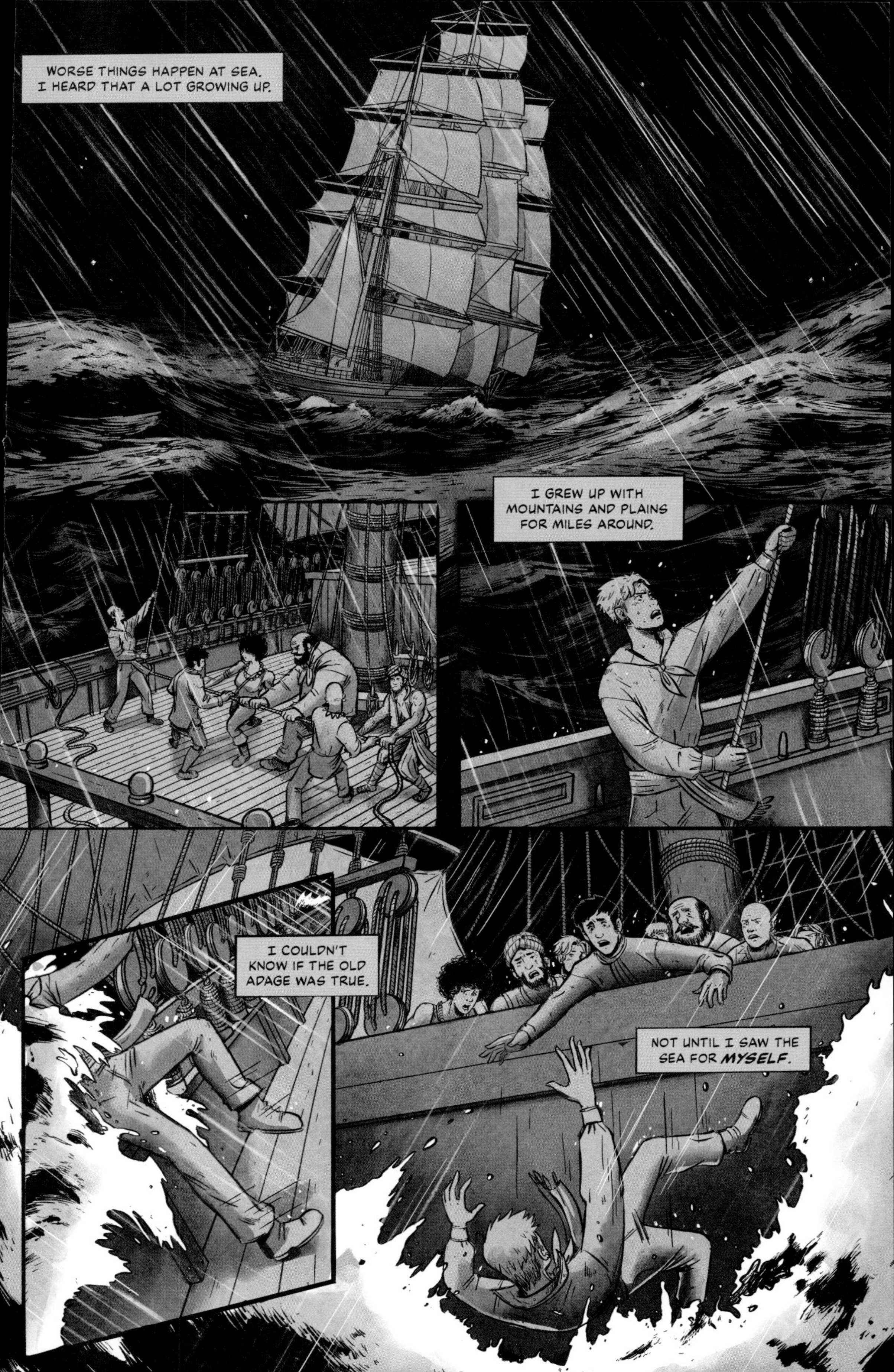
WORSE THINGS HAPPEN AT SEA. I HEARD THAT A LOT GROWING UP.
I GREW UP WITH MOUNTAINS AND PLAINS FOR MILES AROUND.
I COULDN'T KNOW IF THE OLD ADAGE WAS TRUE.
NOT UNTIL I SAW THE SEA FOR *MYSELF*.

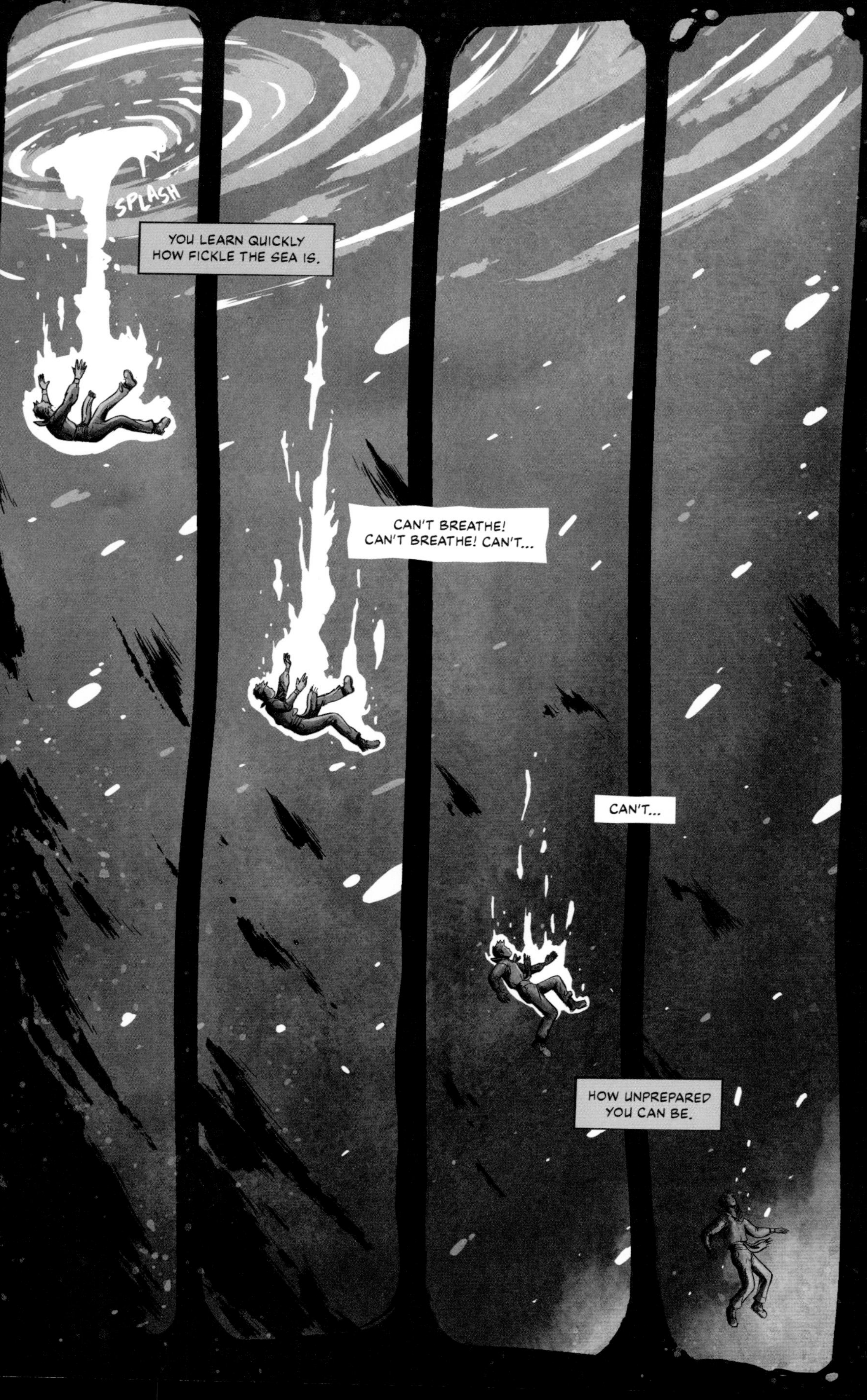
SPLASH
YOU LEARN QUICKLY HOW FICKLE THE SEA IS.
CAN'T BREATHE! CAN'T BREATHE! CAN'T...
CAN'T...
HOW UNPREPARED YOU CAN BE.

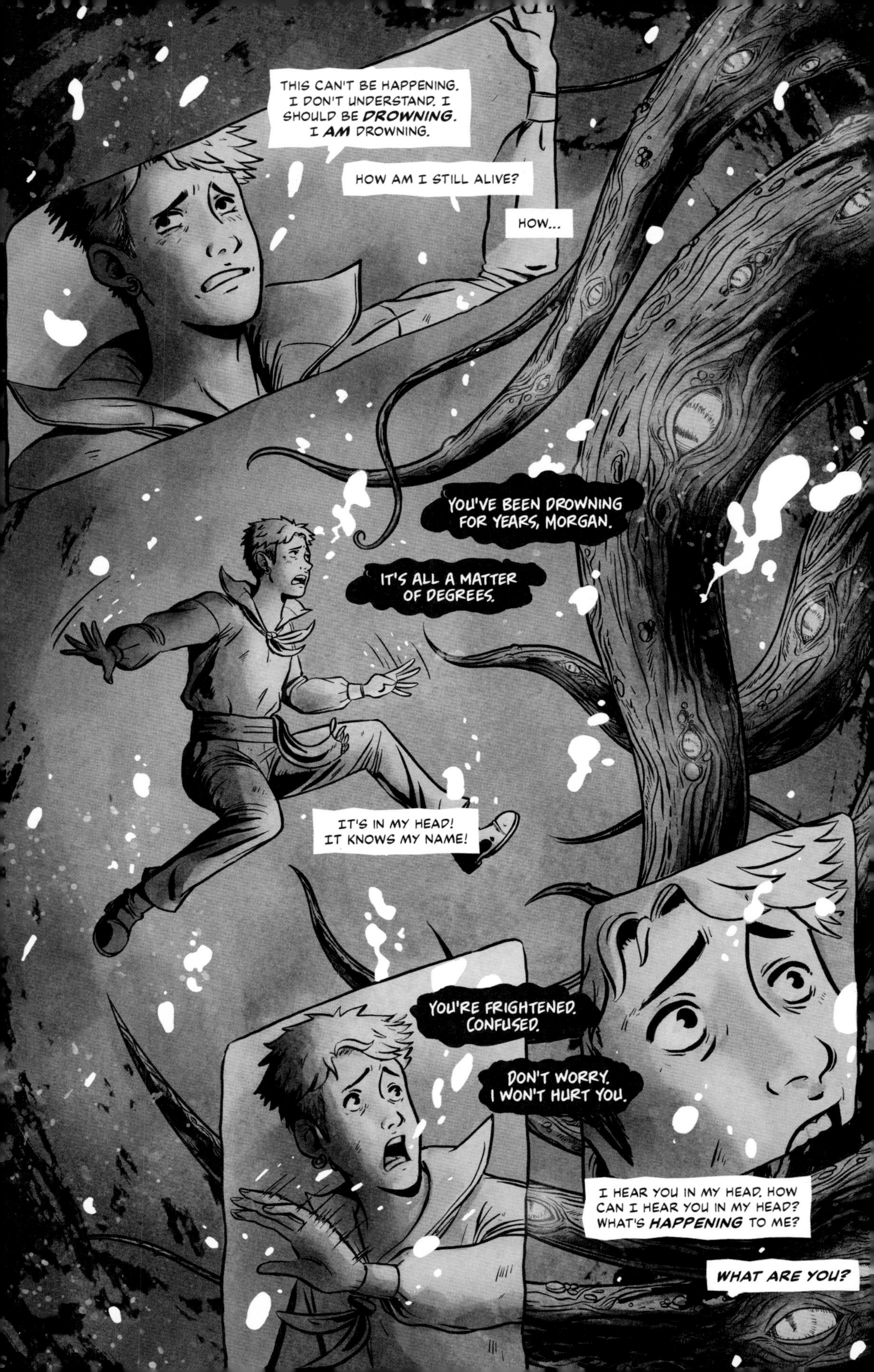
THIS CAN'T BE HAPPENING. I DON'T UNDERSTAND. I SHOULD BE DROWNING. I AM DROWNING.
HOW AM I STILL ALIVE?
HOW...
YOU'VE BEEN DROWNING FOR YEARS, MORGAN.
IT'S ALL A MATTER OF DEGREES.
IT'S IN MY HEAD! IT KNOWS MY NAME!
YOU'RE FRIGHTENED. CONFUSED.
DON'T WORRY. I WON'T HURT YOU.
I HEAR YOU IN MY HEAD. HOW CAN I HEAR YOU IN MY HEAD? WHAT'S HAPPENING TO ME?
WHAT ARE YOU?

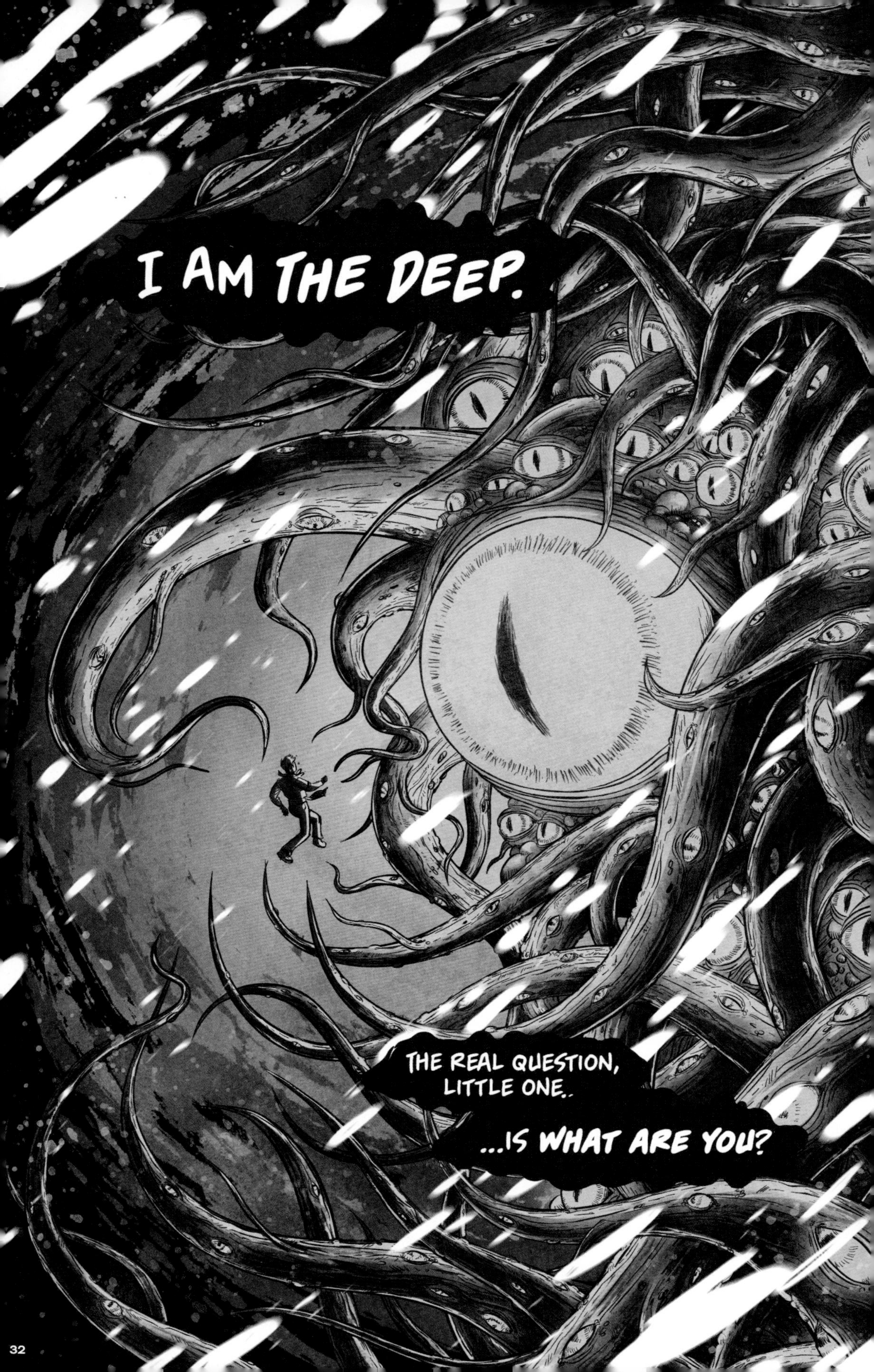
I AM THE DEEP.
THE REAL QUESTION, LITTLE ONE..
...IS WHAT ARE YOU?

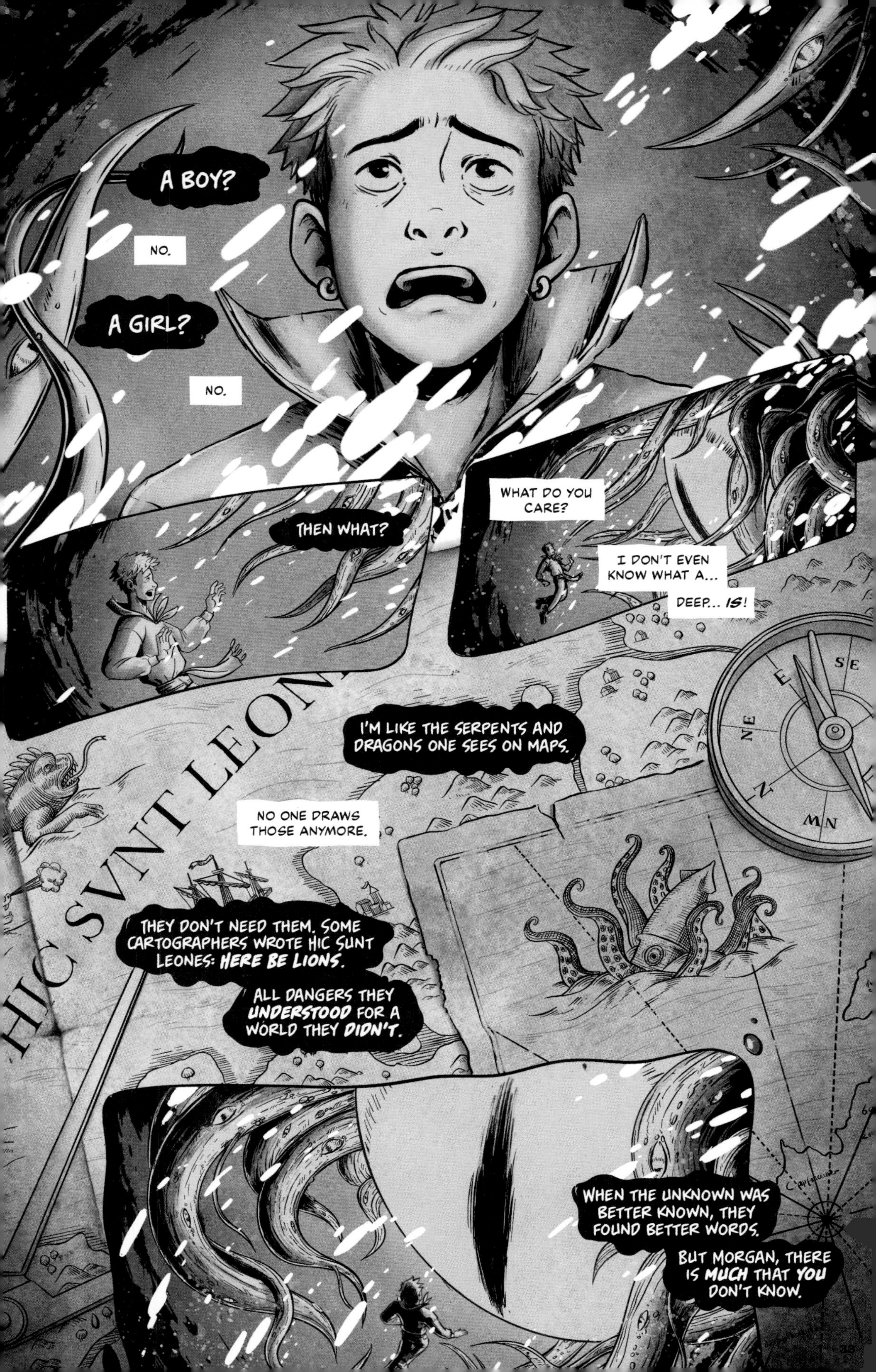
A BOY?
NO.
A GIRL?
NO.
THEN WHAT?
WHAT DO YOU CARE?
I DON'T EVEN KNOW WHAT A...
DEEP... IS!
HIC SVNT LEON
I'M LIKE THE SERPENTS AND DRAGONS ONE SEES ON MAPS.
NO ONE DRAWS THOSE ANYMORE.
THEY DON'T NEED THEM. SOME CARTOGRAPHERS WROTE HIC SUNT LEONES: HERE BE LIONS.
ALL DANGERS THEY UNDERSTOOD FOR A WORLD THEY DIDN'T.
WHEN THE UNKNOWN WAS BETTER KNOWN, THEY FOUND BETTER WORDS.
BUT MORGAN, THERE IS MUCH THAT YOU DON'T KNOW.

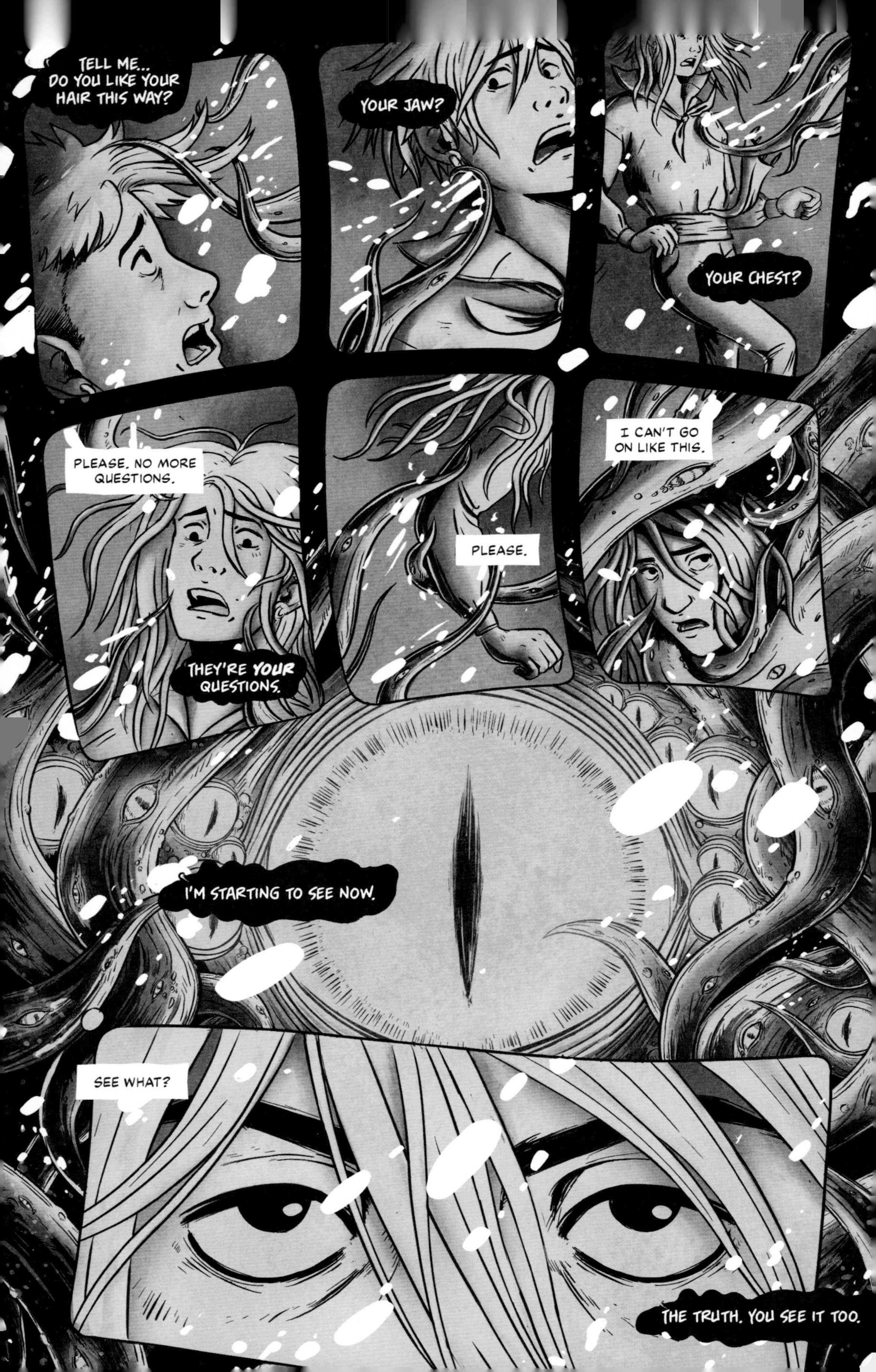

TELL ME... DO YOU LIKE YOUR HAIR THIS WAY?
YOUR JAW?
YOUR CHEST?
PLEASE. NO MORE QUESTIONS.
THEY'RE YOUR QUESTIONS.
PLEASE.
I CAN'T GO ON LIKE THIS.
I'M STARTING TO SEE NOW.
SEE WHAT?
THE TRUTH. YOU SEE IT TOO.

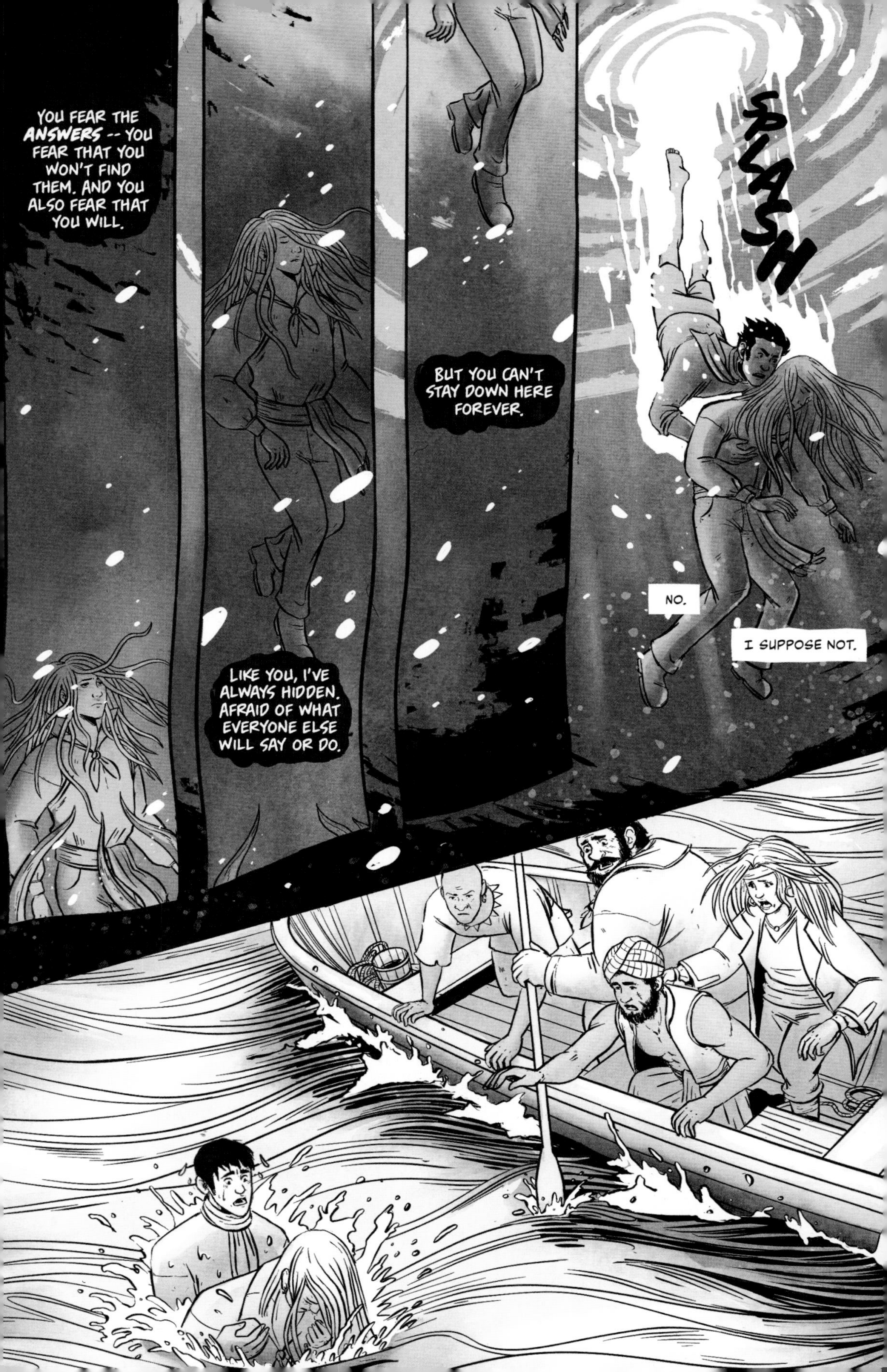
YOU FEAR THE ANSWERS -- YOU FEAR THAT YOU WON'T FIND THEM. AND YOU ALSO FEAR THAT YOU WILL.
LIKE YOU, I'VE ALWAYS HIDDEN. AFRAID OF WHAT EVERYONE ELSE WILL SAY OR DO.
BUT YOU CAN'T STAY DOWN HERE FOREVER.
SPLASH
NO.
I SUPPOSE NOT.

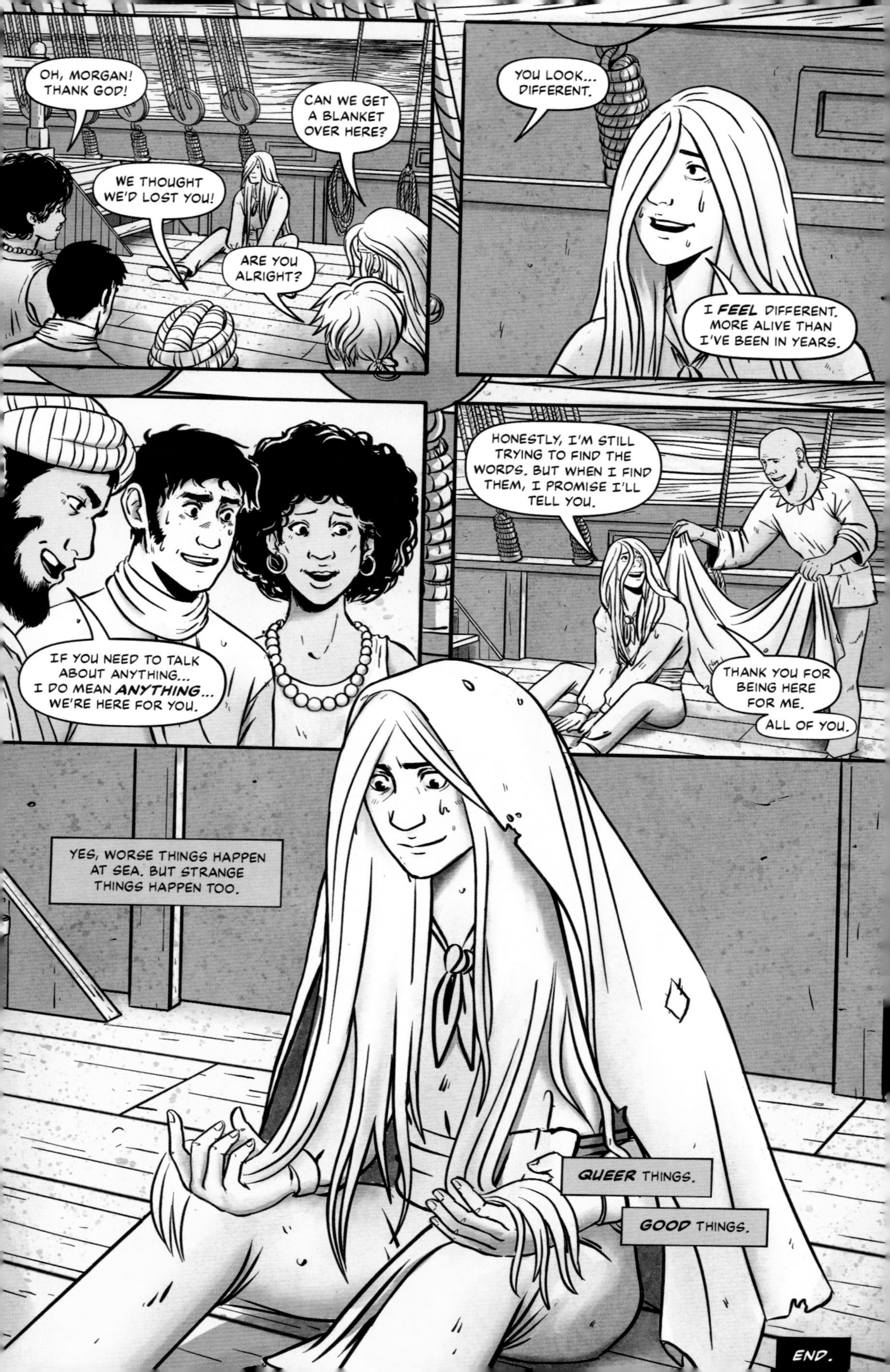
OH, MORGAN! THANK GOD!
WE THOUGHT WE'D LOST YOU!
CAN WE GET A BLANKET OVER HERE?
ARE YOU ALRIGHT?
YOU LOOK... DIFFERENT.
I FEEL DIFFERENT. MORE ALIVE THAN I'VE BEEN IN YEARS.
IF YOU NEED TO TALK ABOUT ANYTHING... I DO MEAN ANYTHING... WE'RE HERE FOR YOU.
HONESTLY, I'M STILL TRYING TO FIND THE WORDS. BUT WHEN I FIND THEM, I PROMISE I'LL TELL YOU.
THANK YOU FOR BEING HERE FOR ME.
ALL OF YOU.
YES, WORSE THINGS HAPPEN AT SEA. BUT STRANGE THINGS HAPPEN TOO.
QUEER THINGS.
GOOD THINGS.
END.

ALWAYS

"Letting It Fall"

WRITER-Priya Saxena • Artist-Jenny Fleming

EVERY TAROT CARD SERVES A PURPOSE.

BUT THERE IS ONE CARD TAROT READERS DREAD THE MOST.

THE TOWER WARNS OF IMMINENT DOOM.

THE TOWER

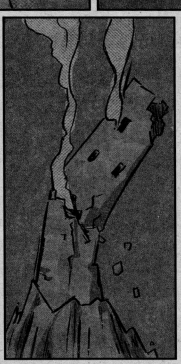

EVERYTHING YOU HAVE BUILT WILL CRUMBLE TO ASH.

THOUGH DESTRUCTION MAY MAKE WAY FOR SOMETHING NEW,

SOMETHING BETTER...

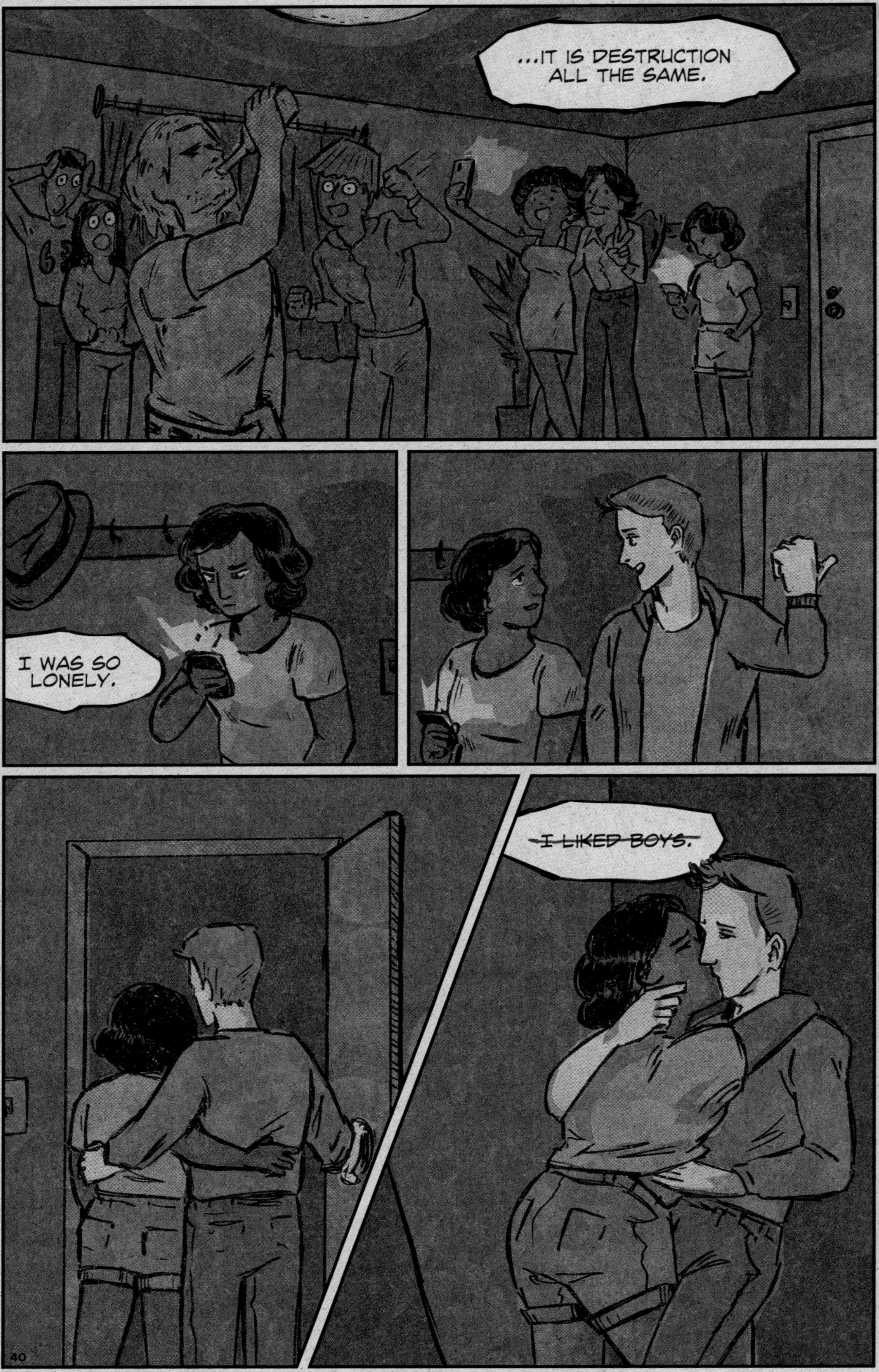
...IT IS DESTRUCTION ALL THE SAME.
I WAS SO LONELY.
~~I LIKED BOYS.~~

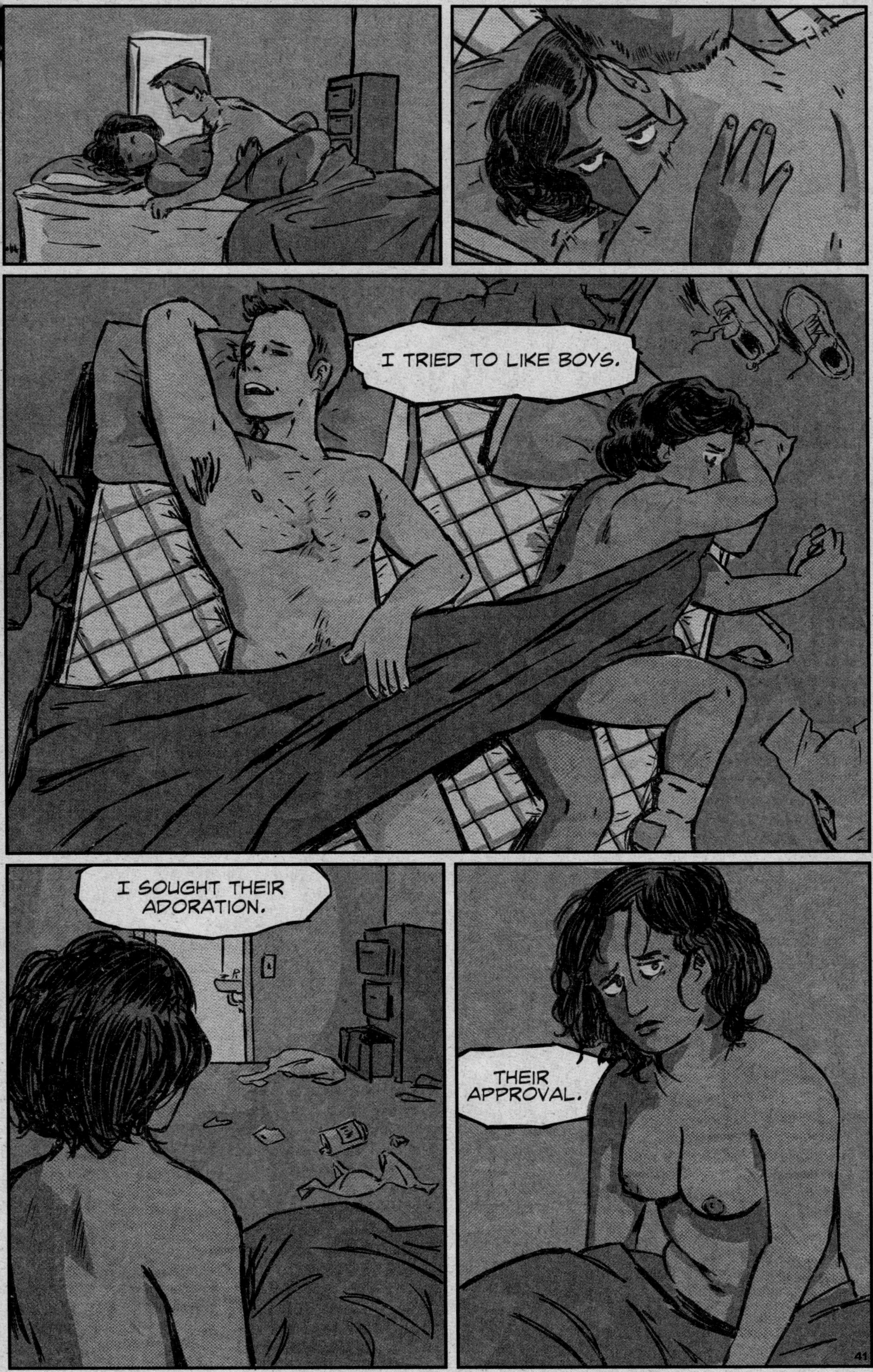
I TRIED TO LIKE BOYS.
I SOUGHT THEIR ADORATION.
THEIR APPROVAL.

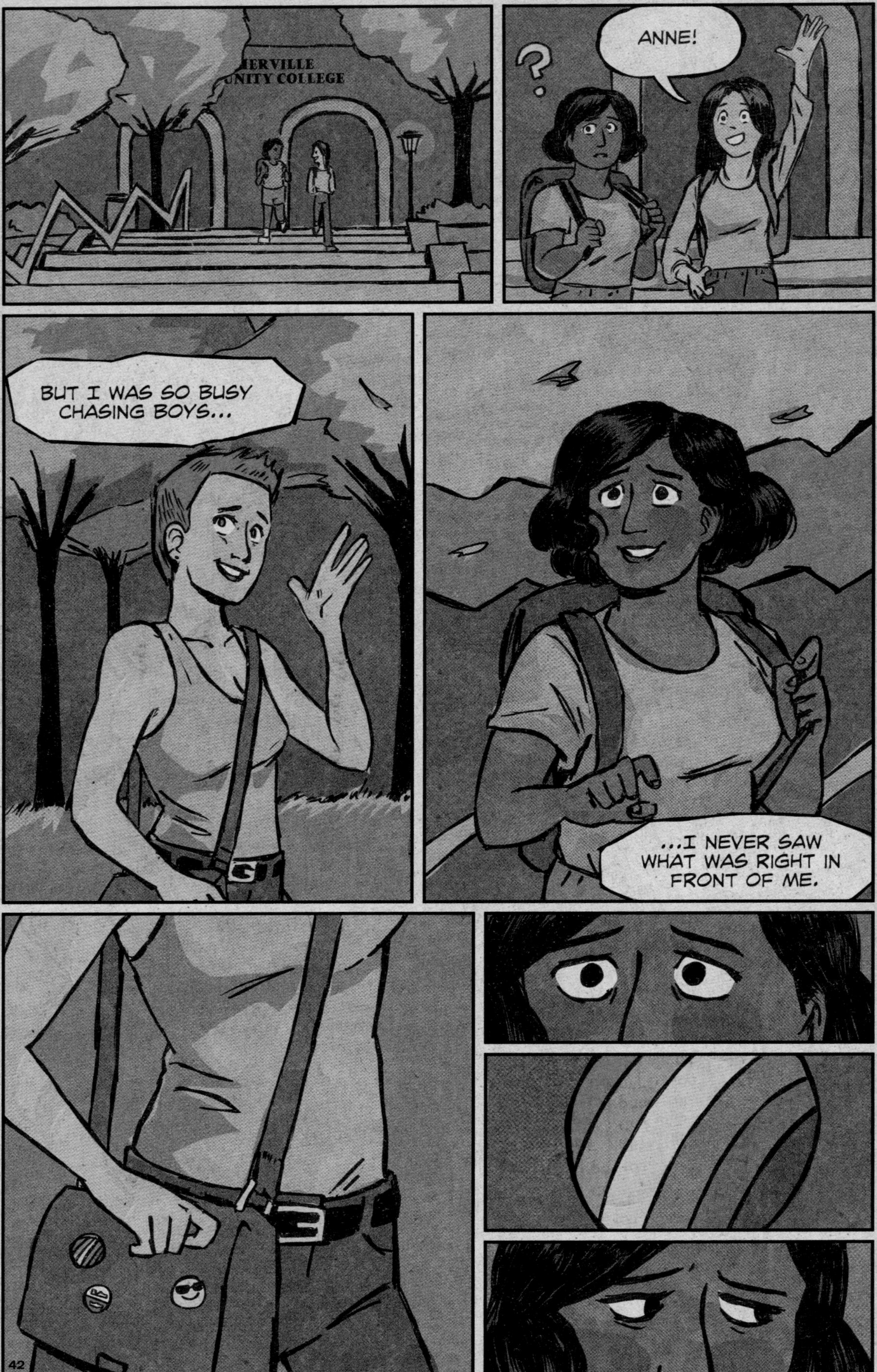
ERVILLE
UNITY COLLEGE
ANNE!
?
BUT I WAS SO BUSY CHASING BOYS...
...I NEVER SAW WHAT WAS RIGHT IN FRONT OF ME.

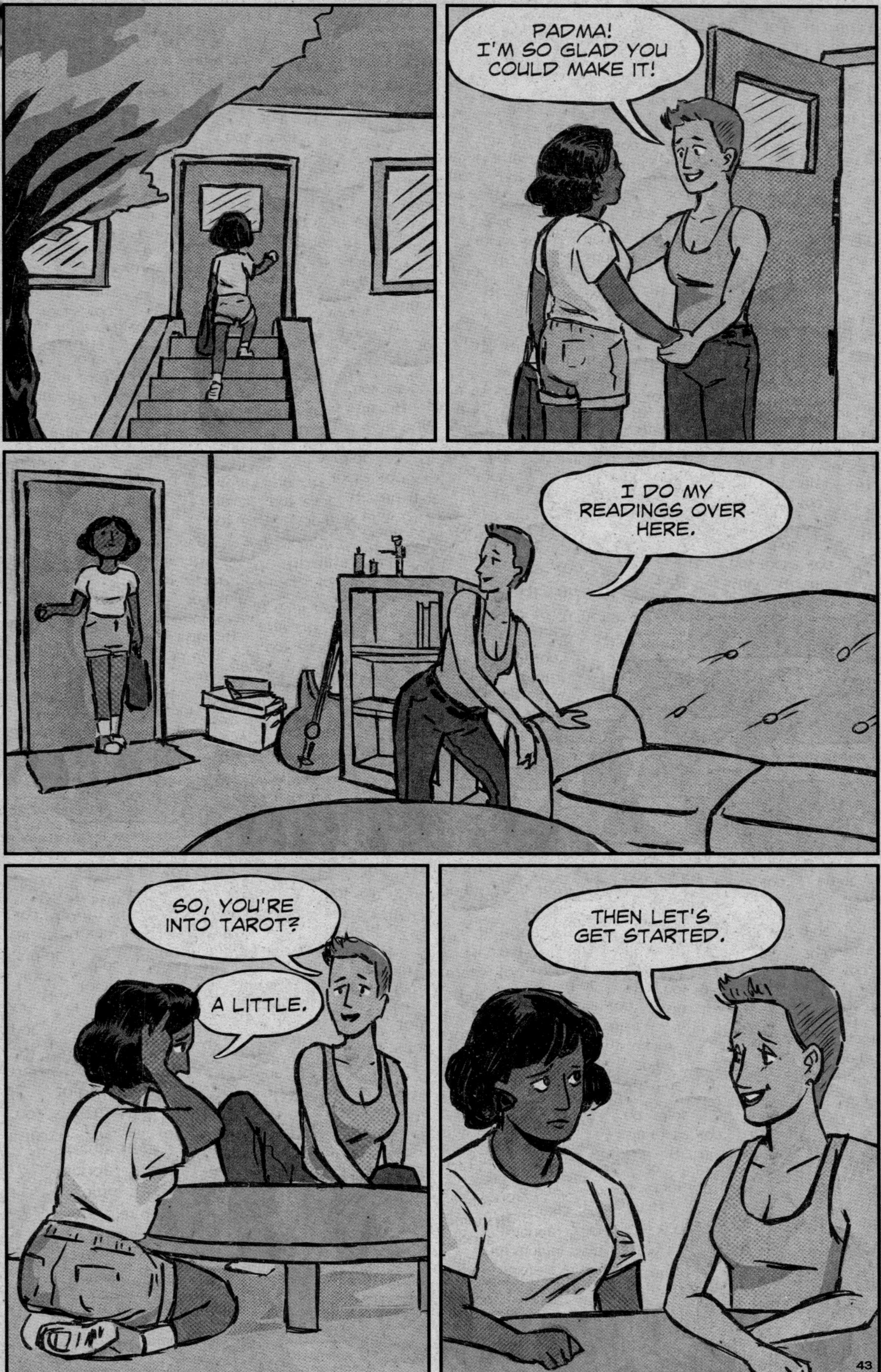
PADMA!
I'M SO GLAD YOU COULD MAKE IT!
I DO MY READINGS OVER HERE.
SO, YOU'RE INTO TAROT?
A LITTLE.
THEN LET'S GET STARTED.

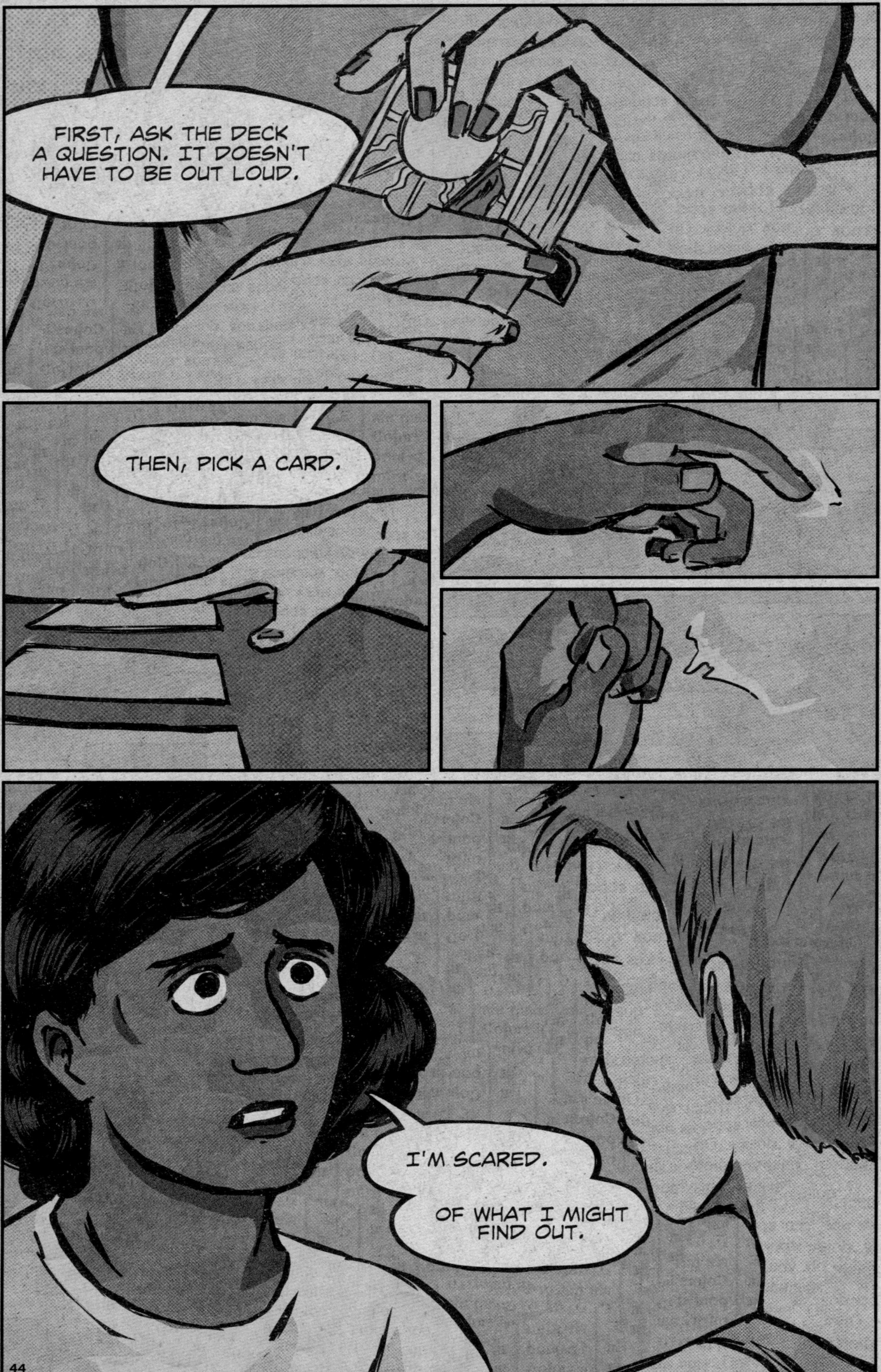
FIRST, ASK THE DECK A QUESTION. IT DOESN'T HAVE TO BE OUT LOUD.
THEN, PICK A CARD.
I'M SCARED.
OF WHAT I MIGHT FIND OUT.

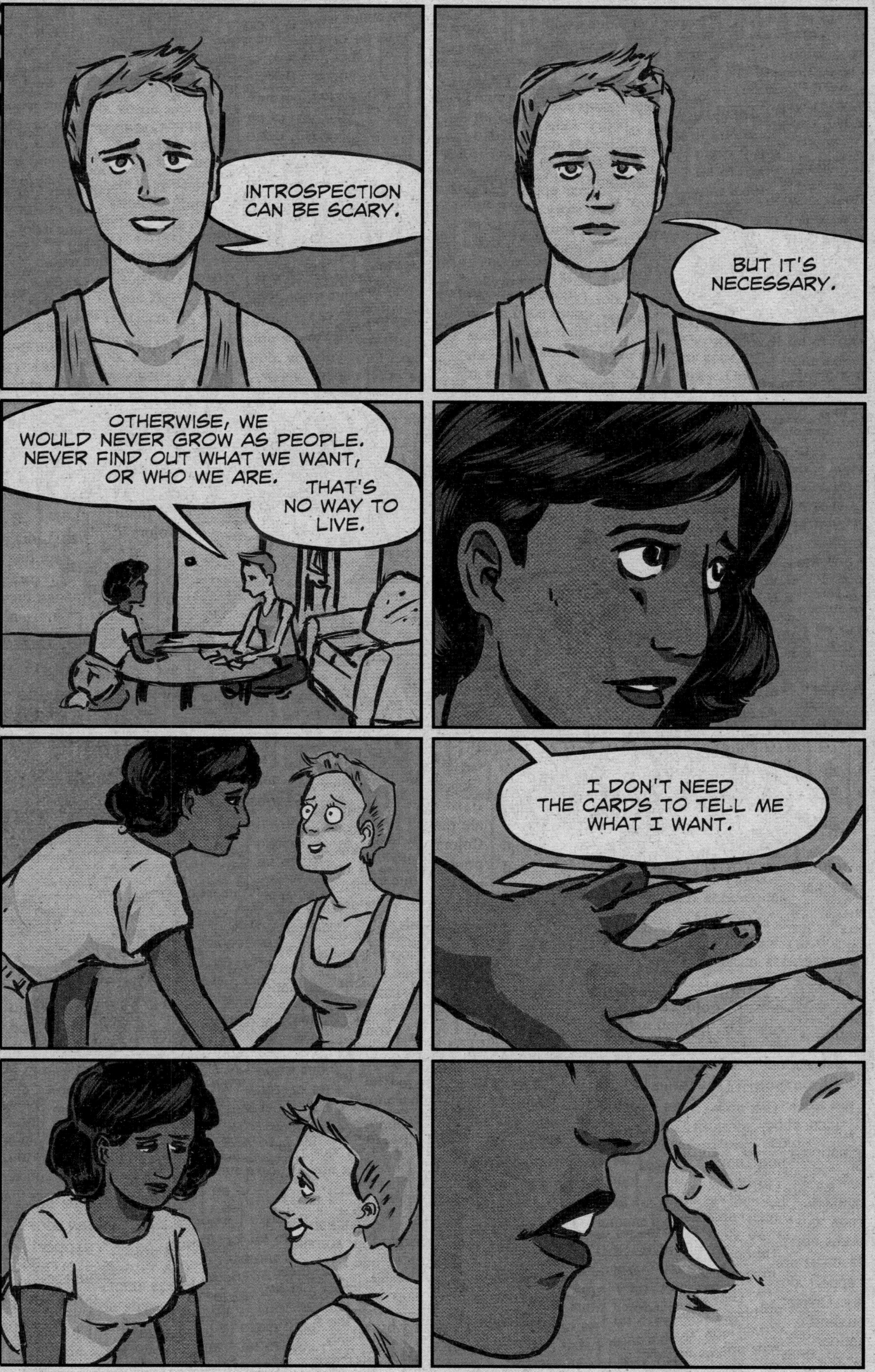
INTROSPECTION CAN BE SCARY.
BUT IT'S NECESSARY.
OTHERWISE, WE WOULD NEVER GROW AS PEOPLE. NEVER FIND OUT WHAT WE WANT, OR WHO WE ARE.
THAT'S NO WAY TO LIVE.
I DON'T NEED THE CARDS TO TELL ME WHAT I WANT.

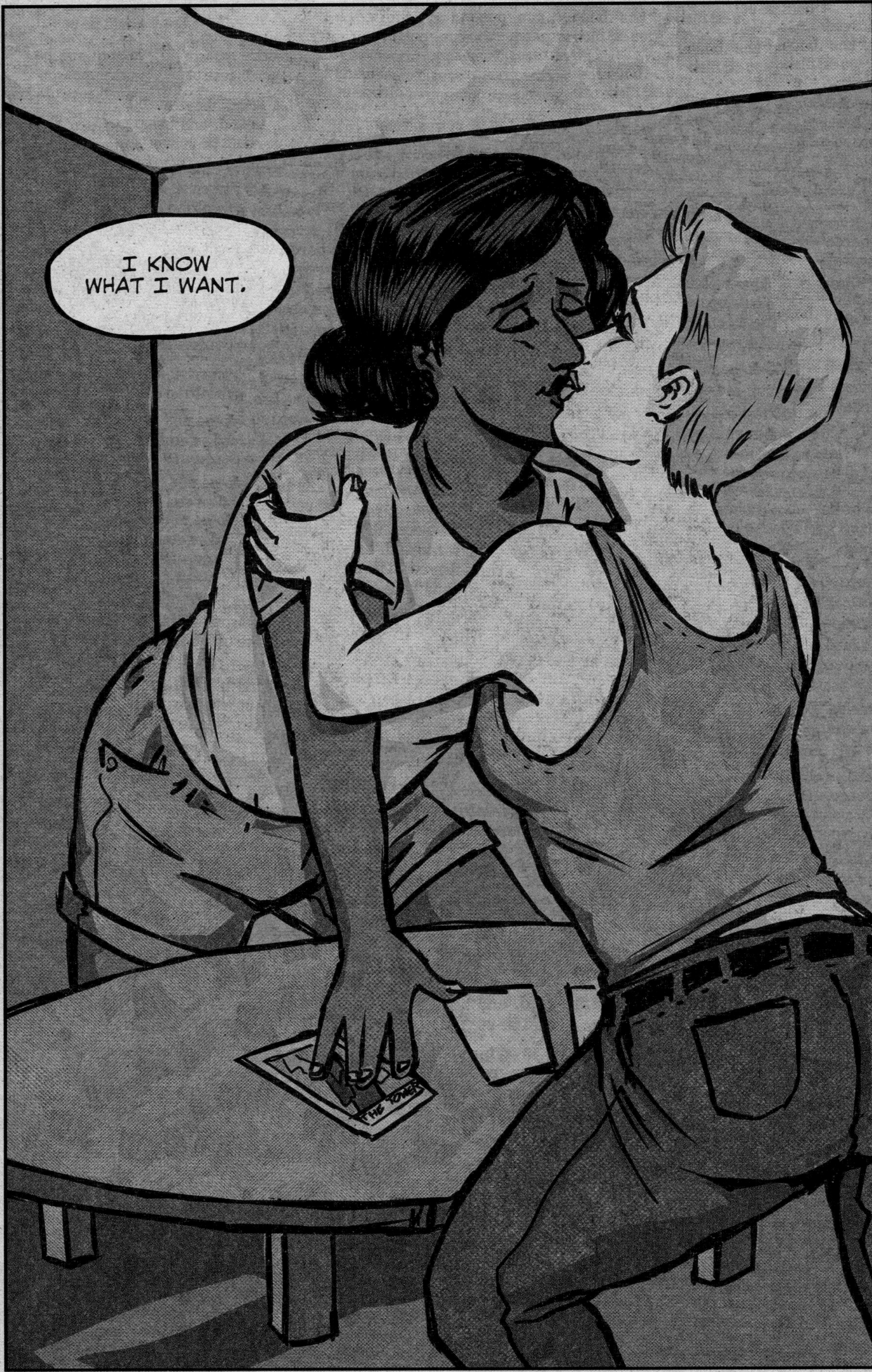
I KNOW WHAT I WANT.
THE TOWER

ALWAYS

"Long Away"

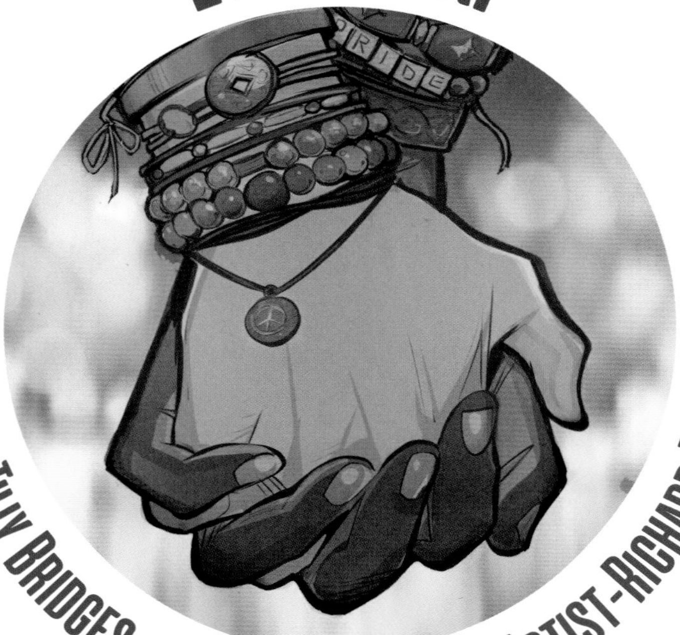
PRIDE

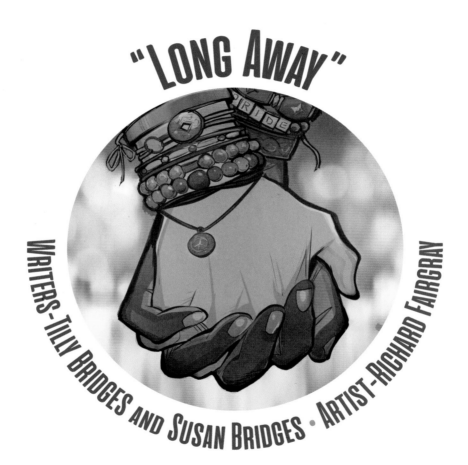

Writers-Tilly Bridges and Susan Bridges • Artist-Richard Fairgray

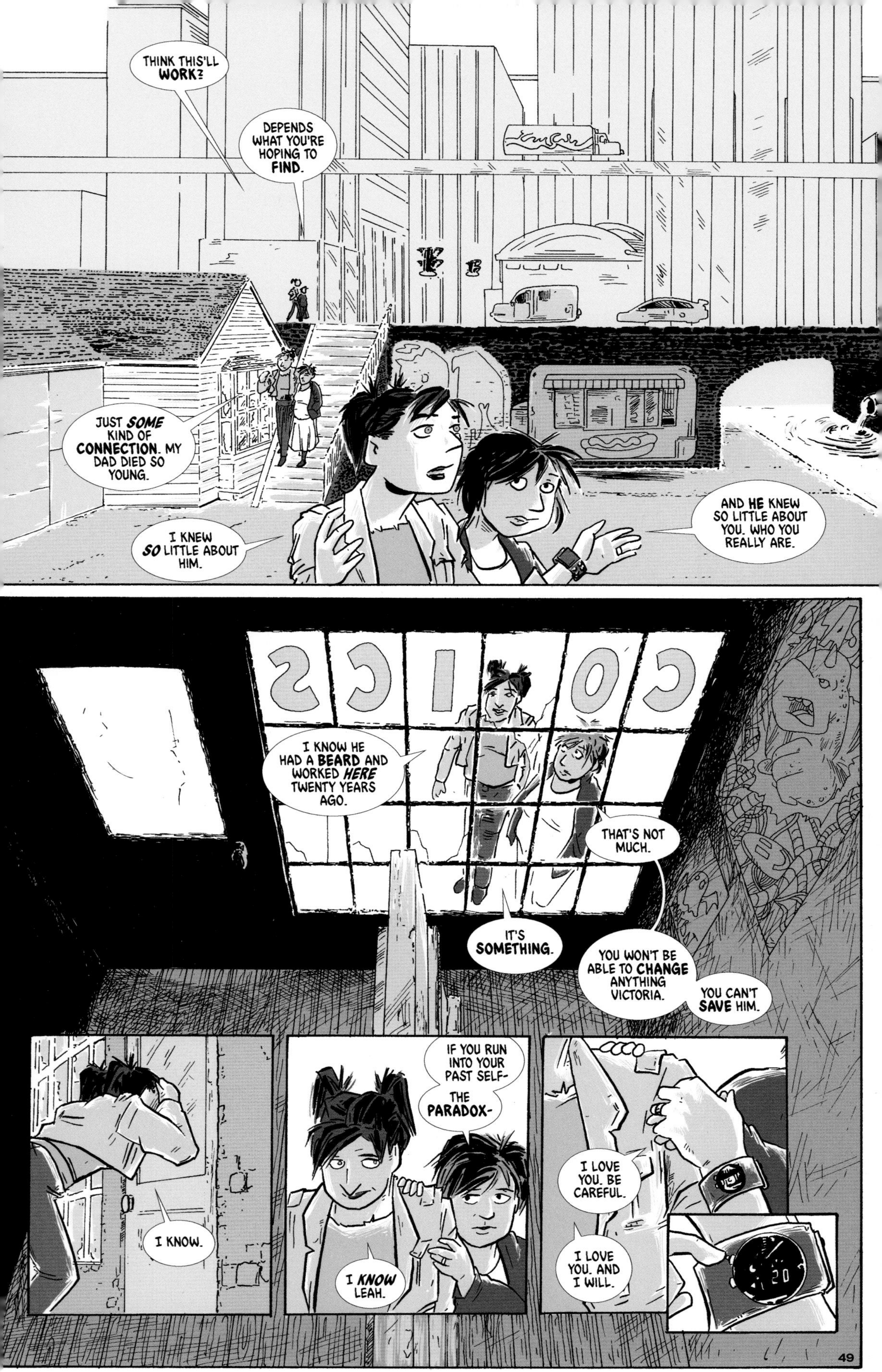
THINK THIS'LL WORK?
DEPENDS WHAT YOU'RE HOPING TO FIND.
JUST SOME KIND OF CONNECTION. MY DAD DIED SO YOUNG.
I KNEW SO LITTLE ABOUT HIM.
AND HE KNEW SO LITTLE ABOUT YOU. WHO YOU REALLY ARE.
I KNOW HE HAD A BEARD AND WORKED HERE TWENTY YEARS AGO.
THAT'S NOT MUCH.
IT'S SOMETHING.
YOU WON'T BE ABLE TO CHANGE ANYTHING VICTORIA.
YOU CAN'T SAVE HIM.
I KNOW.
IF YOU RUN INTO YOUR PAST SELF-
THE PARADOX-
I KNOW LEAH.
I LOVE YOU. BE CAREFUL.
I LOVE YOU. AND I WILL.

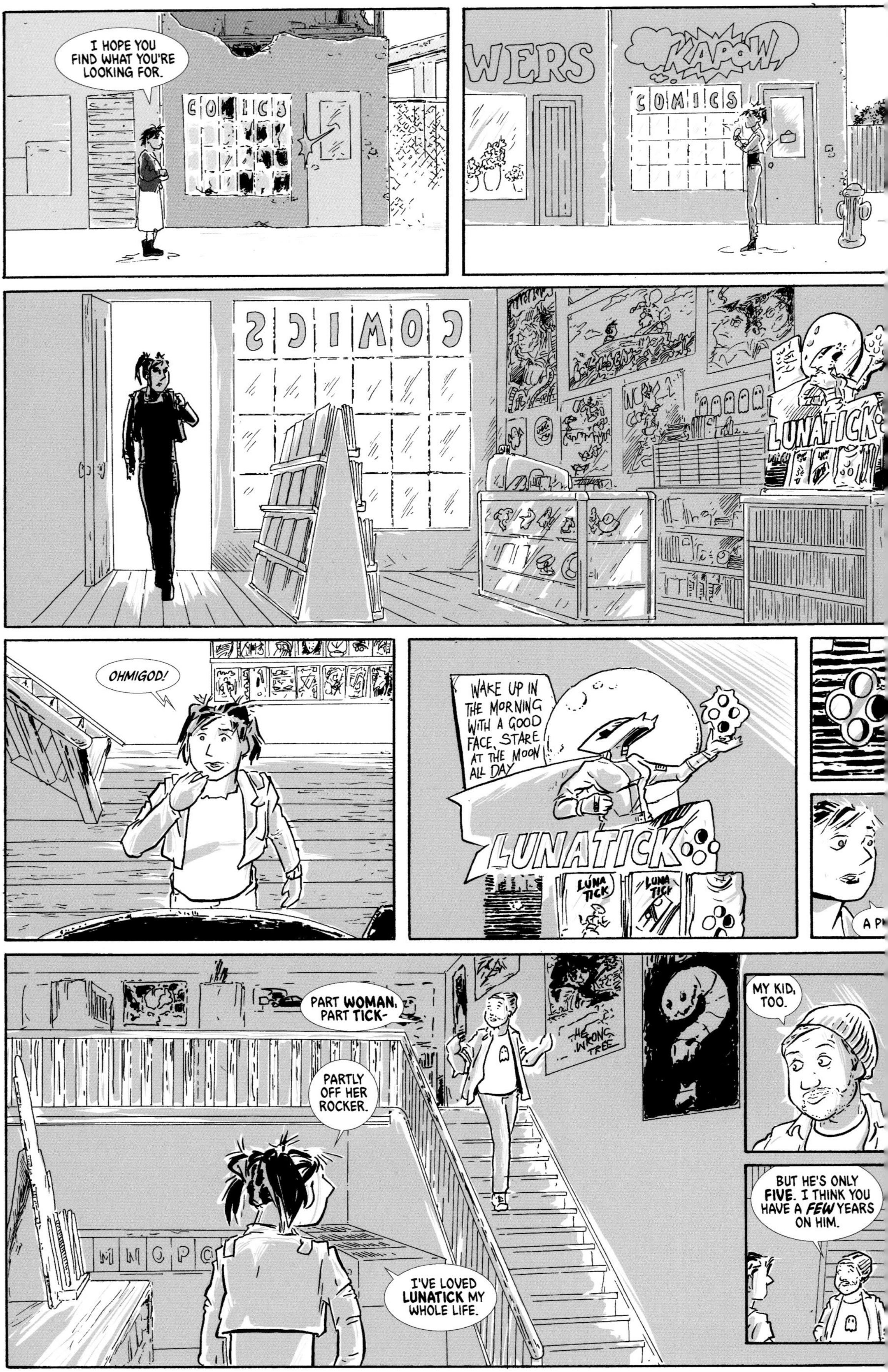
I HOPE YOU FIND WHAT YOU'RE LOOKING FOR.
COMICS
WERS
KAPOW
COMICS
COMICS
LUNATICK
OHMIGOD!
WAKE UP IN THE MORNING WITH A GOOD FACE, STARE AT THE MOON ALL DAY
LUNATICK
LUNA TICK
LUNA TICK
PART WOMAN, PART TICK-
PARTLY OFF HER ROCKER.
THE WRONG TREE
I'VE LOVED LUNATICK MY WHOLE LIFE.
MY KID, TOO.
BUT HE'S ONLY FIVE. I THINK YOU HAVE A FEW YEARS ON HIM.
M N O P Q

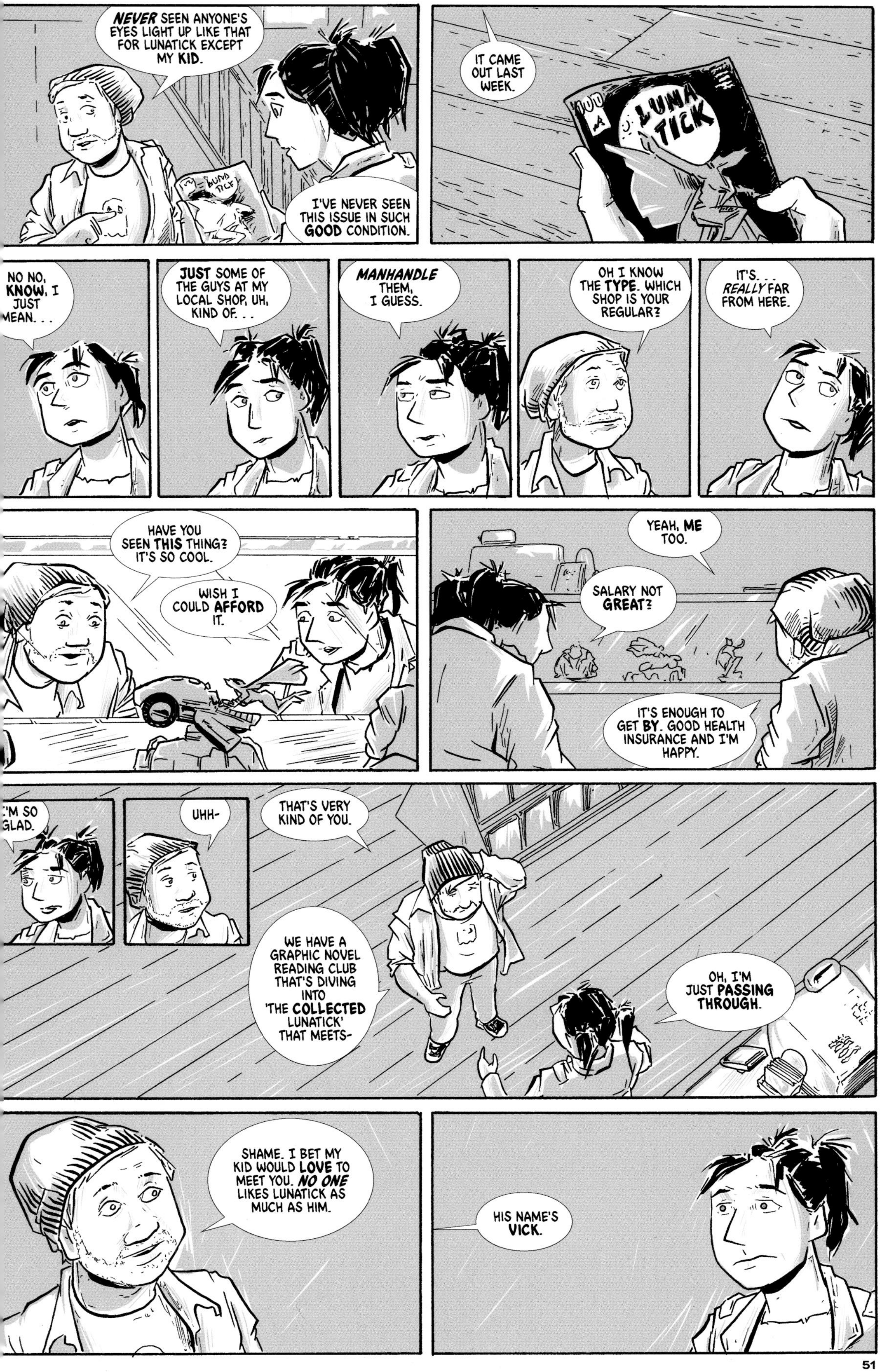

NEVER SEEN ANYONE'S EYES LIGHT UP LIKE THAT FOR LUNATICK EXCEPT MY KID.
I'VE NEVER SEEN THIS ISSUE IN SUCH GOOD CONDITION.
IT CAME OUT LAST WEEK.
LUNA TICK
NO NO, KNOW, I JUST MEAN. . .
JUST SOME OF THE GUYS AT MY LOCAL SHOP, UH, KIND OF. . .
MANHANDLE THEM, I GUESS.
OH I KNOW THE TYPE. WHICH SHOP IS YOUR REGULAR?
IT'S. . . REALLY FAR FROM HERE.
HAVE YOU SEEN THIS THING? IT'S SO COOL.
WISH I COULD AFFORD IT.
YEAH, ME TOO.
SALARY NOT GREAT?
IT'S ENOUGH TO GET BY. GOOD HEALTH INSURANCE AND I'M HAPPY.
I'M SO GLAD.
UHH-
THAT'S VERY KIND OF YOU.
WE HAVE A GRAPHIC NOVEL READING CLUB THAT'S DIVING INTO 'THE COLLECTED LUNATICK' THAT MEETS-
OH, I'M JUST PASSING THROUGH.
SHAME. I BET MY KID WOULD LOVE TO MEET YOU. NO ONE LIKES LUNATICK AS MUCH AS HIM.
HIS NAME'S VICK.

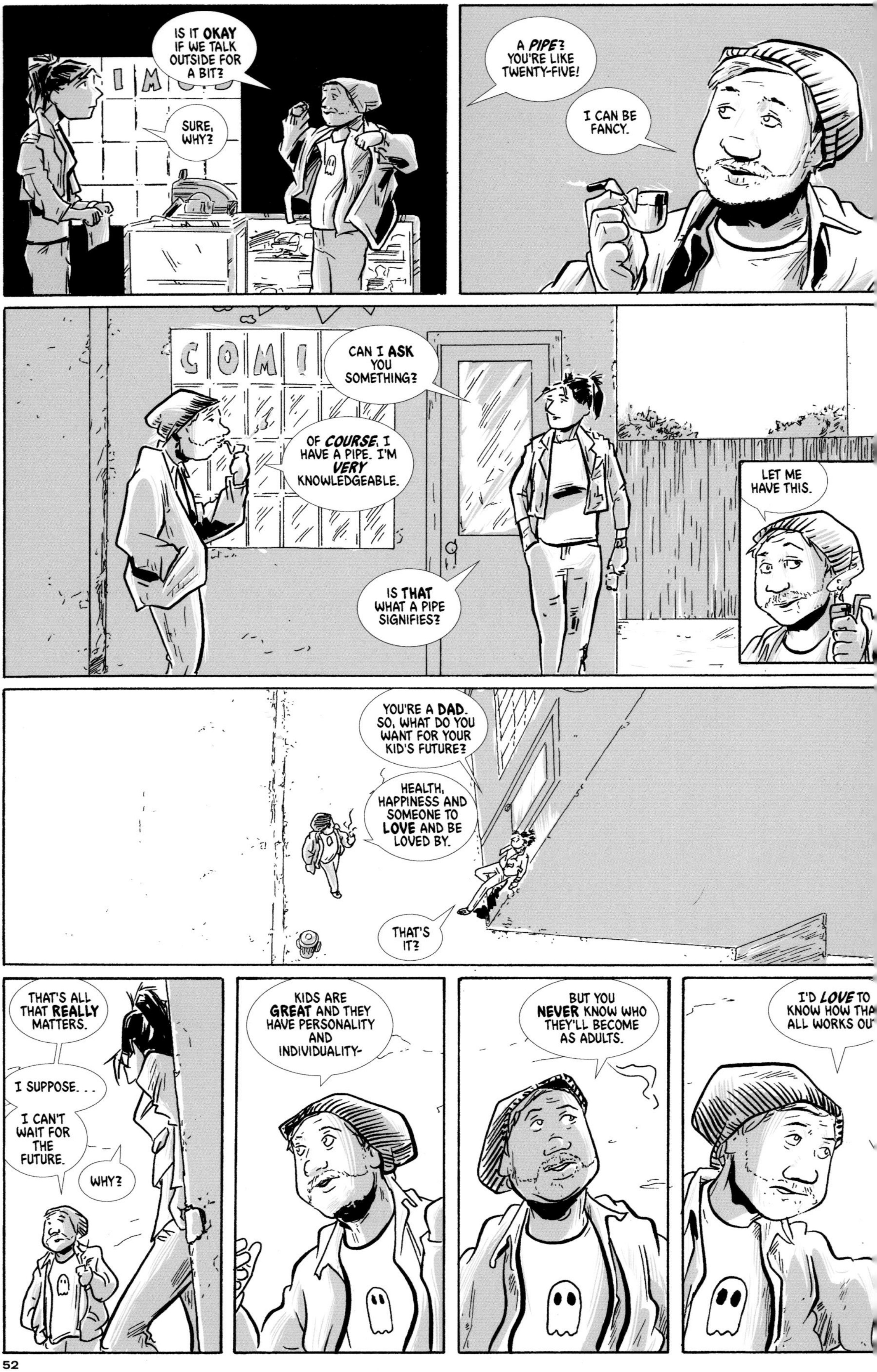
IS IT **OKAY** IF WE TALK OUTSIDE FOR A BIT?
SURE, WHY?
A *PIPE*? YOU'RE LIKE TWENTY-FIVE!
I CAN BE FANCY.
CAN I **ASK** YOU SOMETHING?
OF *COURSE*. I HAVE A PIPE. I'M *VERY* KNOWLEDGEABLE.
IS **THAT** WHAT A PIPE SIGNIFIES?
LET ME HAVE THIS.
YOU'RE A **DAD**. SO, WHAT DO YOU WANT FOR YOUR KID'S FUTURE?
HEALTH, HAPPINESS AND SOMEONE TO **LOVE** AND BE LOVED BY.
THAT'S IT?
THAT'S ALL THAT **REALLY** MATTERS.
I SUPPOSE. . .
I CAN'T WAIT FOR THE FUTURE.
WHY?
KIDS ARE **GREAT** AND THEY HAVE PERSONALITY AND INDIVIDUALITY-
BUT YOU **NEVER** KNOW WHO THEY'LL BECOME AS ADULTS.
I'D *LOVE* TO KNOW HOW THA
ALL WORKS OU

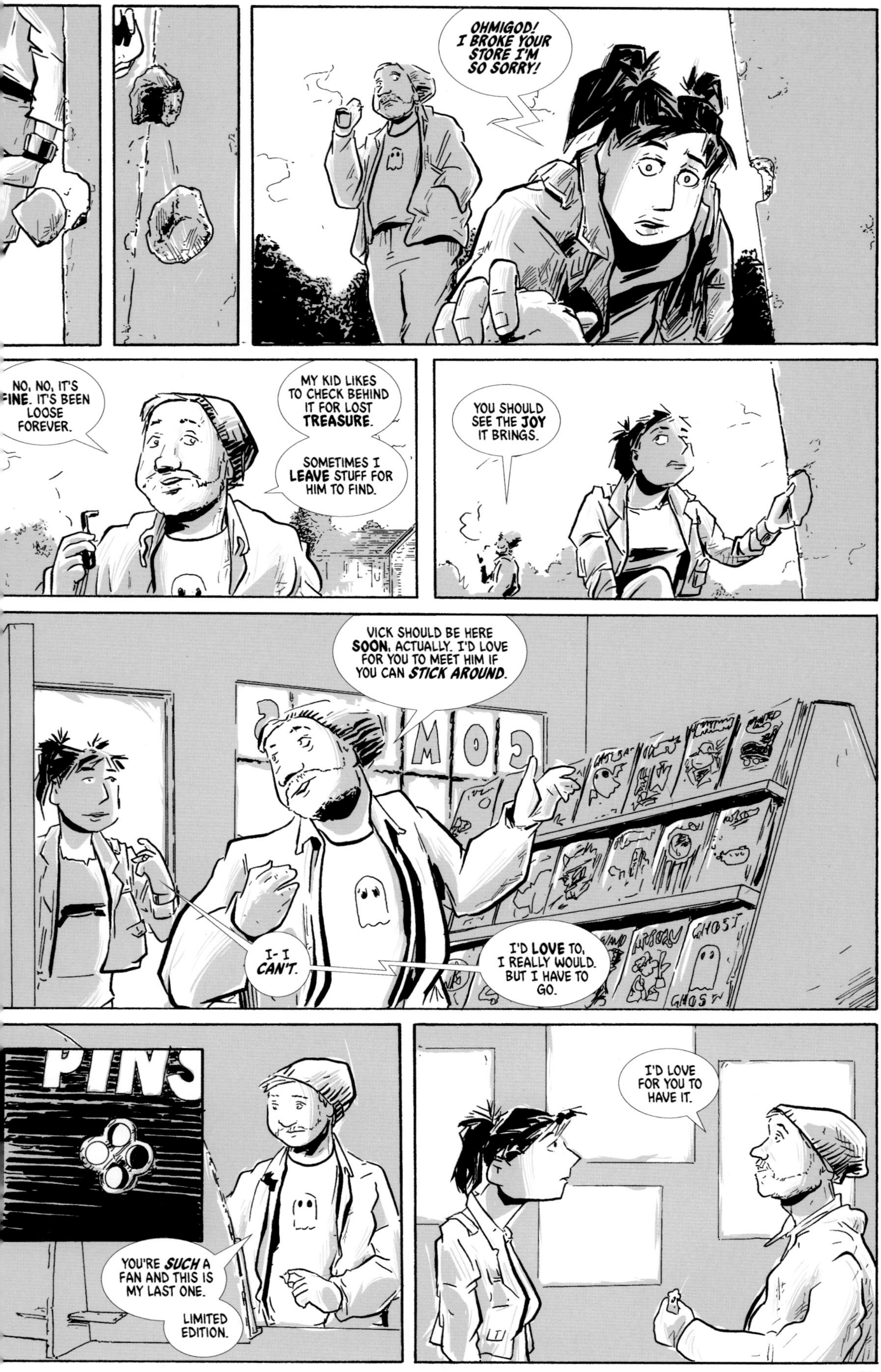
OHMIGOD! I BROKE YOUR STORE I'M SO SORRY!
NO, NO, IT'S FINE. IT'S BEEN LOOSE FOREVER.
MY KID LIKES TO CHECK BEHIND IT FOR LOST TREASURE.
SOMETIMES I LEAVE STUFF FOR HIM TO FIND.
YOU SHOULD SEE THE JOY IT BRINGS.
VICK SHOULD BE HERE SOON, ACTUALLY. I'D LOVE FOR YOU TO MEET HIM IF YOU CAN STICK AROUND.
I- I CAN'T.
I'D LOVE TO, I REALLY WOULD. BUT I HAVE TO GO.
GHOST
PINS
YOU'RE SUCH A FAN AND THIS IS MY LAST ONE.
LIMITED EDITION.
I'D LOVE FOR YOU TO HAVE IT.

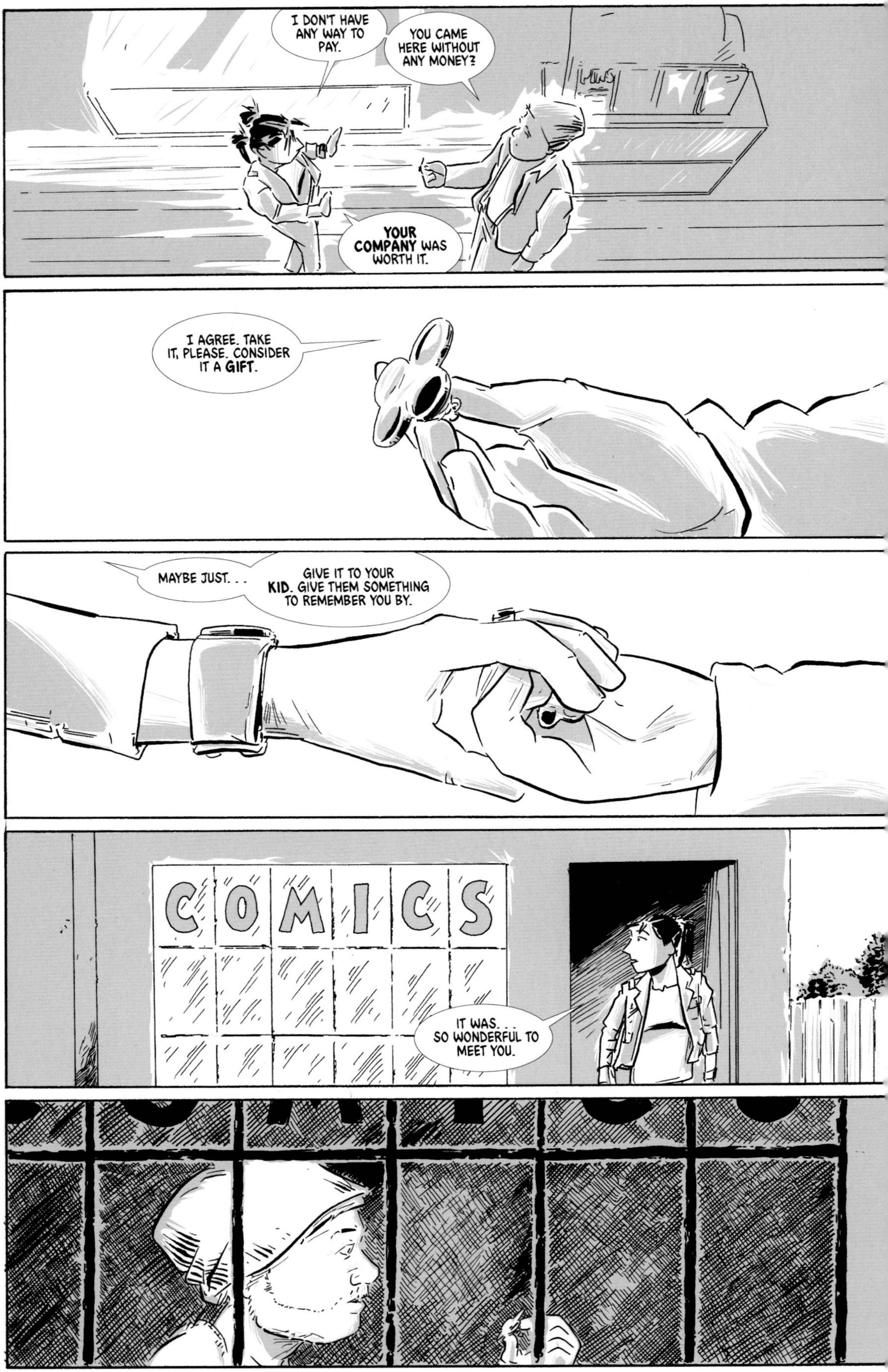
I DON'T HAVE ANY WAY TO PAY.
YOU CAME HERE WITHOUT ANY MONEY?
YOUR COMPANY WAS WORTH IT.
I AGREE. TAKE IT, PLEASE. CONSIDER IT A GIFT.
MAYBE JUST. . .
GIVE IT TO YOUR KID. GIVE THEM SOMETHING TO REMEMBER YOU BY.
COMICS
IT WAS. . . SO WONDERFUL TO MEET YOU.

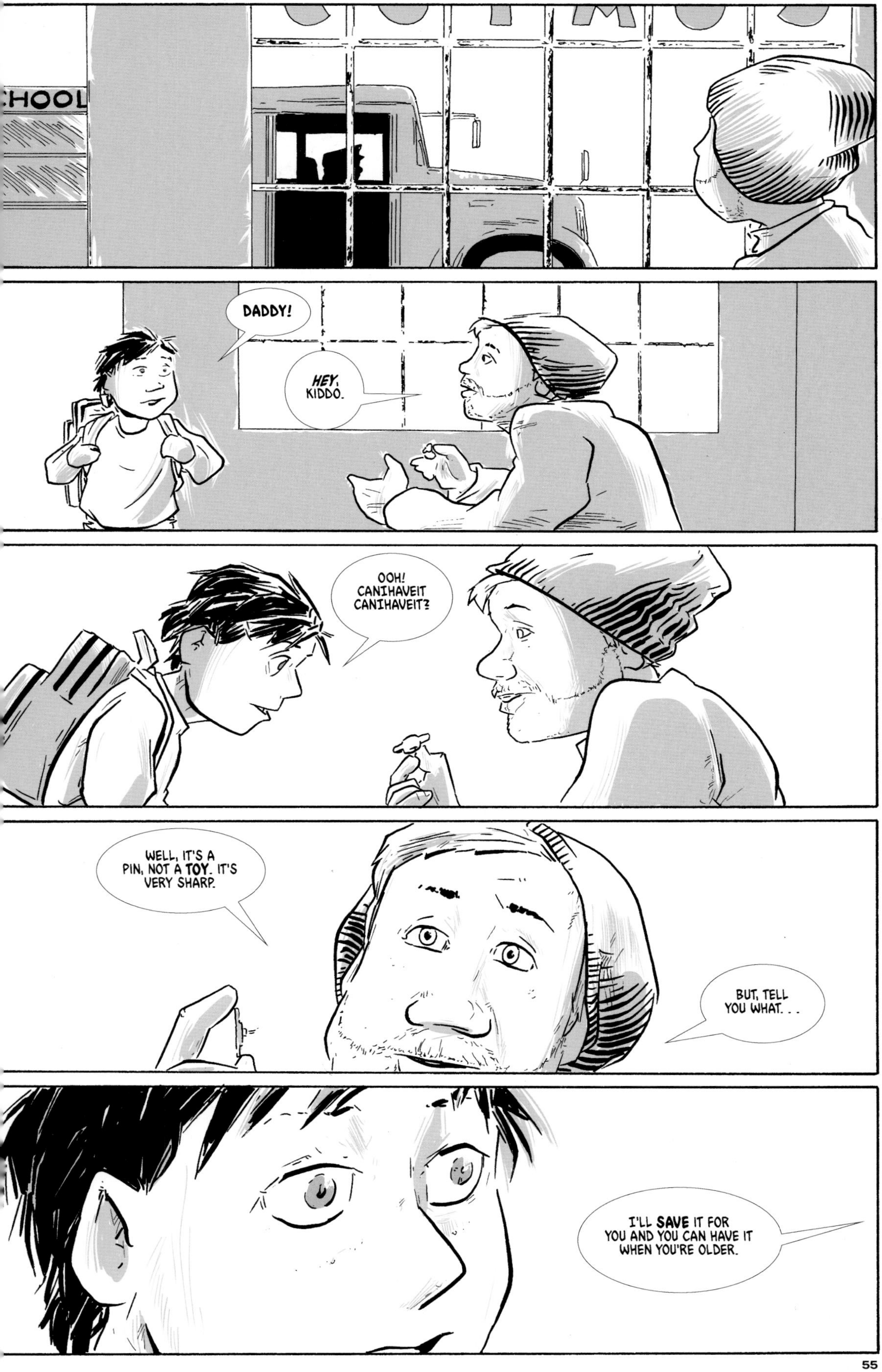

CHOOL
DADDY!
HEY, KIDDO.
OOH! CANIHAVEIT CANIHAVEIT?
WELL, IT'S A PIN, NOT A TOY. IT'S VERY SHARP.
BUT, TELL YOU WHAT. . .
I'LL SAVE IT FOR YOU AND YOU CAN HAVE IT WHEN YOU'RE OLDER.

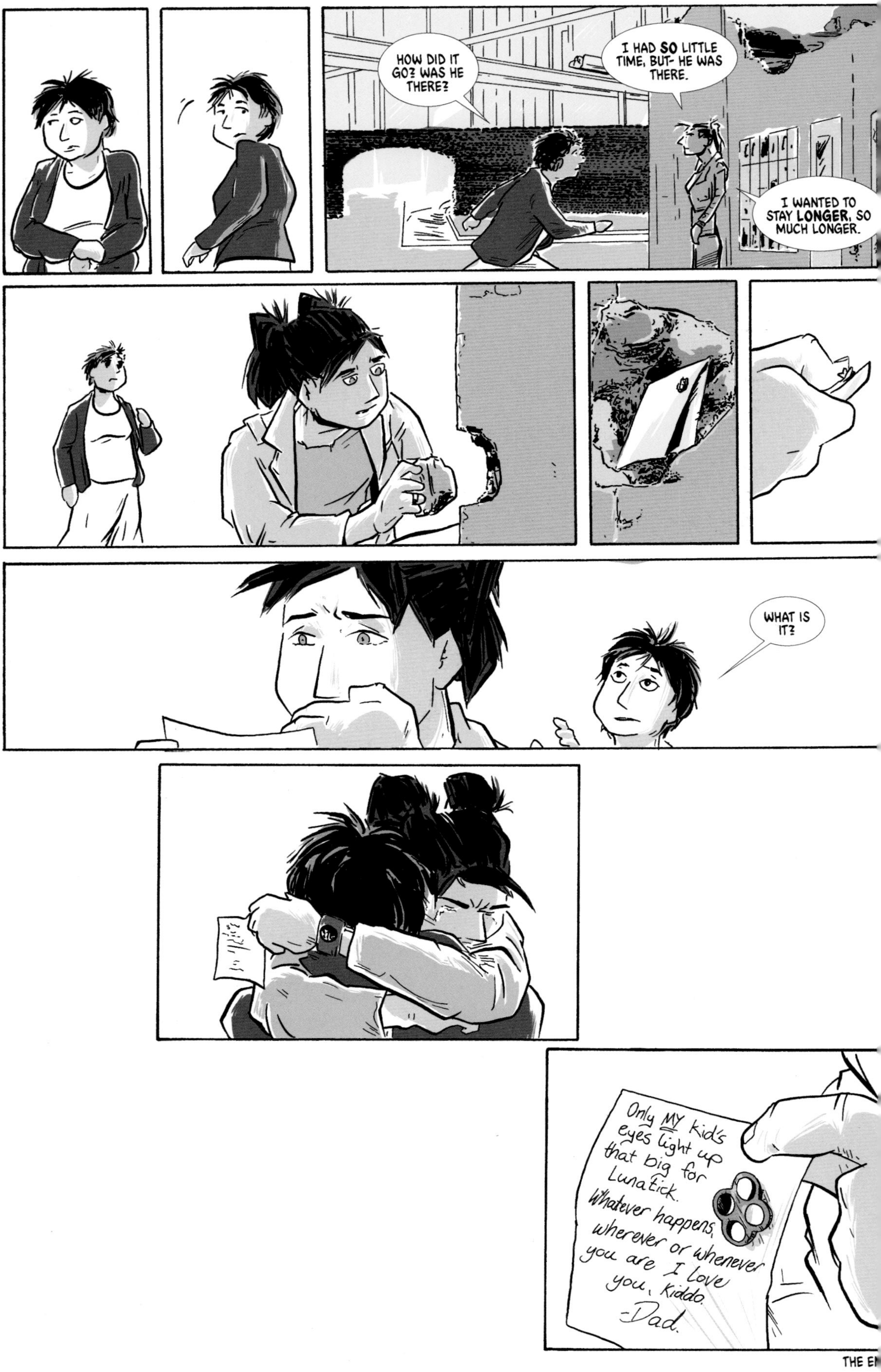
HOW DID IT GO? WAS HE THERE?
I HAD SO LITTLE TIME, BUT- HE WAS THERE.
I WANTED TO STAY LONGER, SO MUCH LONGER.
WHAT IS IT?
Only MY kid's eyes light up that big for Lunatick.
Whatever happens, wherever or whenever you are I love you, kiddo.
-Dad.
THE EN

ALWAYS

"All That Glitters"

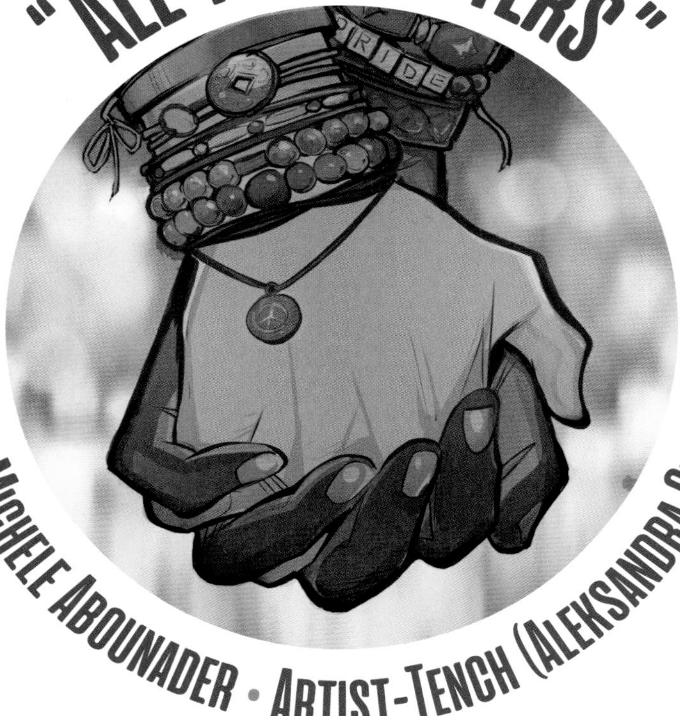
RIDE

Writer-Michele Abounader • Artist-Tench (Aleksandra Orekhova)

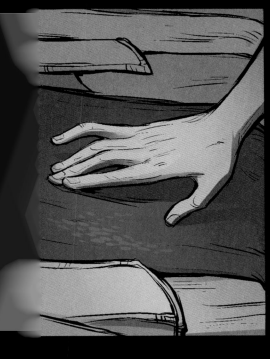

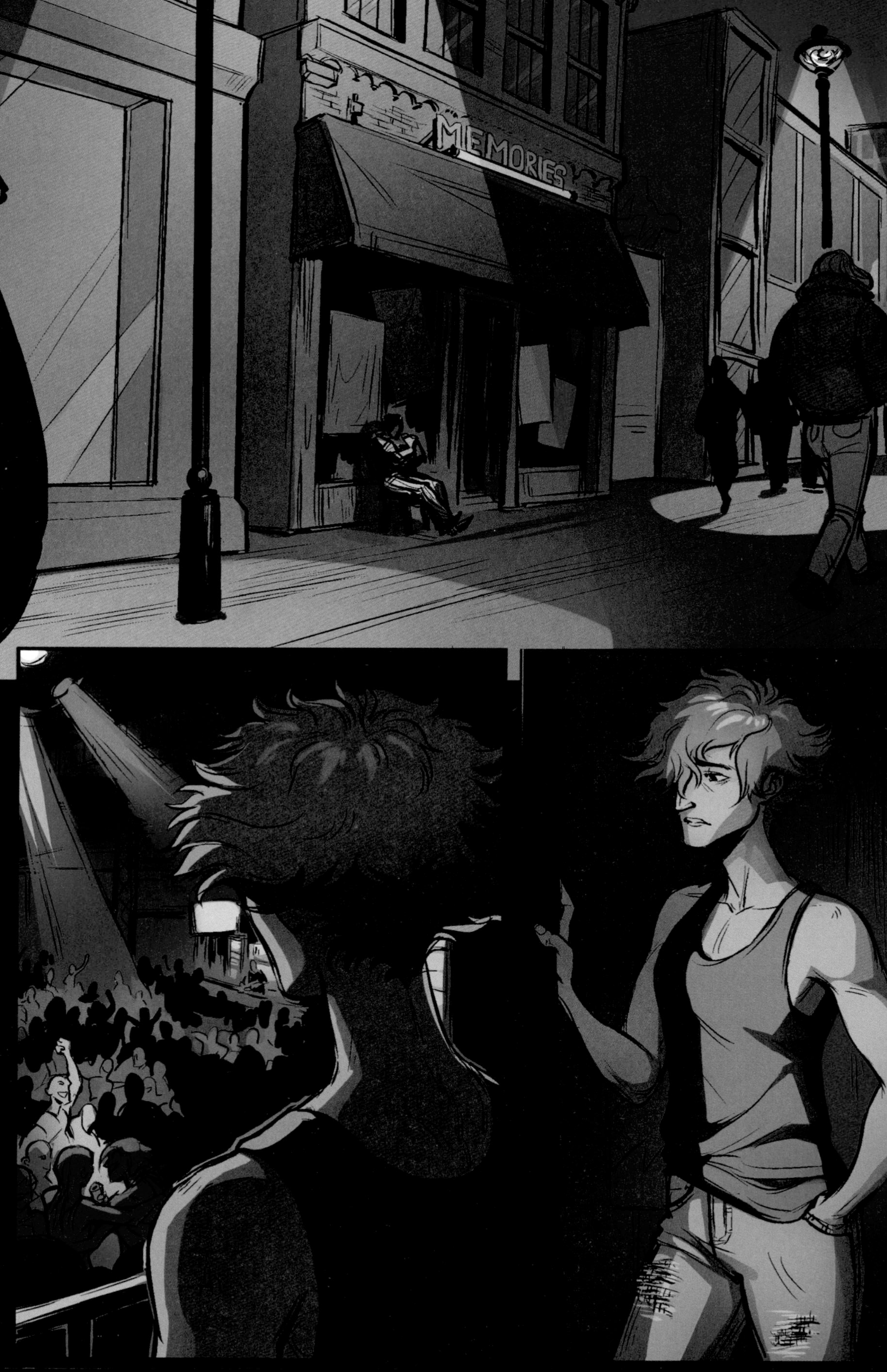
MEMORIES

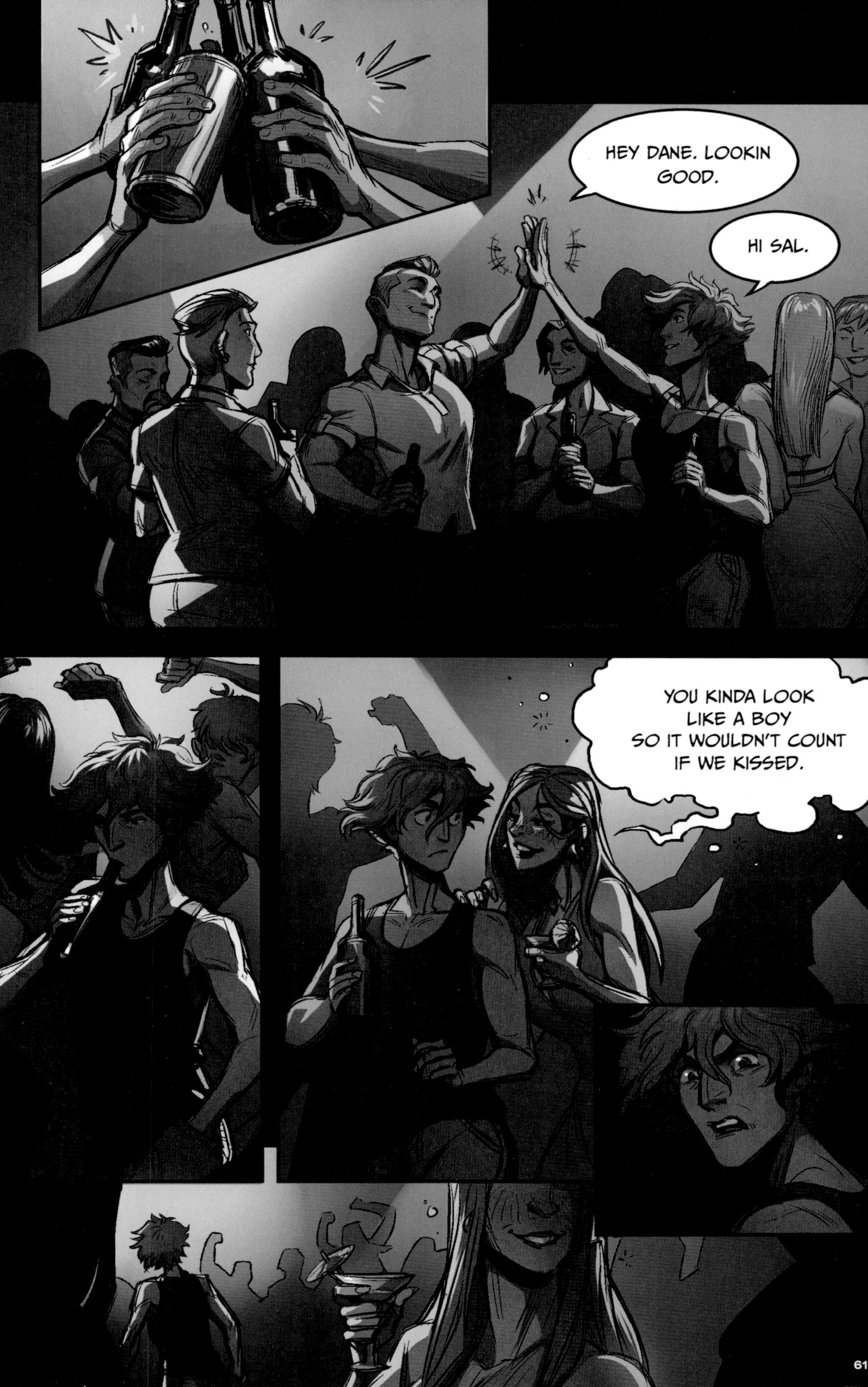
HEY DANE. LOOKIN GOOD.
HI SAL.
YOU KINDA LOOK LIKE A BOY SO IT WOULDN'T COUNT IF WE KISSED.

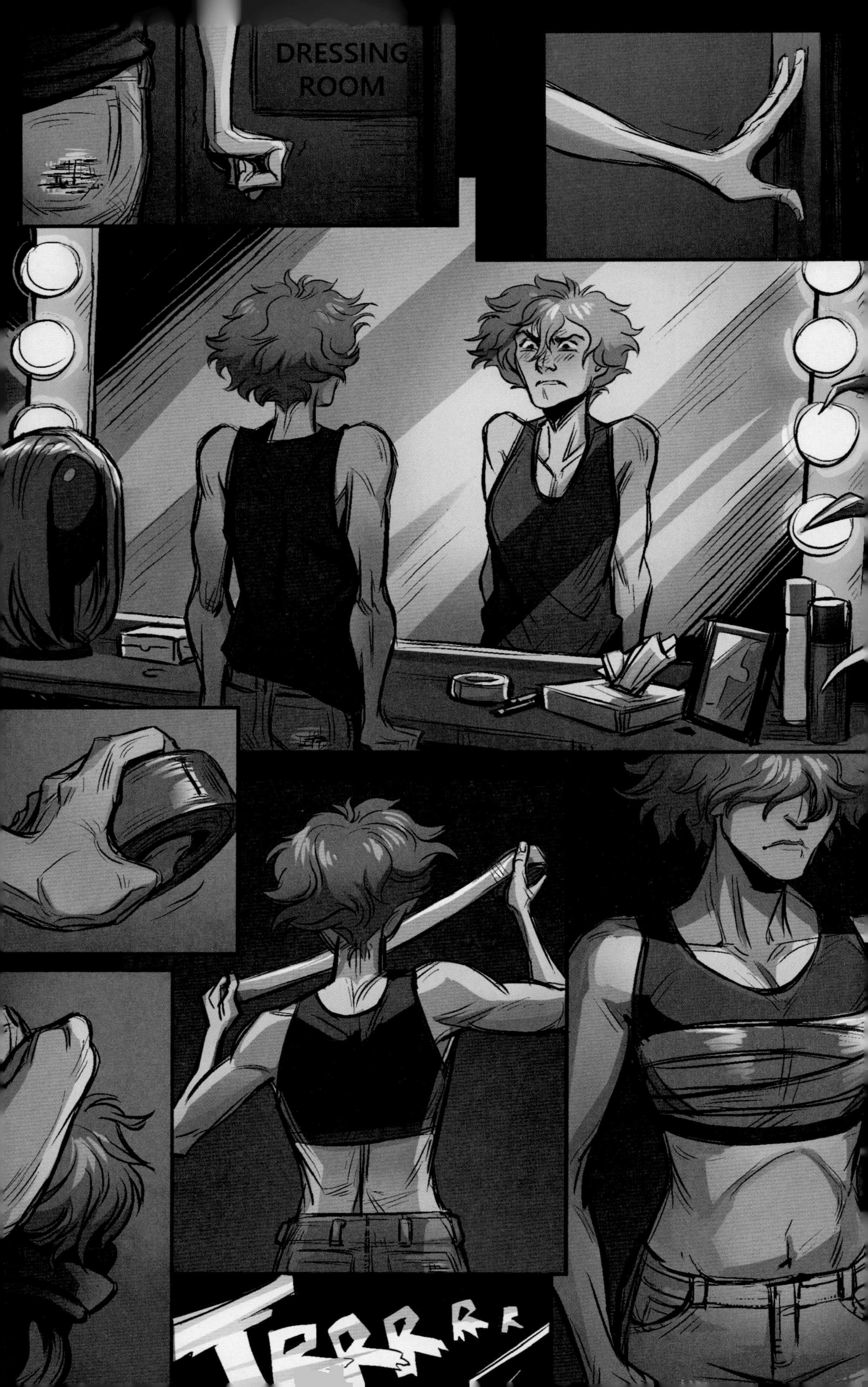
DRESSING
ROOM
TRRRRR

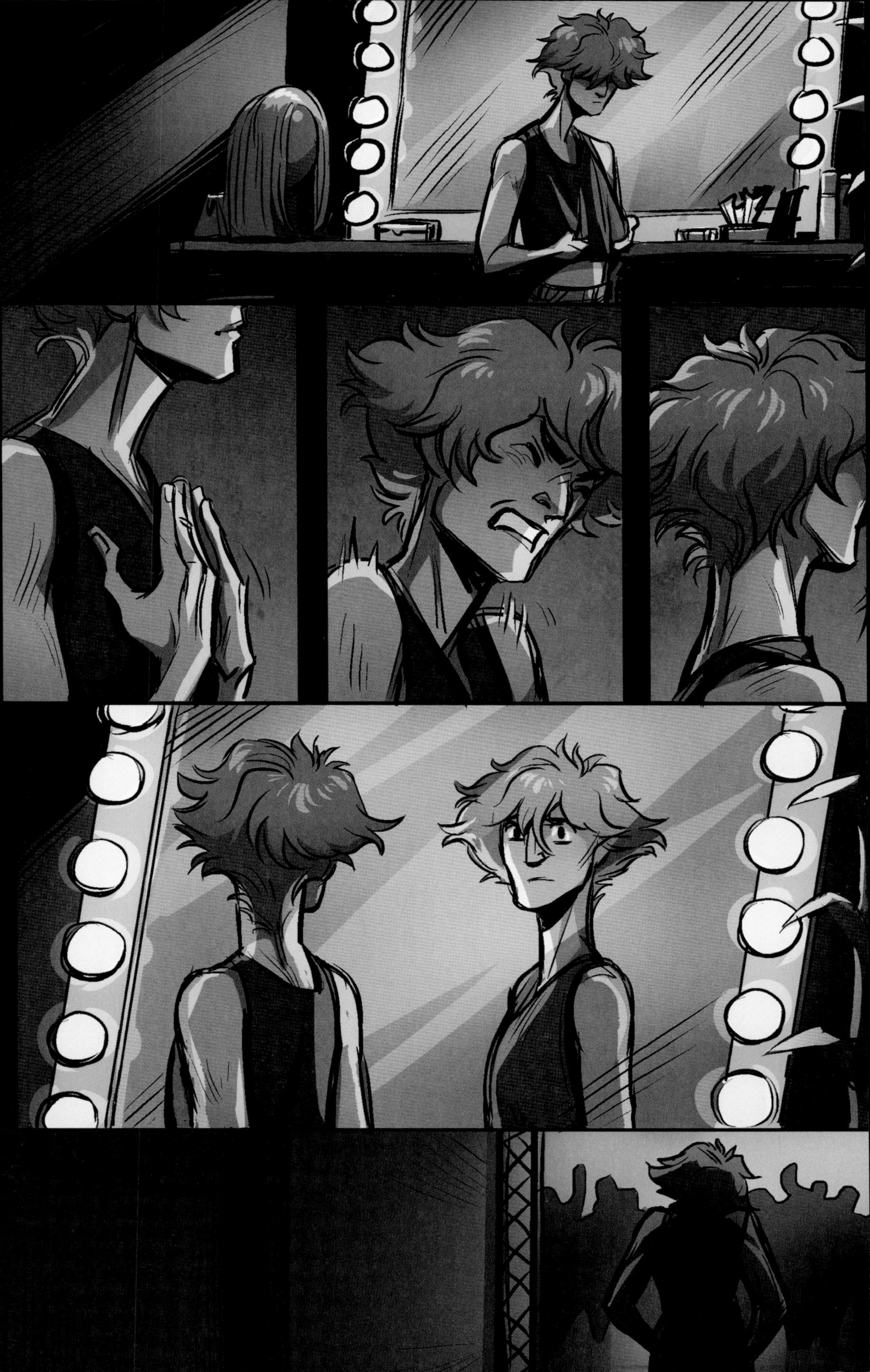

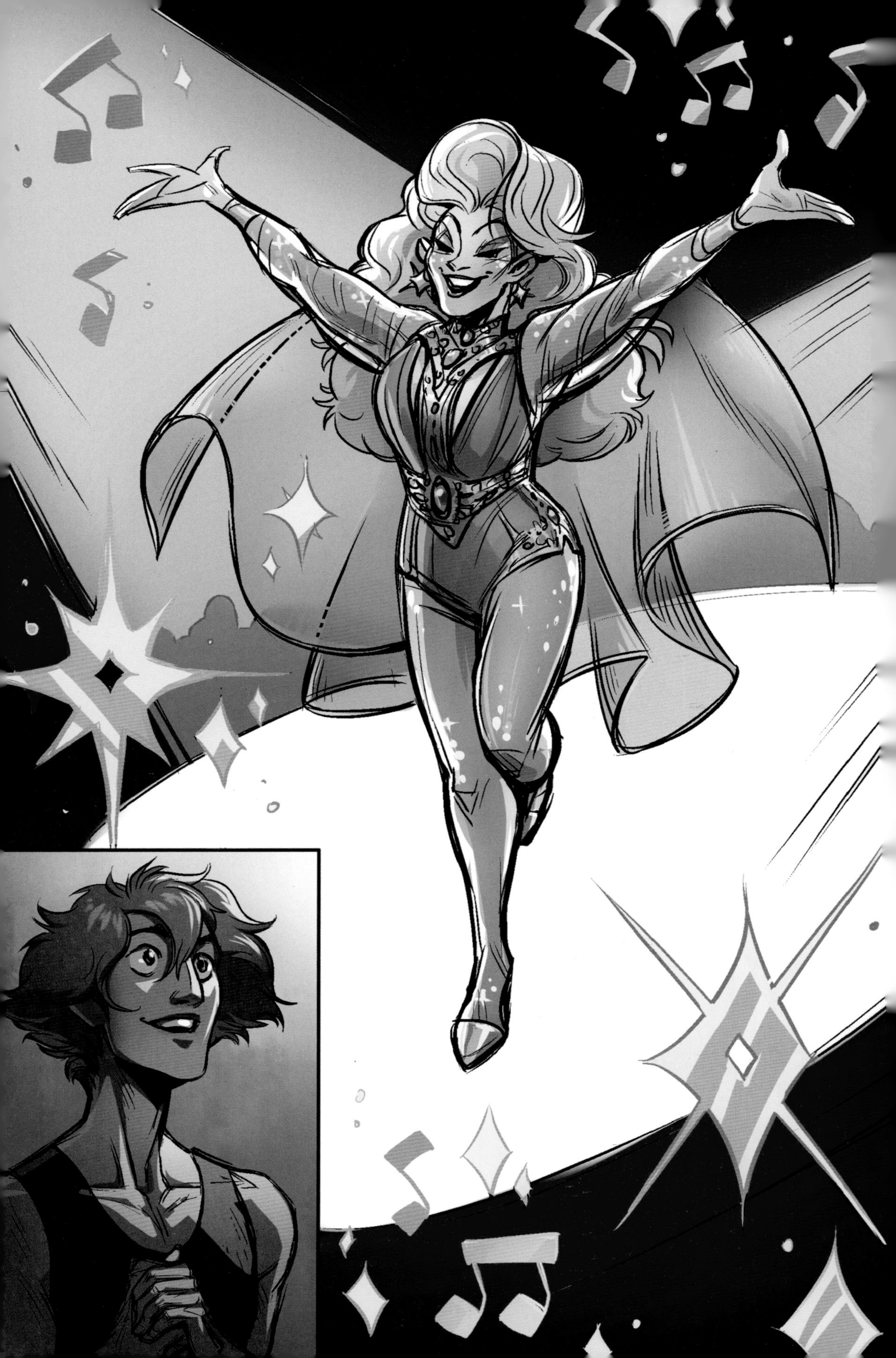

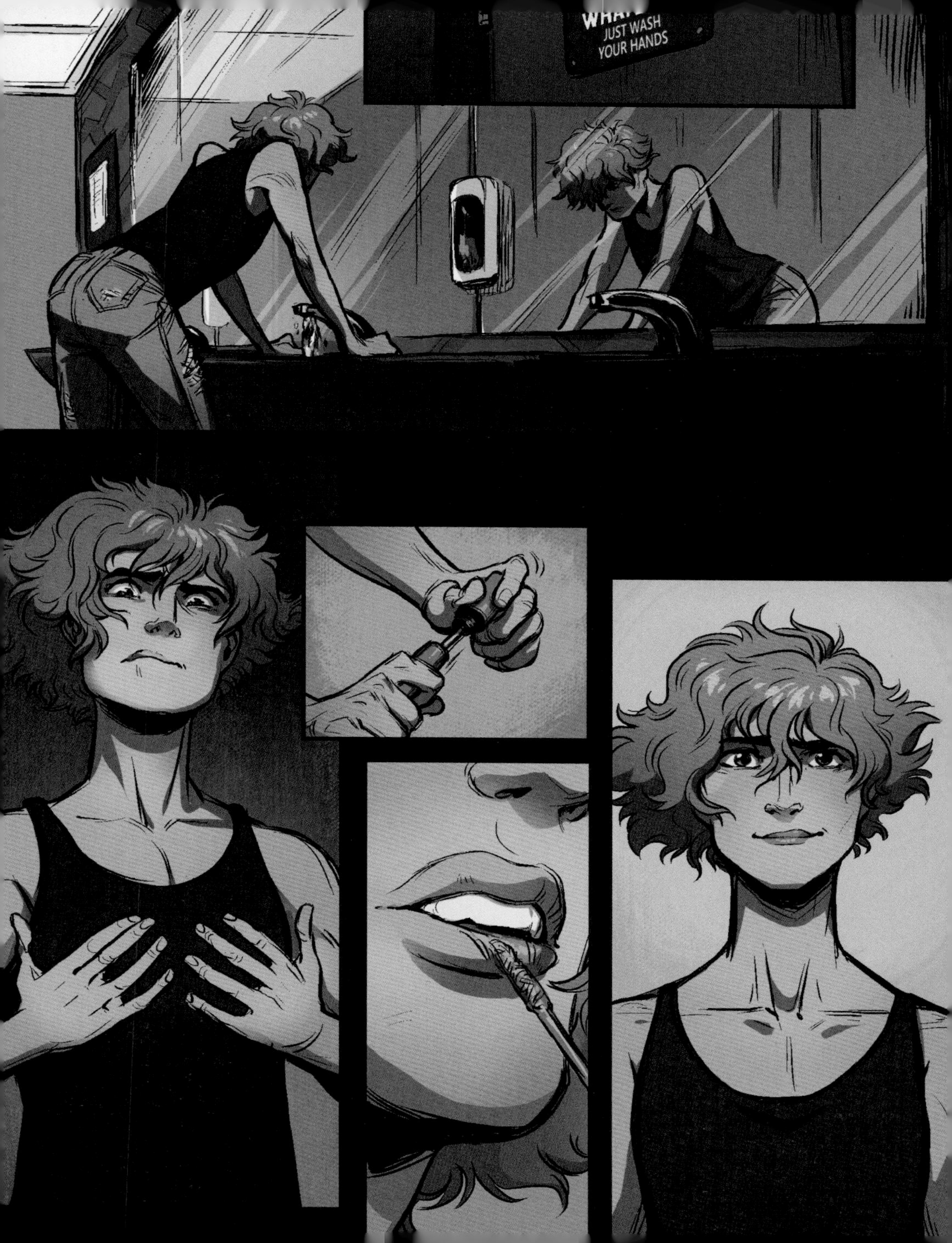
JUST WASH
YOUR HANDS

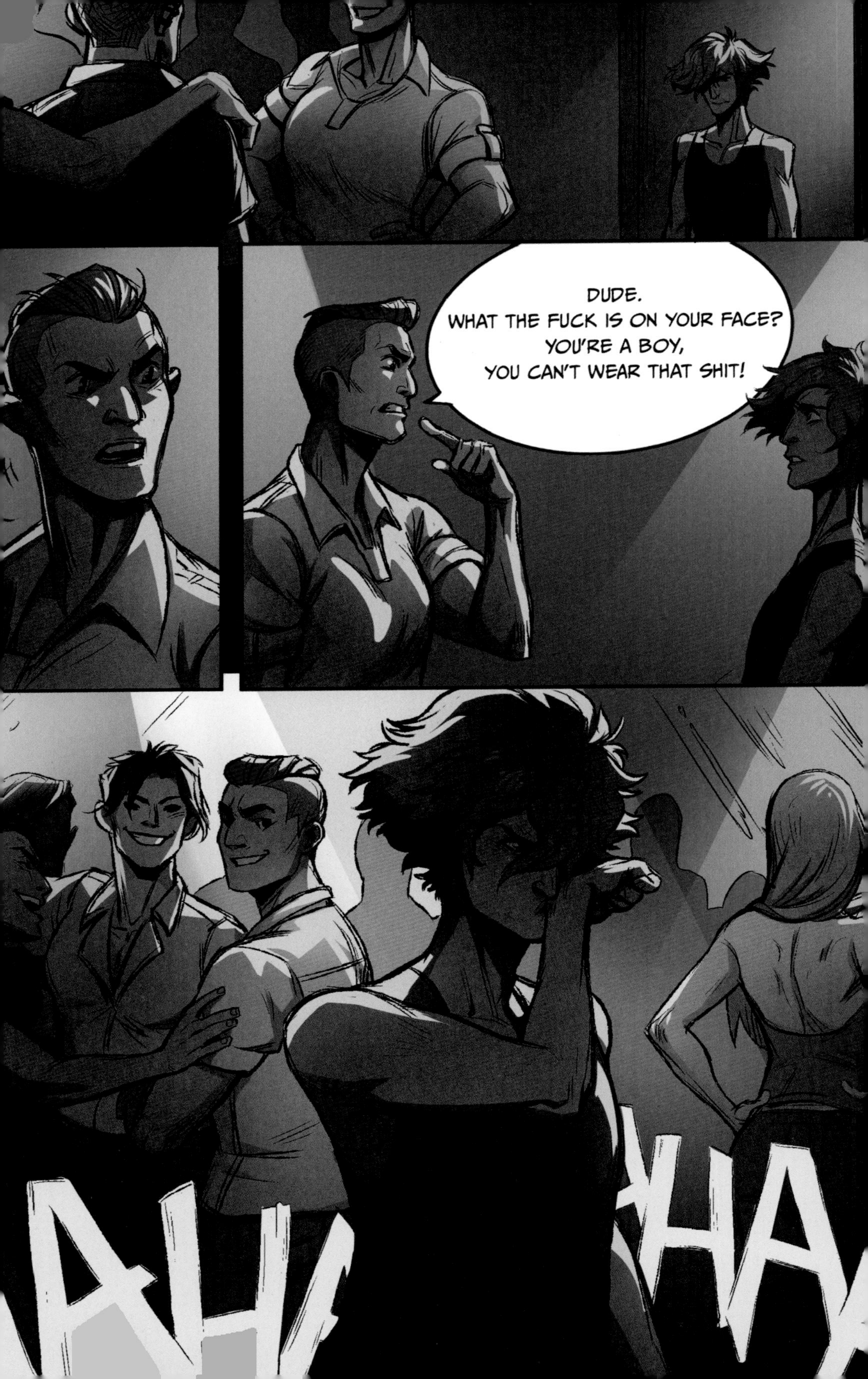
DUDE.
WHAT THE FUCK IS ON YOUR FACE?
YOU'RE A BOY,
YOU CAN'T WEAR THAT SHIT!

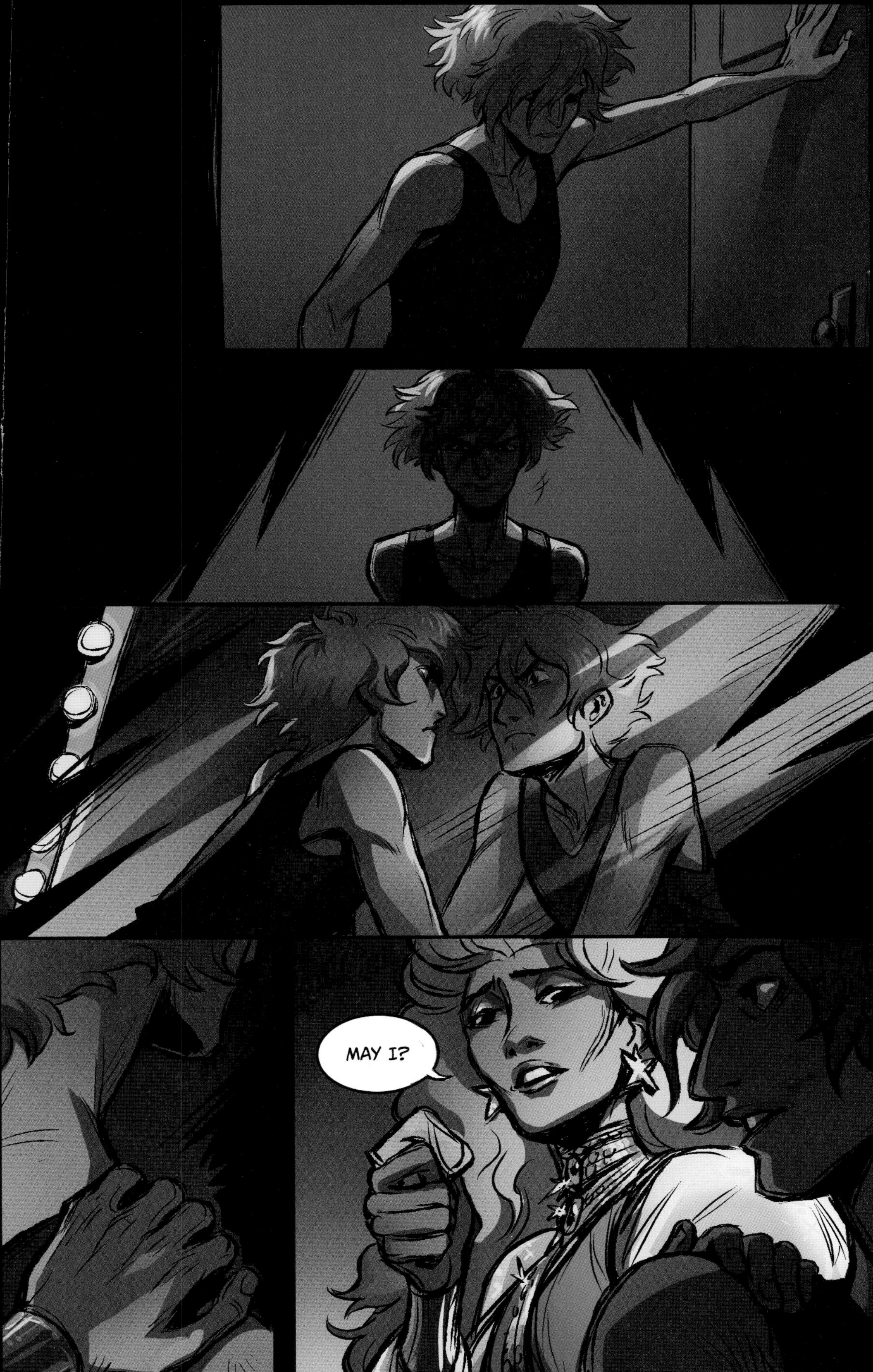
MAY I?

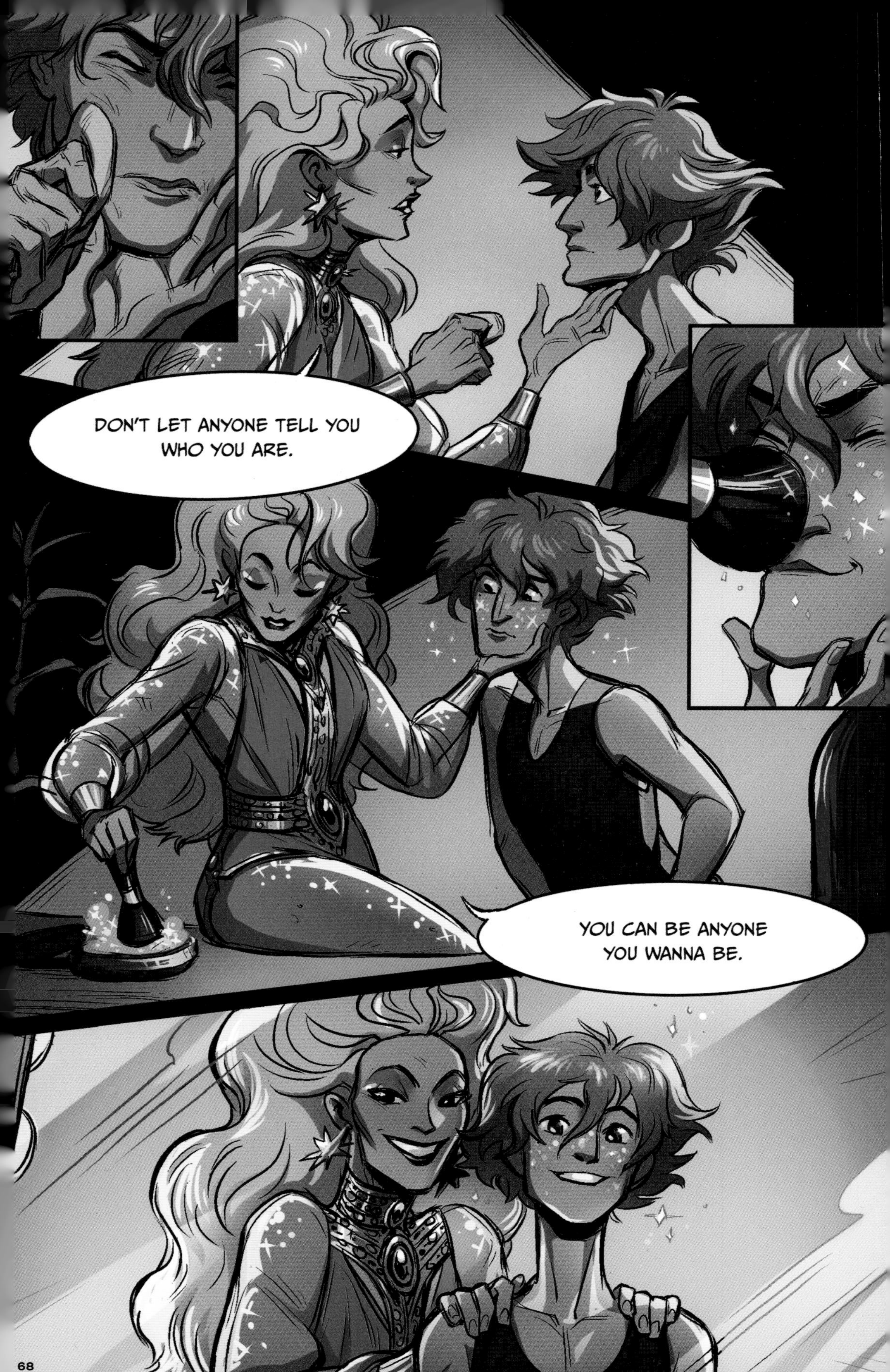
DON'T LET ANYONE TELL YOU WHO YOU ARE.
YOU CAN BE ANYONE YOU WANNA BE.

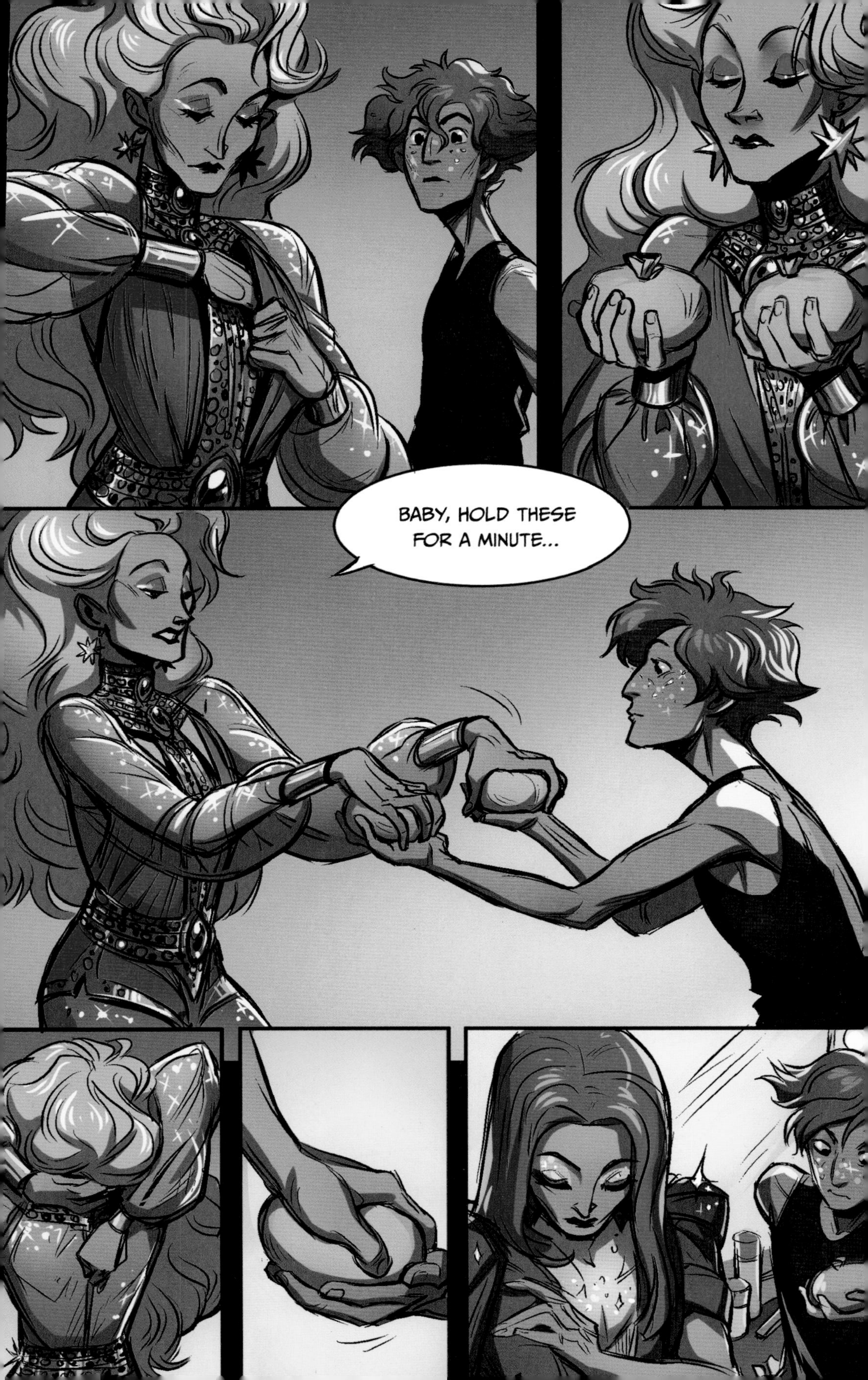
BABY, HOLD THESE
FOR A MINUTE...

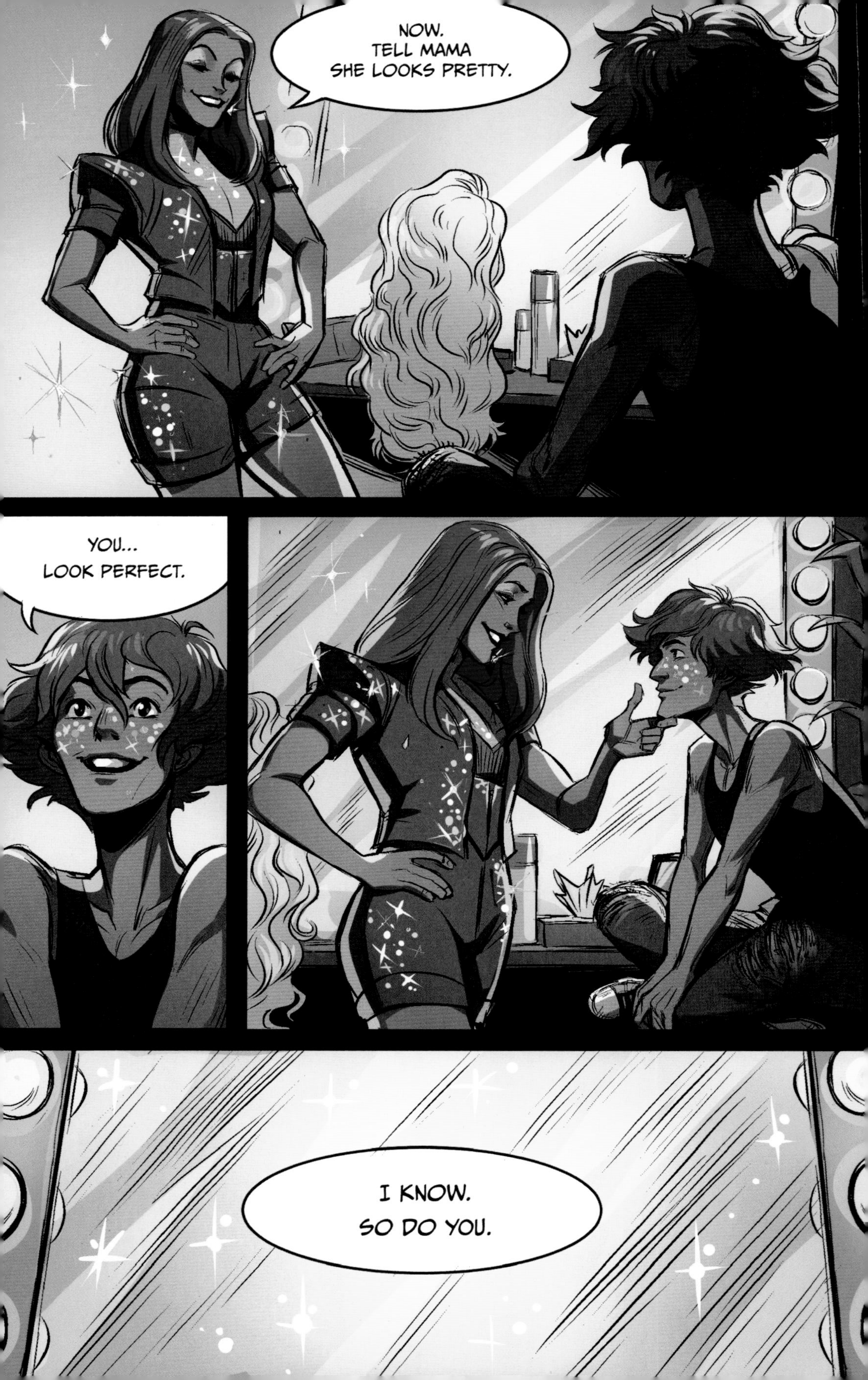
NOW.
TELL MAMA
SHE LOOKS PRETTY.
YOU...
LOOK PERFECT.
I KNOW.
SO DO YOU.

ALWAYS

"HOLLOW WOLF"

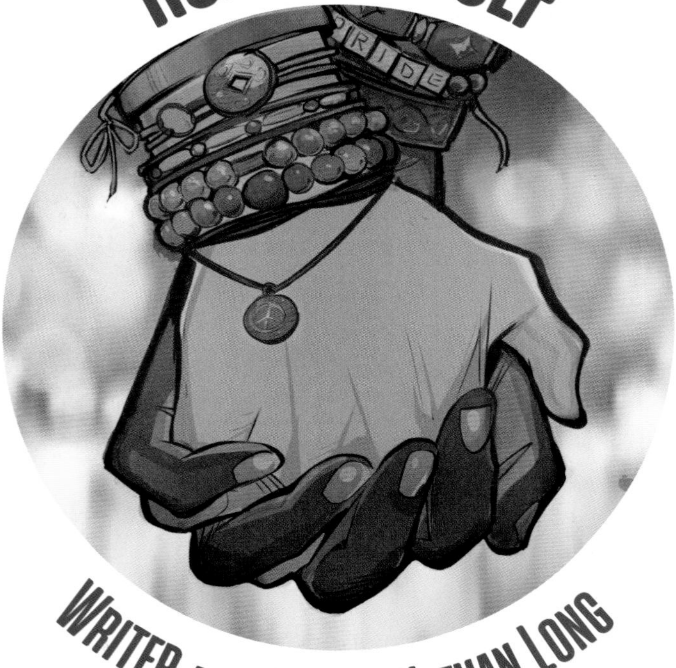
RIDE

WRITER AND ARTIST-NATHAN LONG

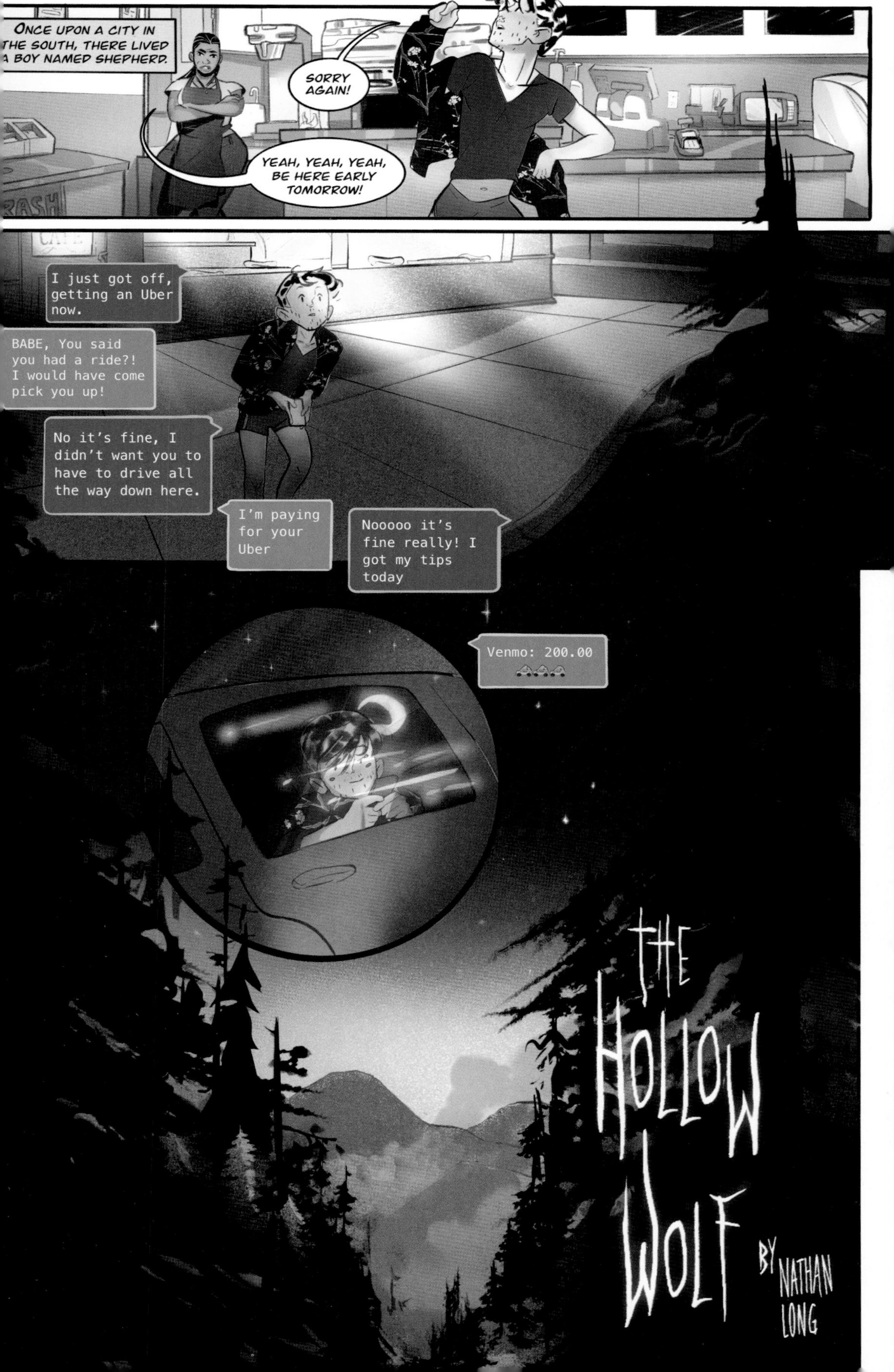
ONCE UPON A CITY IN THE SOUTH, THERE LIVED A BOY NAMED SHEPHERD.
SORRY AGAIN!
YEAH, YEAH, YEAH, BE HERE EARLY TOMORROW!
I just got off, getting an Uber now.
BABE, You said you had a ride?! I would have come pick you up!
No it's fine, I didn't want you to have to drive all the way down here.
I'm paying for your Uber
Nooooo it's fine really! I got my tips today
Venmo: 200.00
THE HOLLOW WOLF
BY NATHAN LONG

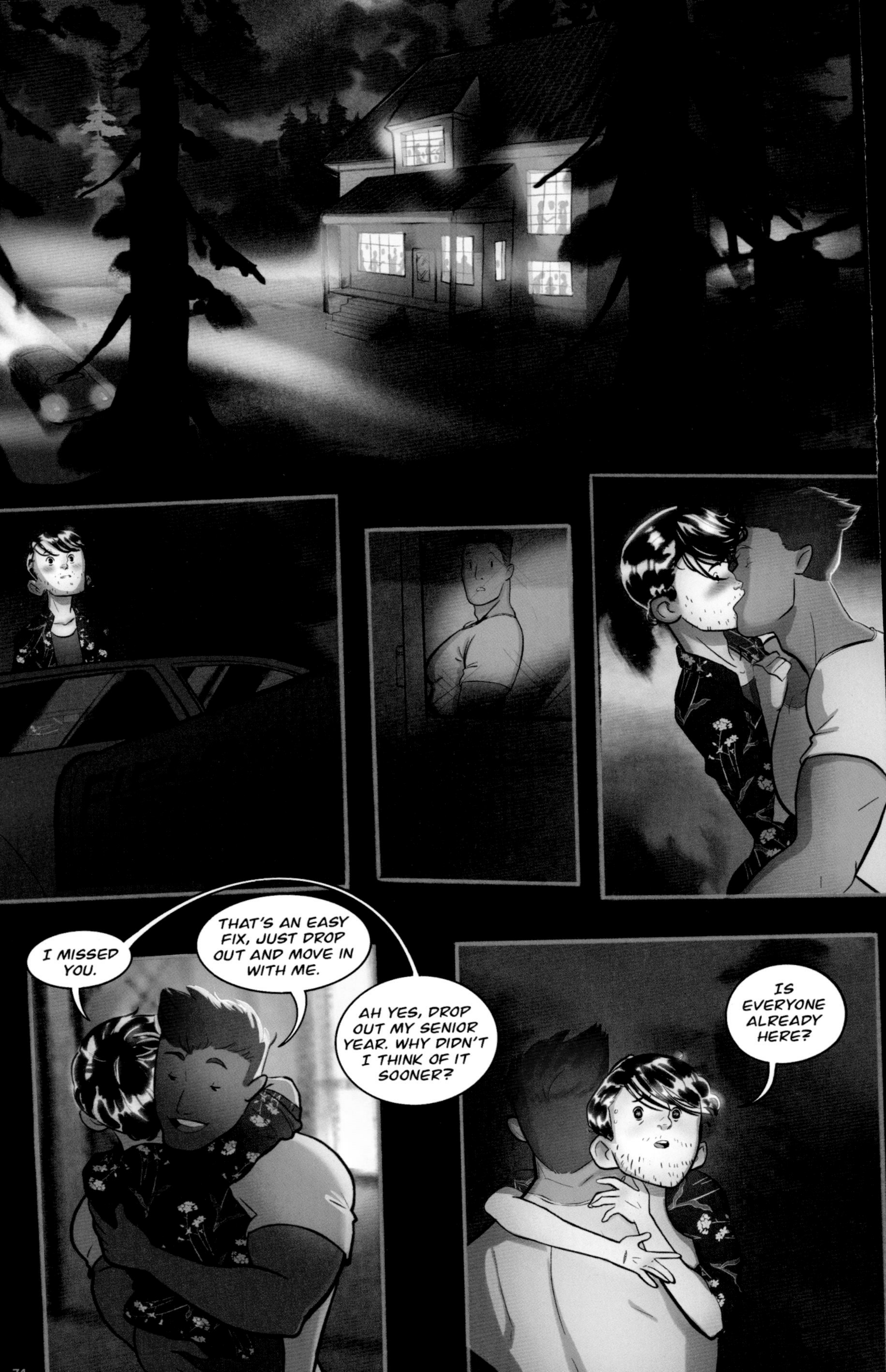
I MISSED YOU.
THAT'S AN EASY FIX, JUST DROP OUT AND MOVE IN WITH ME.
AH YES, DROP OUT MY SENIOR YEAR. WHY DIDN'T I THINK OF IT SOONER?
IS EVERYONE ALREADY HERE?

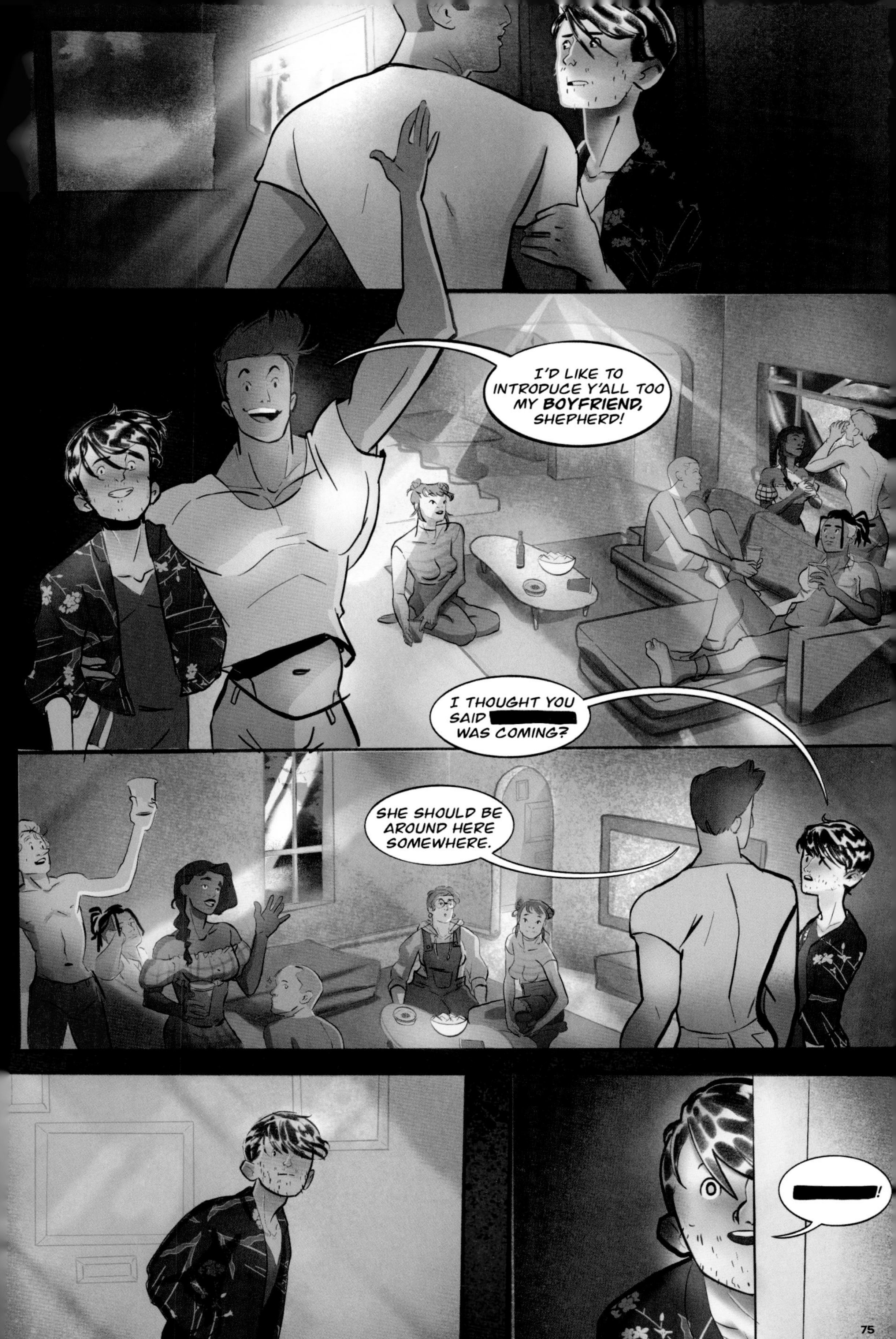
I'D LIKE TO INTRODUCE Y'ALL TOO MY **BOYFRIEND,** SHEPHERD!
I THOUGHT YOU SAID [redacted] WAS COMING?
SHE SHOULD BE AROUND HERE SOMEWHERE.
[redacted]!

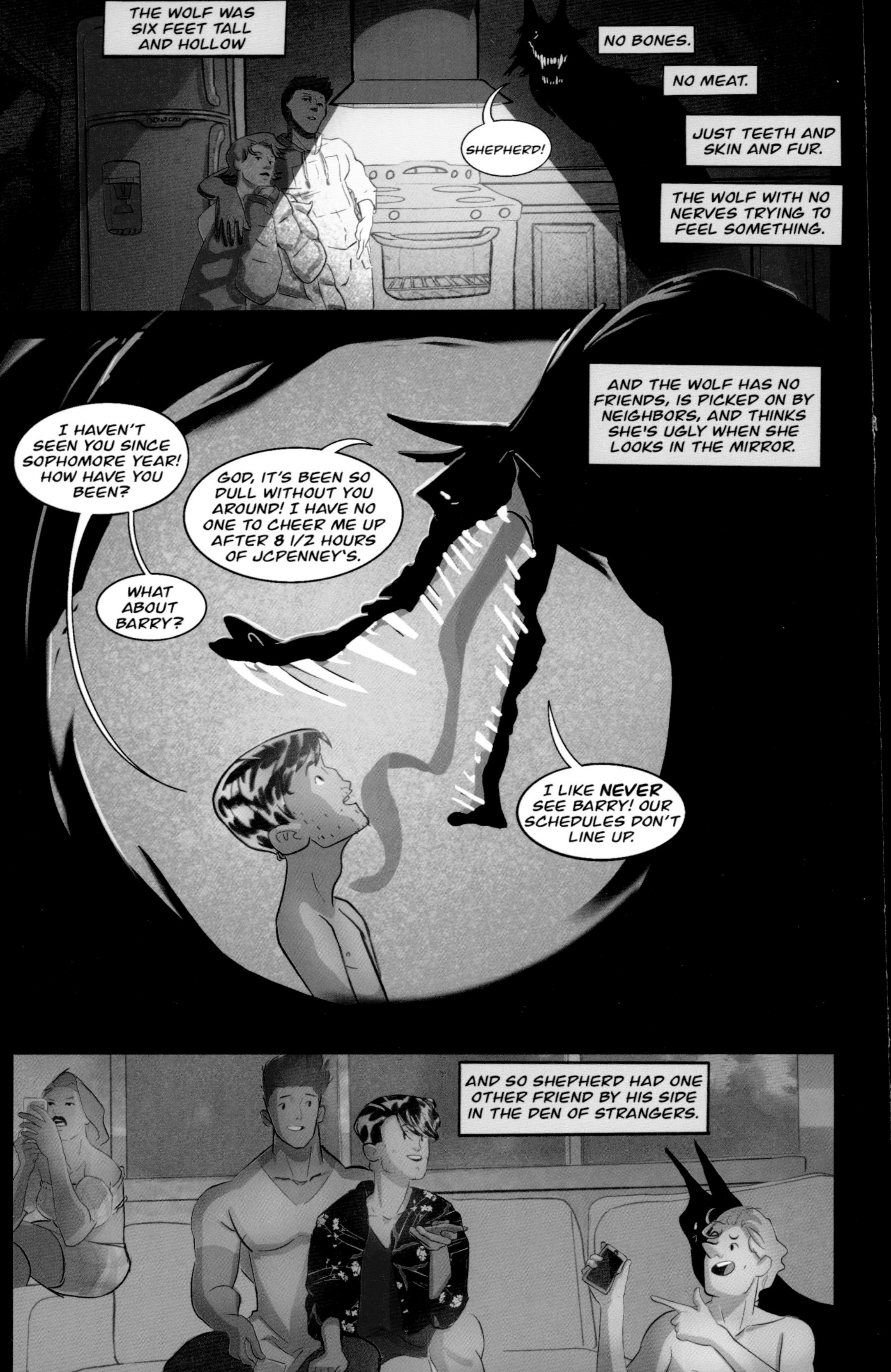
THE WOLF WAS SIX FEET TALL AND HOLLOW
NO BONES.
NO MEAT.
JUST TEETH AND SKIN AND FUR.
THE WOLF WITH NO NERVES TRYING TO FEEL SOMETHING.
SHEPHERD!
AND THE WOLF HAS NO FRIENDS, IS PICKED ON BY NEIGHBORS, AND THINKS SHE'S UGLY WHEN SHE LOOKS IN THE MIRROR.
I HAVEN'T SEEN YOU SINCE SOPHOMORE YEAR! HOW HAVE YOU BEEN?
GOD, IT'S BEEN SO DULL WITHOUT YOU AROUND! I HAVE NO ONE TO CHEER ME UP AFTER 8 1/2 HOURS OF JCPENNEY'S.
WHAT ABOUT BARRY?
I LIKE **NEVER** SEE BARRY! OUR SCHEDULES DON'T LINE UP.
AND SO SHEPHERD HAD ONE OTHER FRIEND BY HIS SIDE IN THE DEN OF STRANGERS.

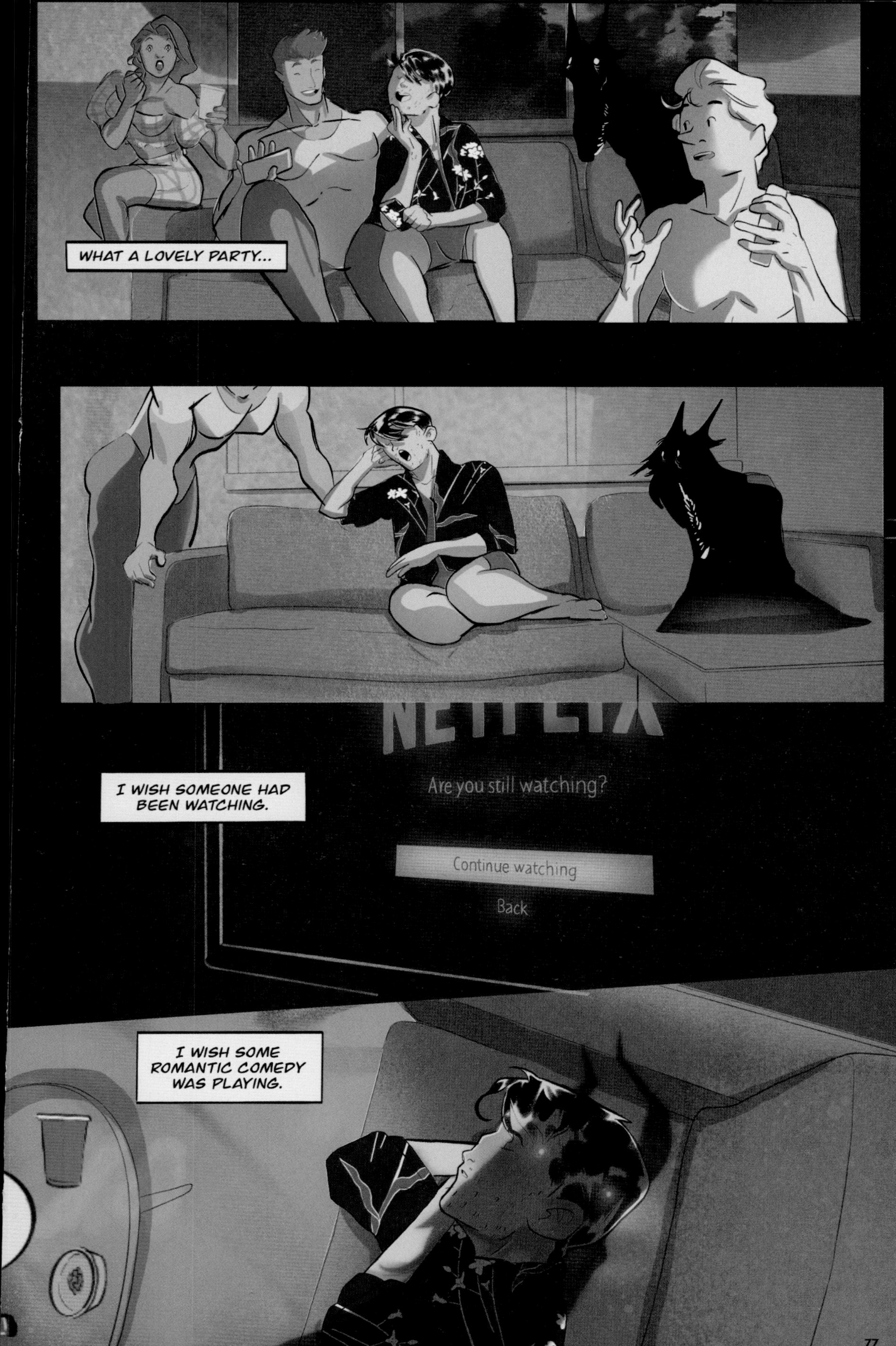
WHAT A LOVELY PARTY...
I WISH SOMEONE HAD BEEN WATCHING.
Are you still watching?
Continue watching
Back
I WISH SOME ROMANTIC COMEDY WAS PLAYING.

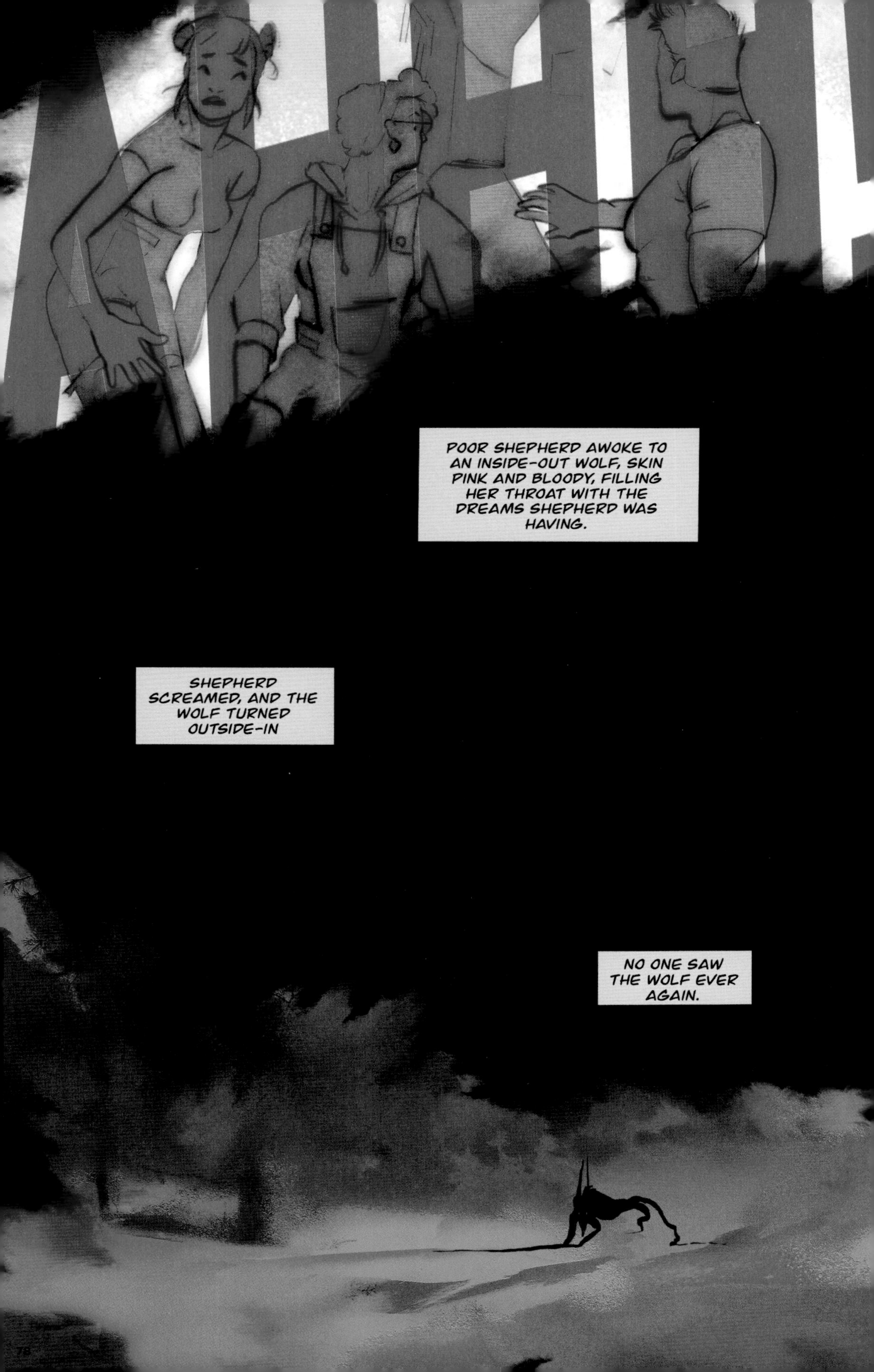
POOR SHEPHERD AWOKE TO AN INSIDE-OUT WOLF, SKIN PINK AND BLOODY, FILLING HER THROAT WITH THE DREAMS SHEPHERD WAS HAVING.
SHEPHERD SCREAMED, AND THE WOLF TURNED OUTSIDE-IN
NO ONE SAW THE WOLF EVER AGAIN.

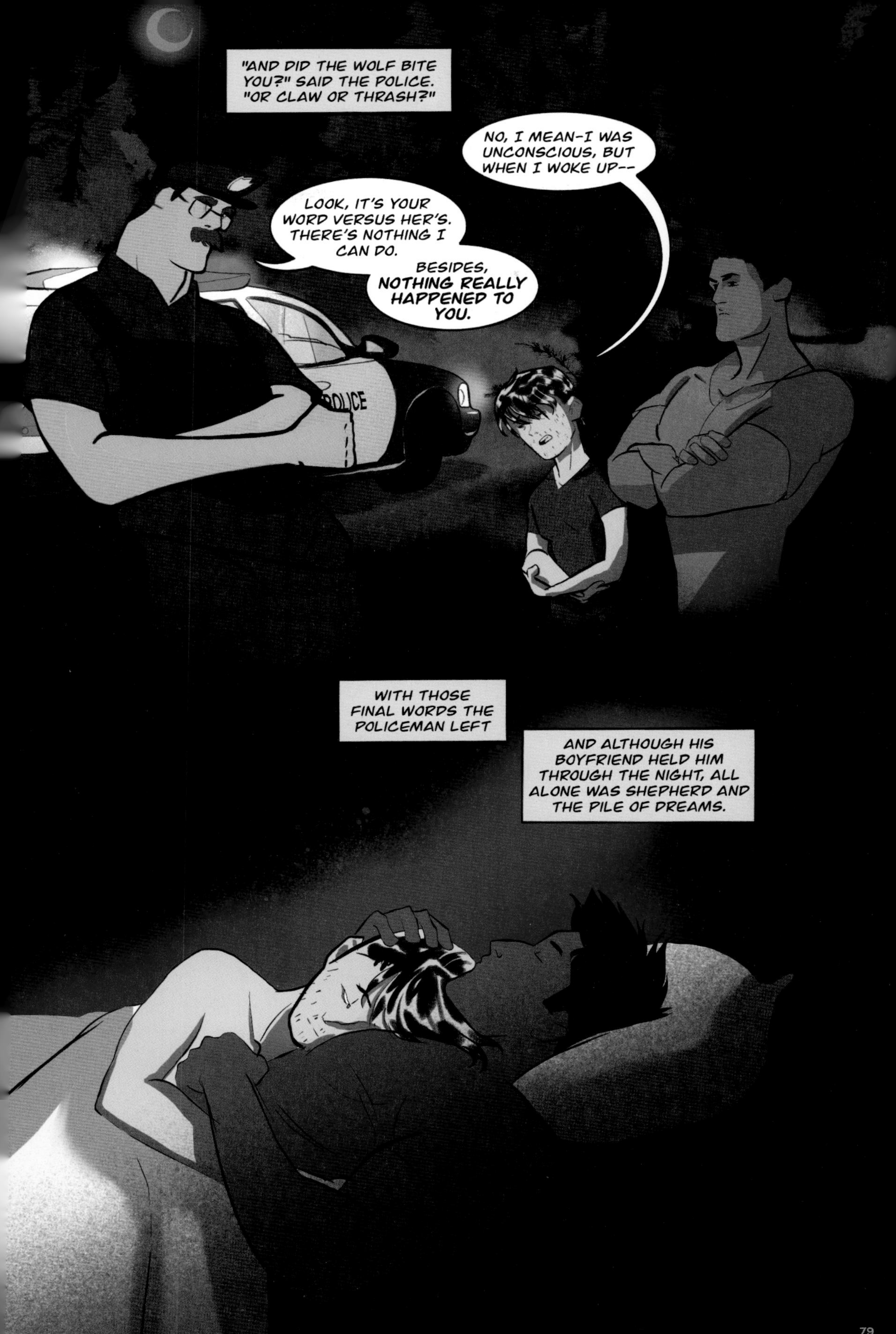
"AND DID THE WOLF BITE YOU?" SAID THE POLICE. "OR CLAW OR THRASH?"
NO, I MEAN-I WAS UNCONSCIOUS, BUT WHEN I WOKE UP--
LOOK, IT'S YOUR WORD VERSUS HER'S. THERE'S NOTHING I CAN DO.
BESIDES, NOTHING REALLY HAPPENED TO YOU.
POLICE
WITH THOSE FINAL WORDS THE POLICEMAN LEFT
AND ALTHOUGH HIS BOYFRIEND HELD HIM THROUGH THE NIGHT, ALL ALONE WAS SHEPHERD AND THE PILE OF DREAMS.

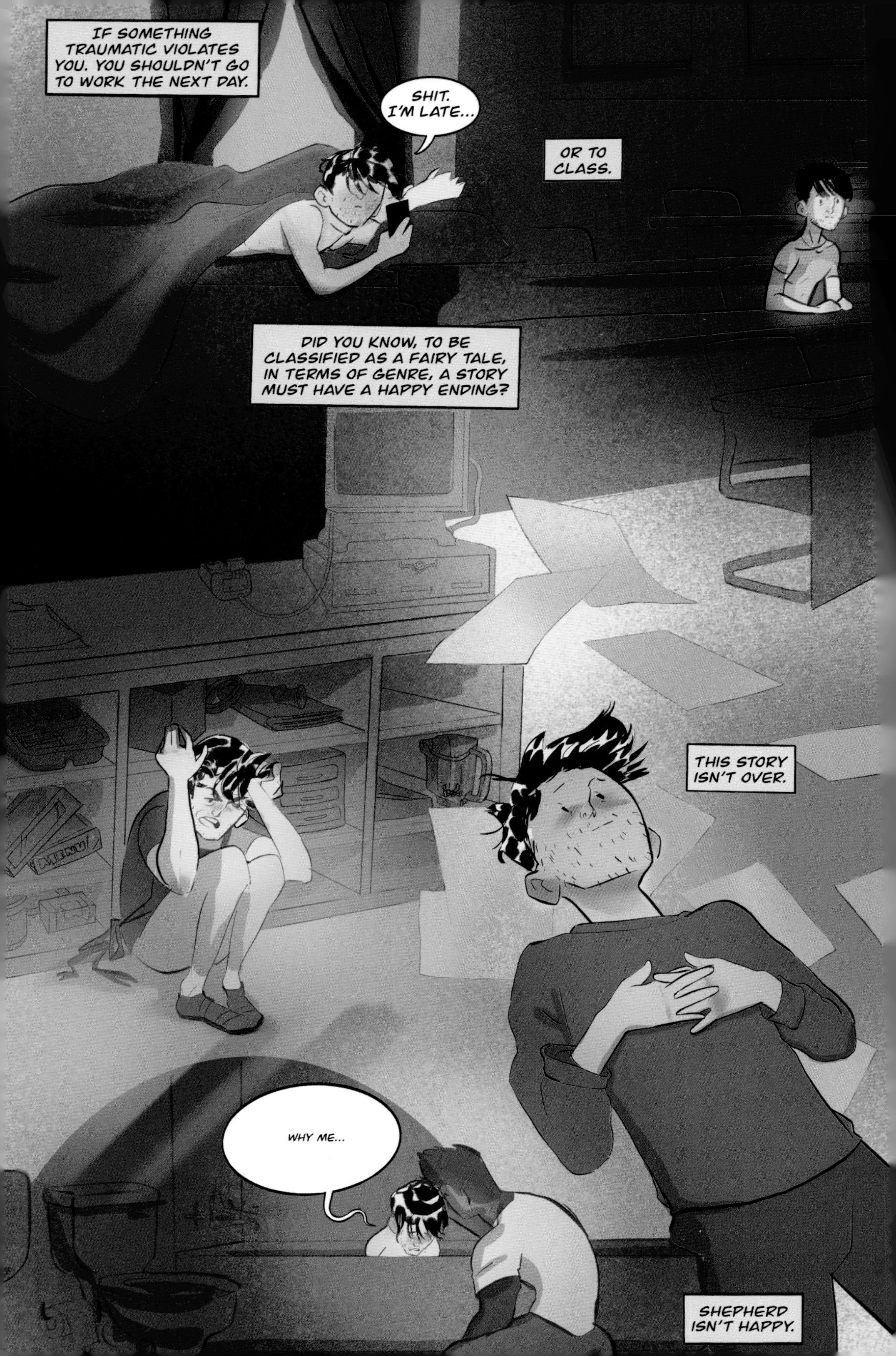
IF SOMETHING TRAUMATIC VIOLATES YOU. YOU SHOULDN'T GO TO WORK THE NEXT DAY.
SHIT. I'M LATE...
OR TO CLASS.
DID YOU KNOW, TO BE CLASSIFIED AS A FAIRY TALE, IN TERMS OF GENRE, A STORY MUST HAVE A HAPPY ENDING?
MENU
THIS STORY ISN'T OVER.
WHY ME...
SHEPHERD ISN'T HAPPY.

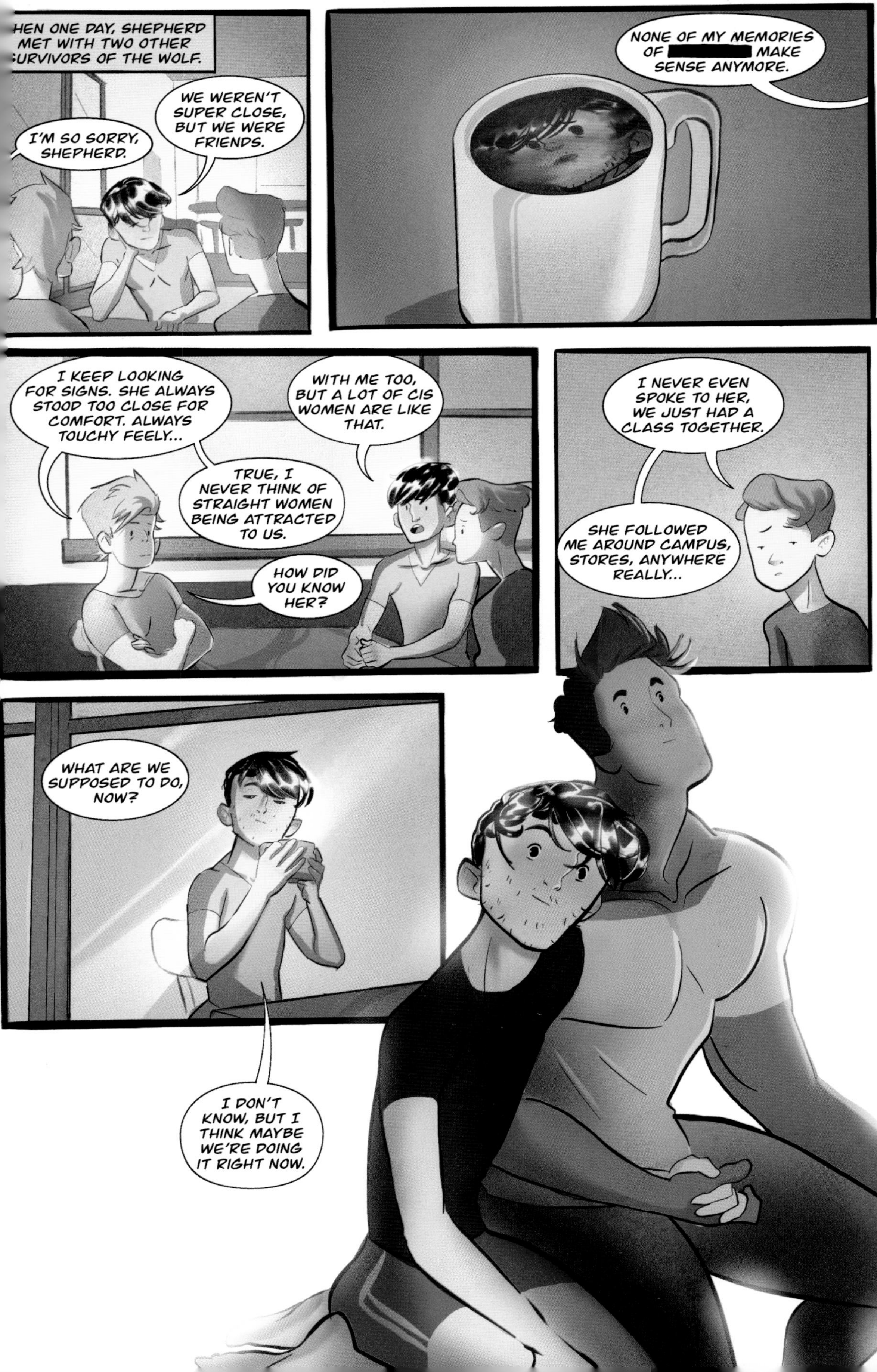
HEN ONE DAY, SHEPHERD MET WITH TWO OTHER URVIVORS OF THE WOLF.
I'M SO SORRY, SHEPHERD.
WE WEREN'T SUPER CLOSE, BUT WE WERE FRIENDS.
NONE OF MY MEMORIES OF [redacted] MAKE SENSE ANYMORE.
I KEEP LOOKING FOR SIGNS. SHE ALWAYS STOOD TOO CLOSE FOR COMFORT. ALWAYS TOUCHY FEELY...
TRUE, I NEVER THINK OF STRAIGHT WOMEN BEING ATTRACTED TO US.
WITH ME TOO, BUT A LOT OF CIS WOMEN ARE LIKE THAT.
HOW DID YOU KNOW HER?
I NEVER EVEN SPOKE TO HER, WE JUST HAD A CLASS TOGETHER.
SHE FOLLOWED ME AROUND CAMPUS, STORES, ANYWHERE REALLY...
WHAT ARE WE SUPPOSED TO DO, NOW?
I DON'T KNOW, BUT I THINK MAYBE WE'RE DOING IT RIGHT NOW.

"EXTRA PAGES"

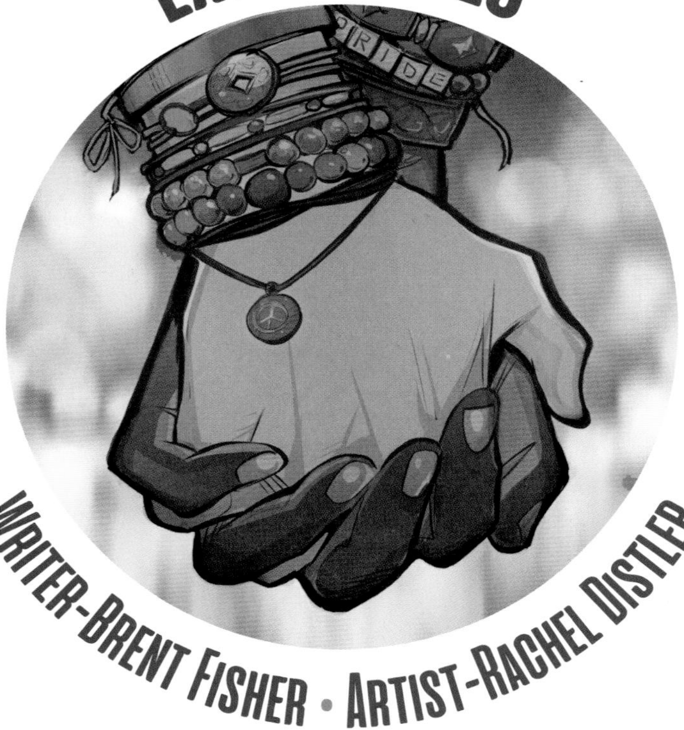
RIDE

WRITER-BRENT FISHER • ARTIST-RACHEL DISTLER

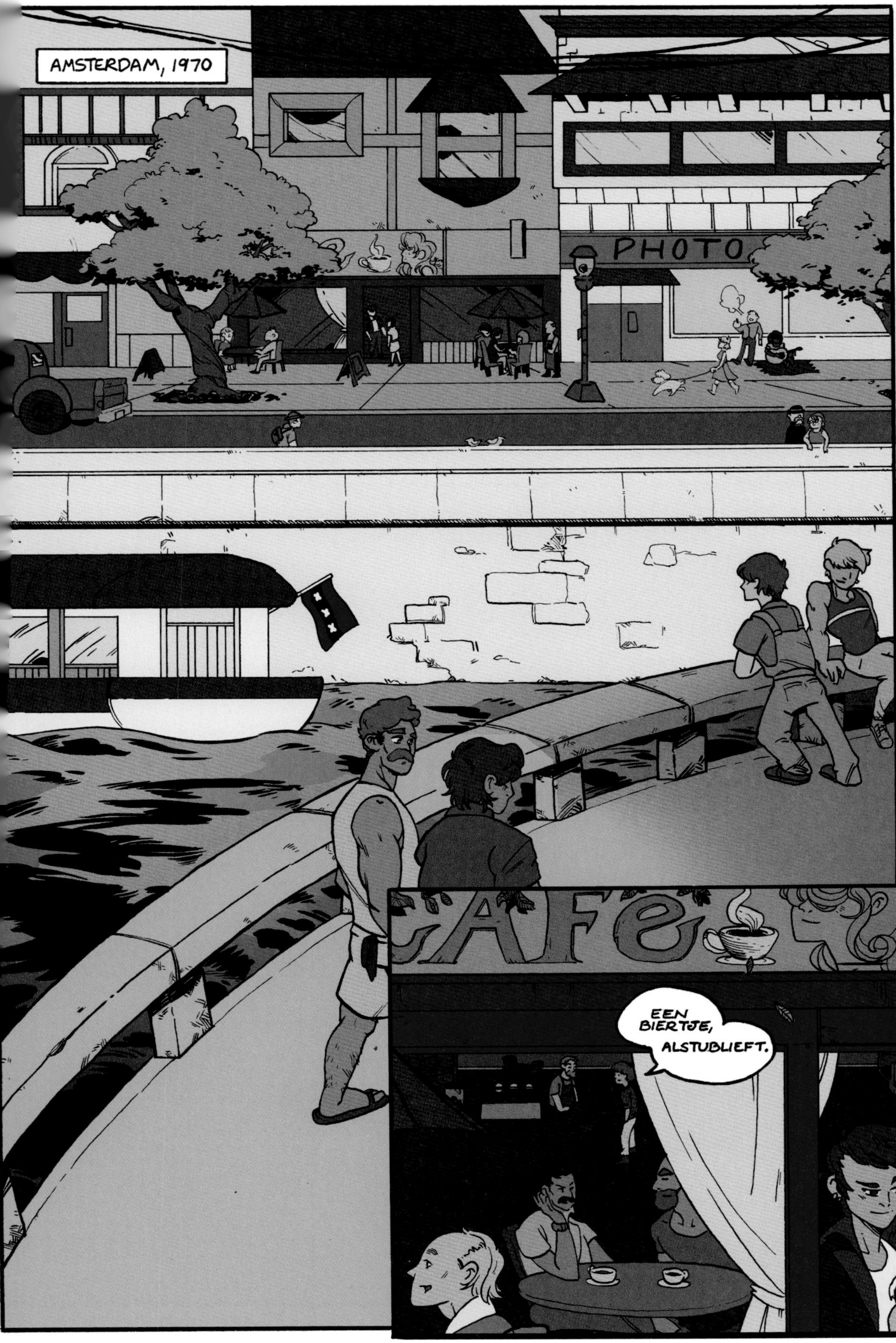
AMSTERDAM, 1970
PHOTO
CAFE
EEN BIERTJE, ALSTUBLIEFT.

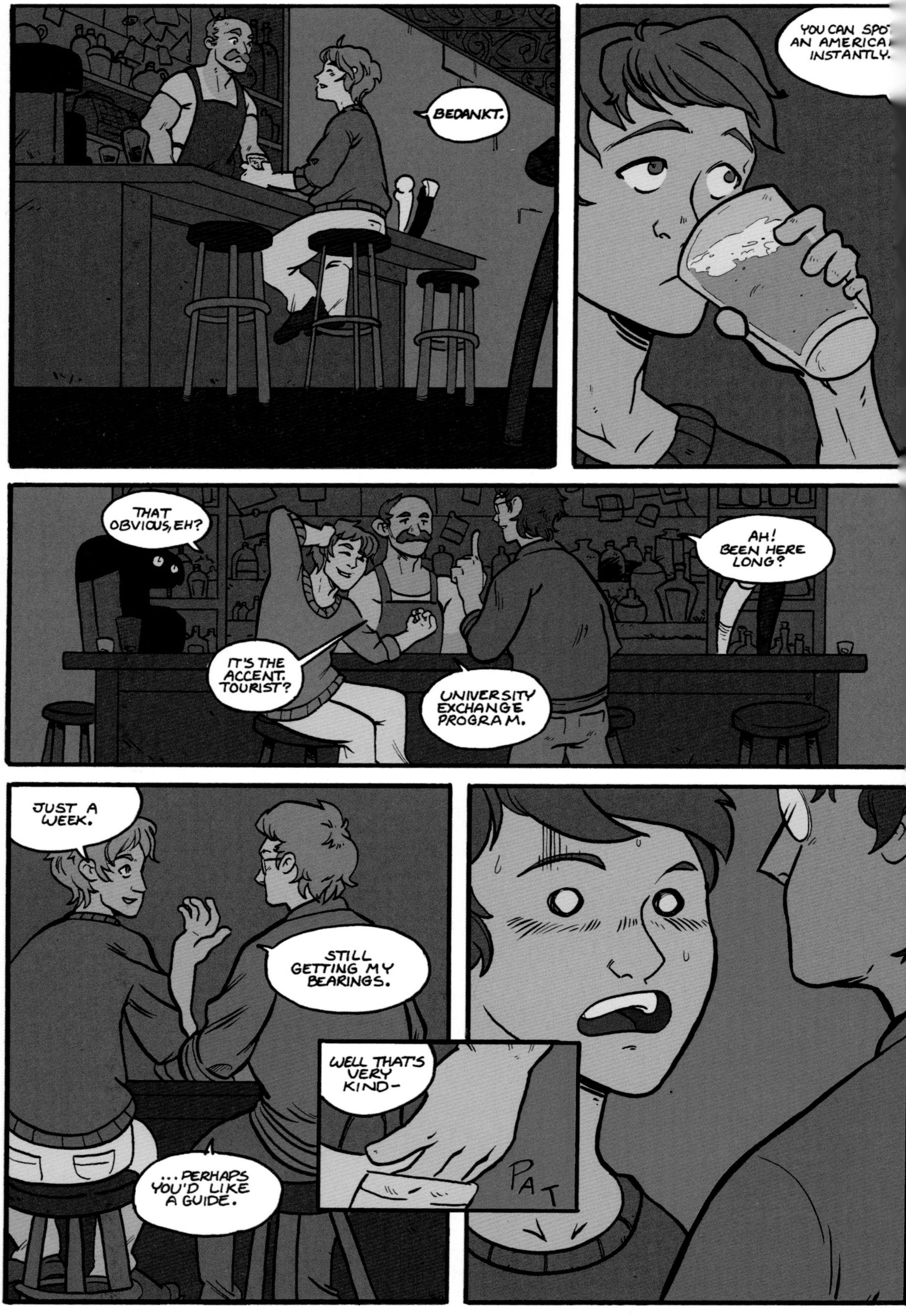
BEDANKT.
YOU CAN SPOT AN AMERICA INSTANTLY.
THAT OBVIOUS, EH?
IT'S THE ACCENT. TOURIST?
AH! BEEN HERE LONG?
UNIVERSITY EXCHANGE PROGRAM.
JUST A WEEK.
STILL GETTING MY BEARINGS.
...PERHAPS YOU'D LIKE A GUIDE.
WELL THAT'S VERY KIND-
PAT

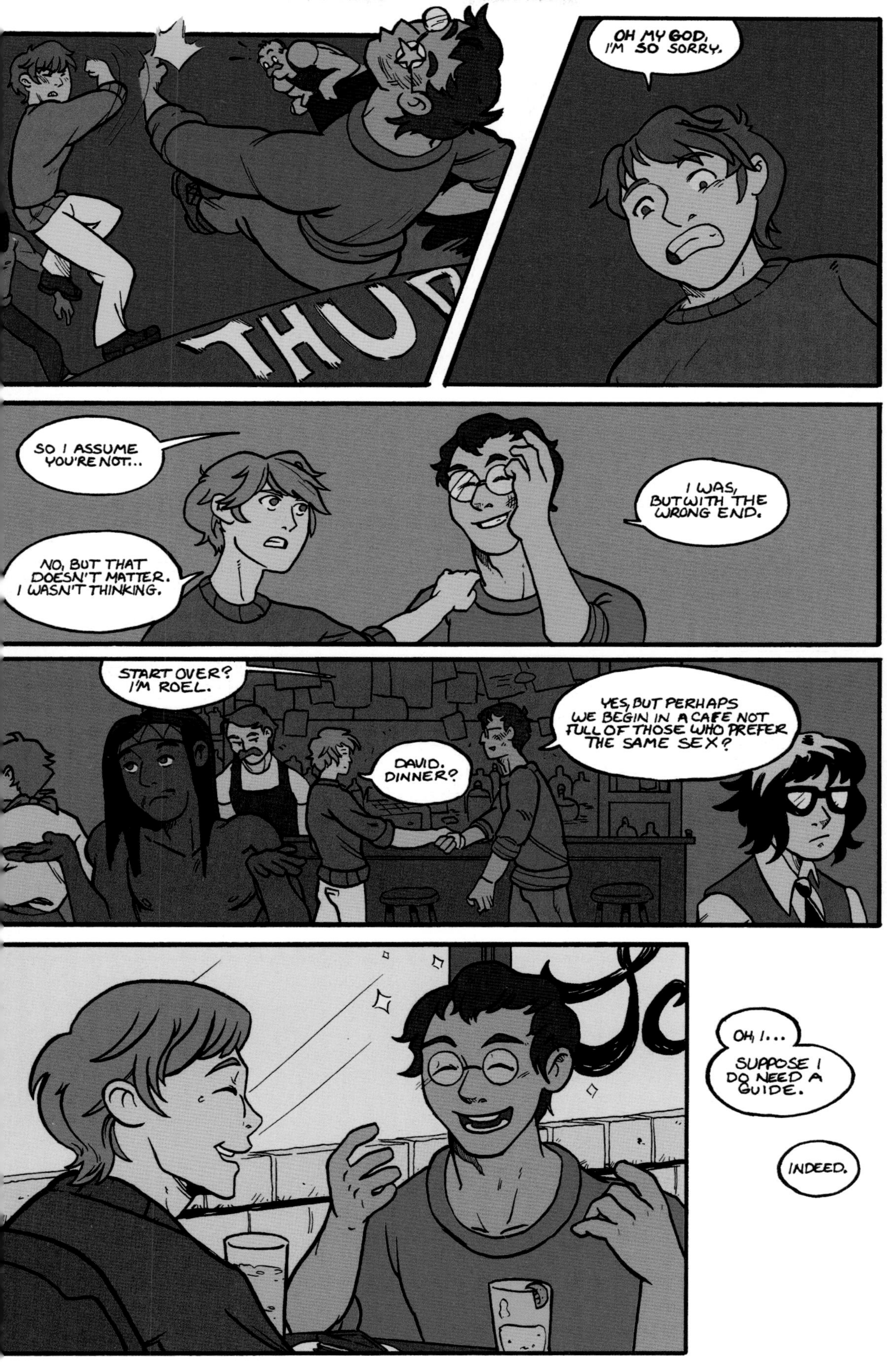
THUD
OH MY GOD, I'M SO SORRY.
SO I ASSUME YOU'RE NOT...
I WAS, BUT WITH THE WRONG END.
NO, BUT THAT DOESN'T MATTER. I WASN'T THINKING.
START OVER? I'M ROEL.
DAVID. DINNER?
YES, BUT PERHAPS WE BEGIN IN A CAFE NOT FULL OF THOSE WHO PREFER THE SAME SEX?
OH, I...
SUPPOSE I DO NEED A GUIDE.
INDEED.

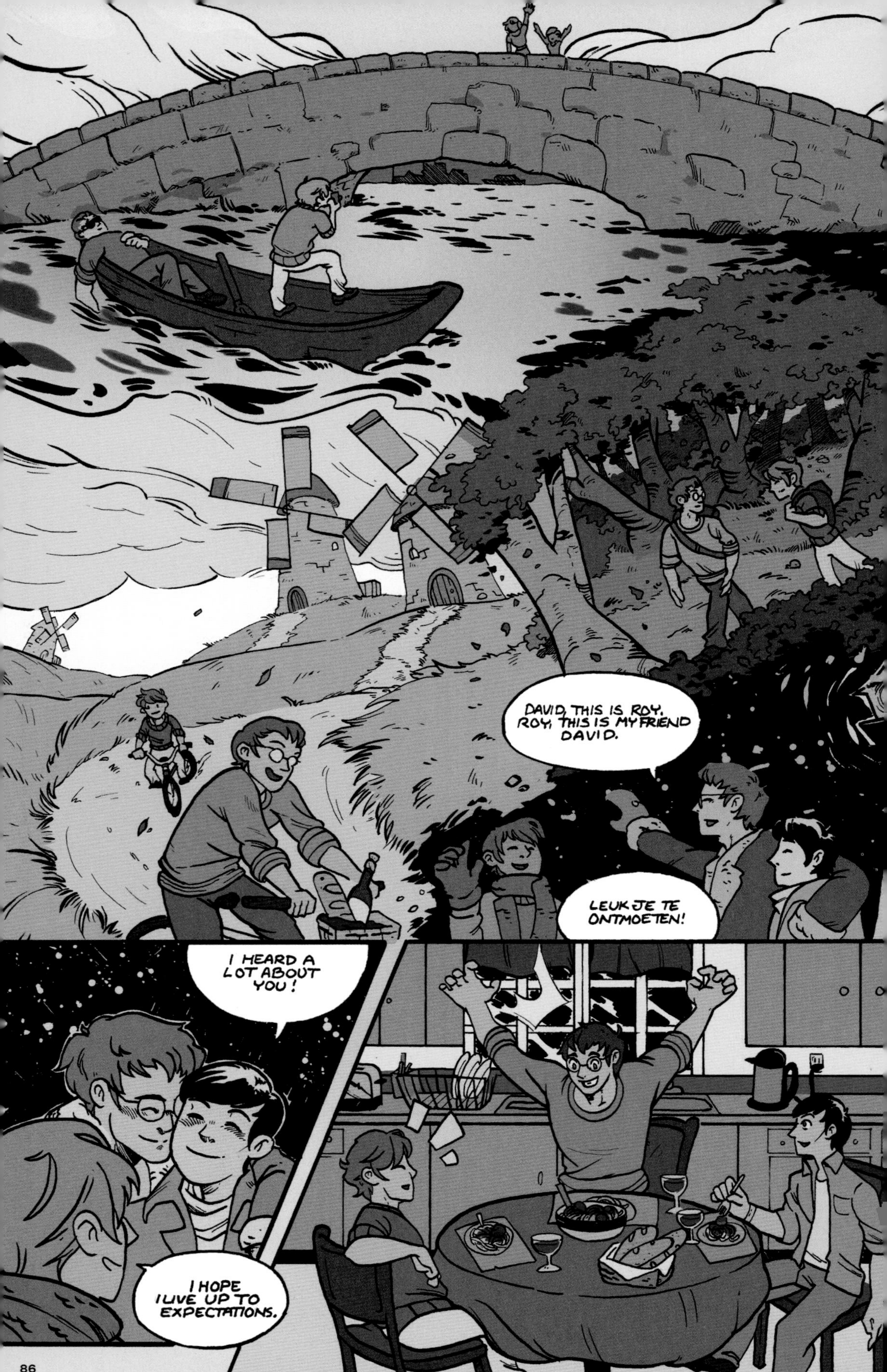
DAVID, THIS IS ROY. ROY, THIS IS MY FRIEND DAVID.
LEUK JE TE ONTMOETEN!
I HEARD A LOT ABOUT YOU!
I HOPE I LIVE UP TO EXPECTATIONS.

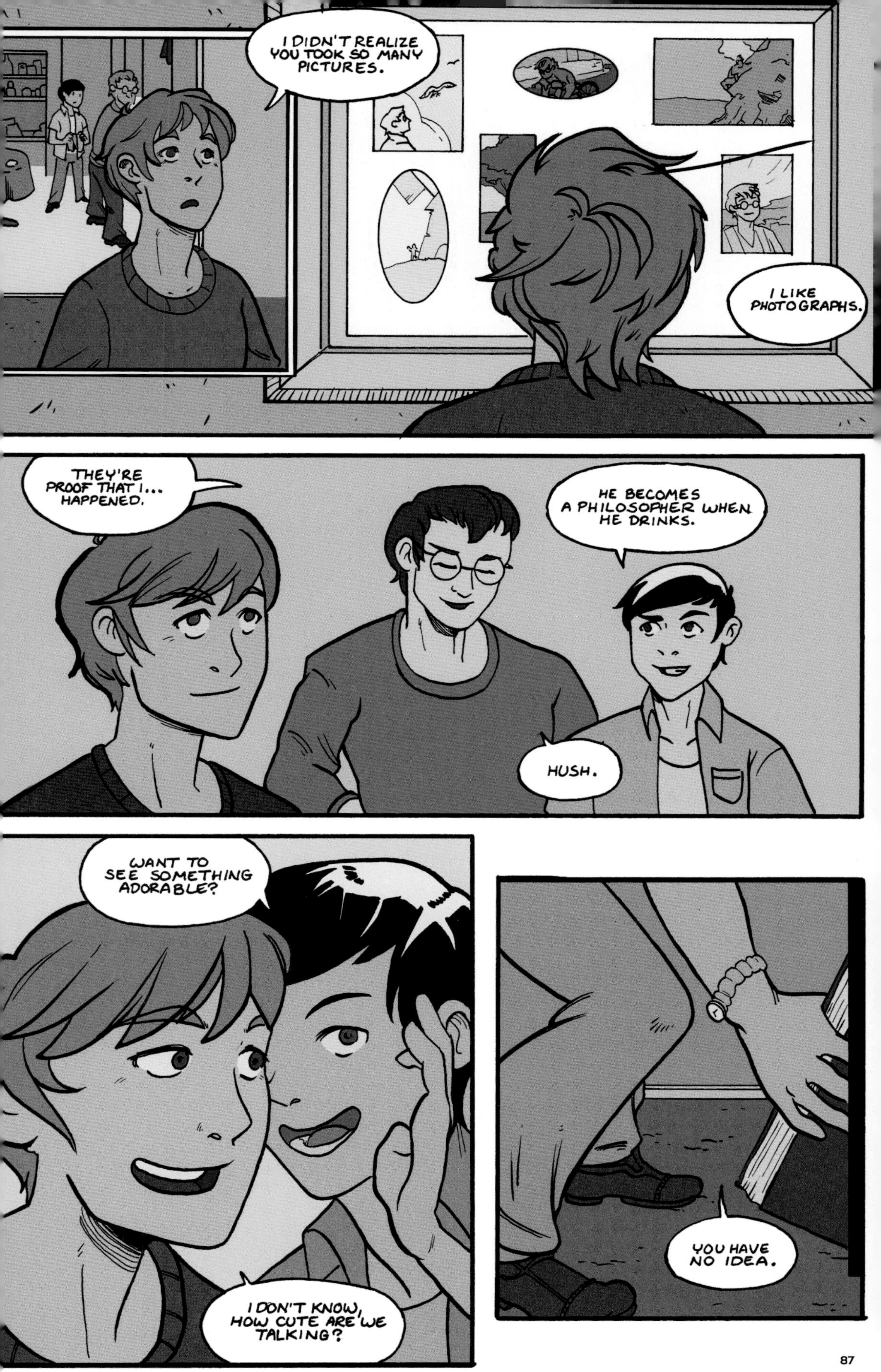

I DIDN'T REALIZE YOU TOOK SO MANY PICTURES.
I LIKE PHOTOGRAPHS.
THEY'RE PROOF THAT I... HAPPENED.
HE BECOMES A PHILOSOPHER WHEN HE DRINKS.
HUSH.
WANT TO SEE SOMETHING ADORABLE?
I DON'T KNOW, HOW CUTE ARE WE TALKING?
YOU HAVE NO IDEA.

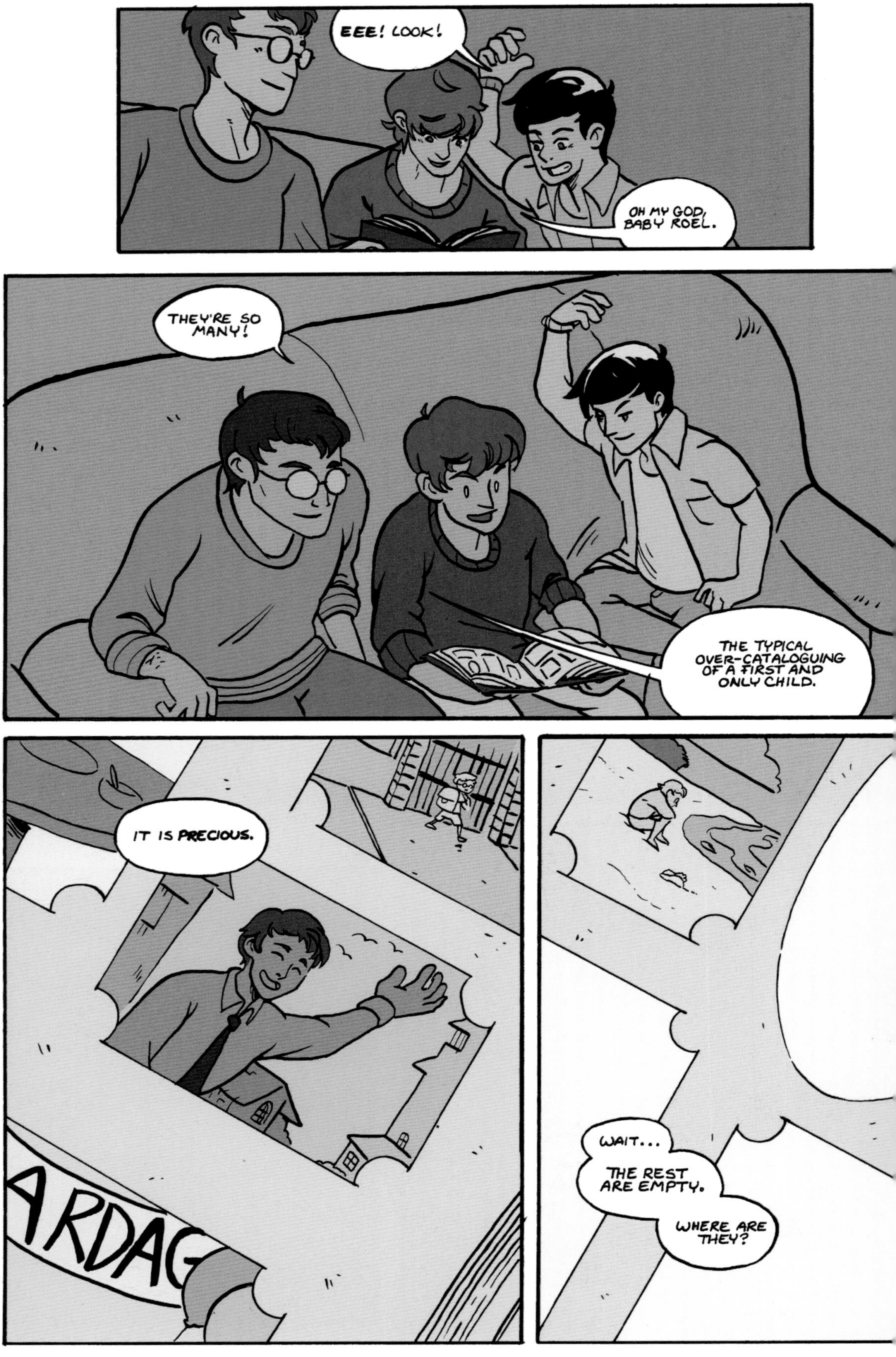
EEE! LOOK!
OH MY GOD, BABY ROEL.
THEY'RE SO MANY!
THE TYPICAL OVER-CATALOGUING OF A FIRST AND ONLY CHILD.
IT IS PRECIOUS.
ARDAG
WAIT...
THE REST ARE EMPTY.
WHERE ARE THEY?

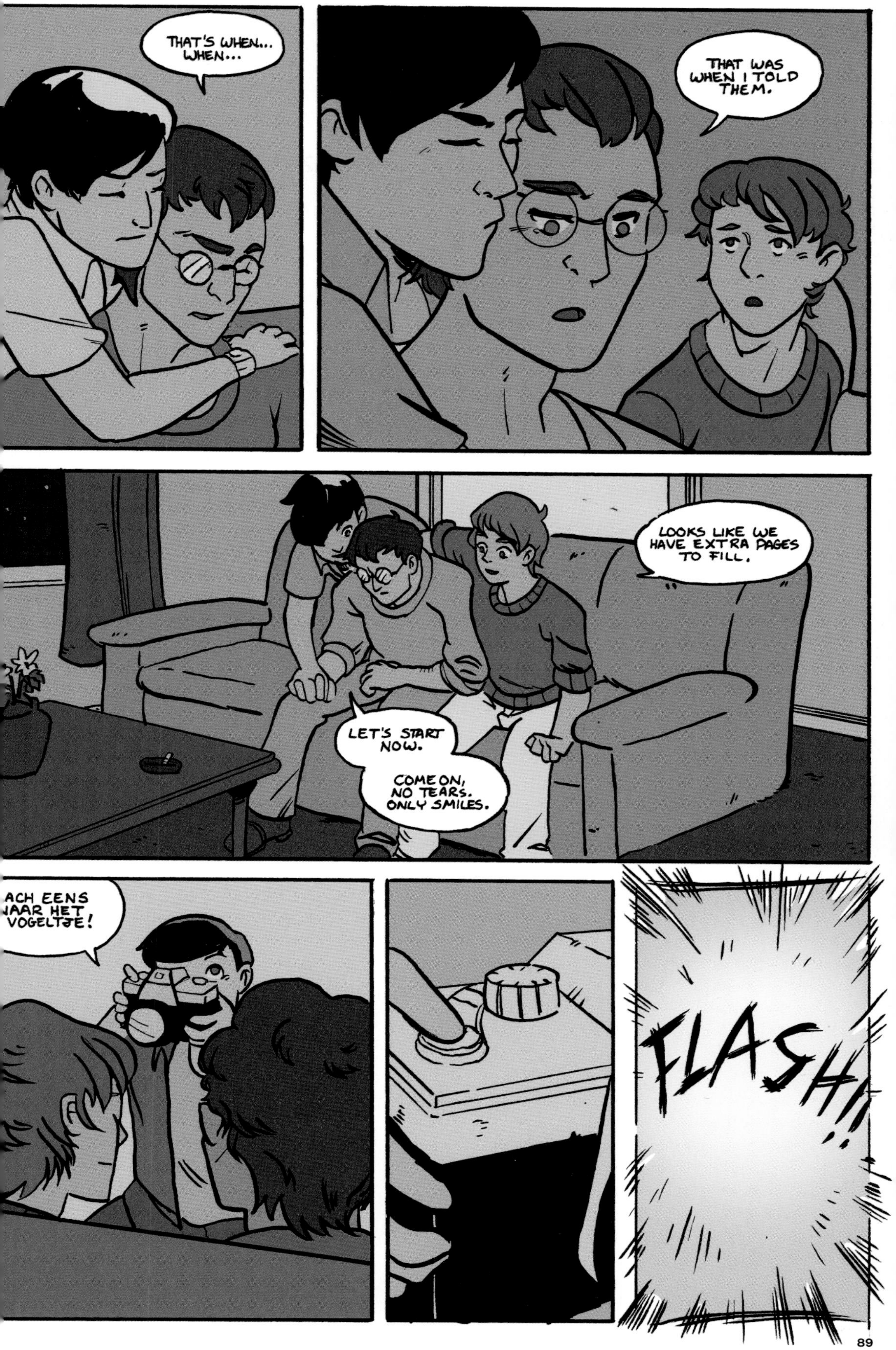

THAT'S WHEN... WHEN...
THAT WAS WHEN I TOLD THEM.
LOOKS LIKE WE HAVE EXTRA PAGES TO FILL.
LET'S START NOW.
COME ON, NO TEARS. ONLY SMILES.
ACH EENS NAAR HET VOGELTJE!
FLASH!!

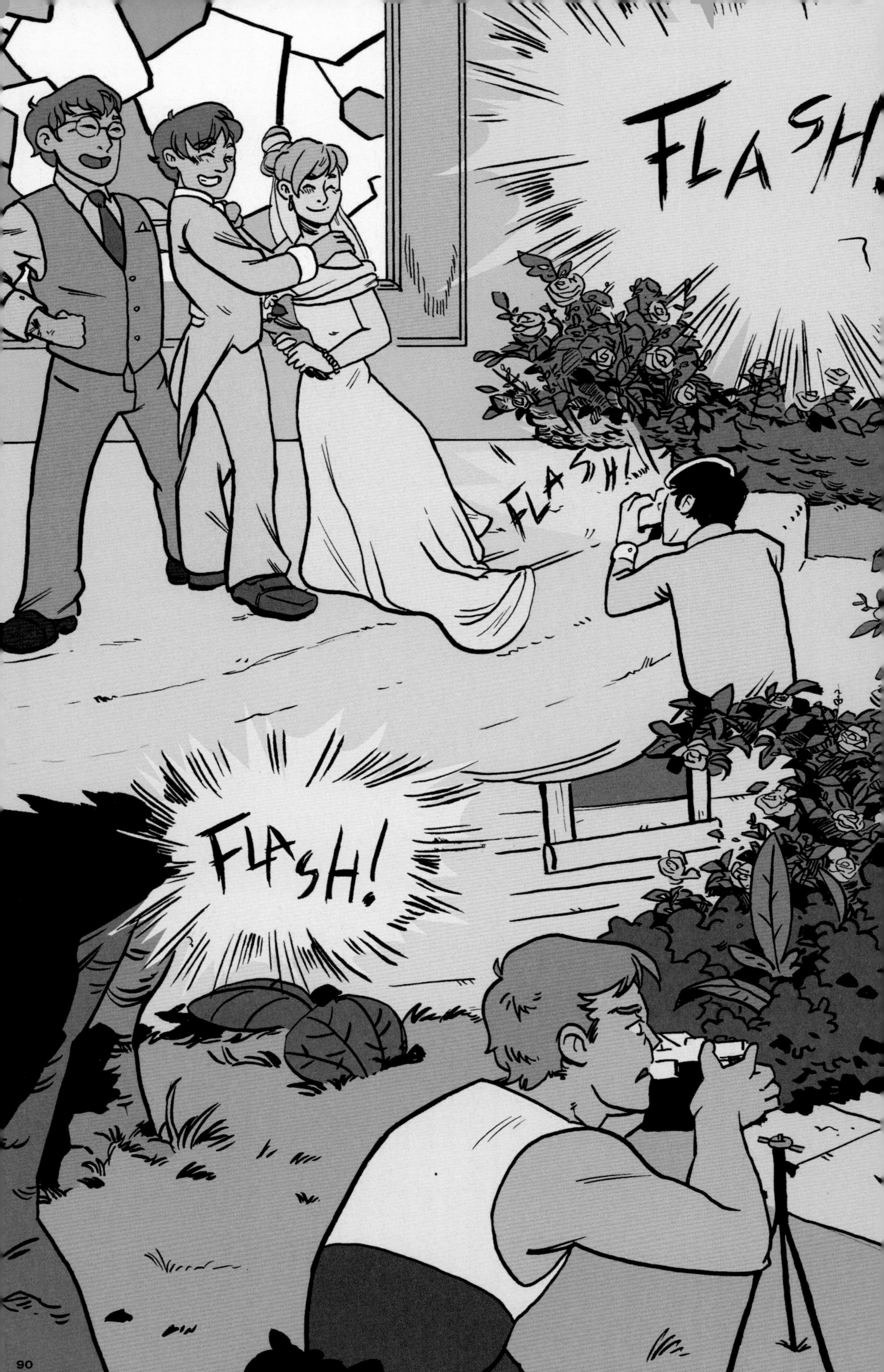
FLASH!
FLASH!
FLASH!

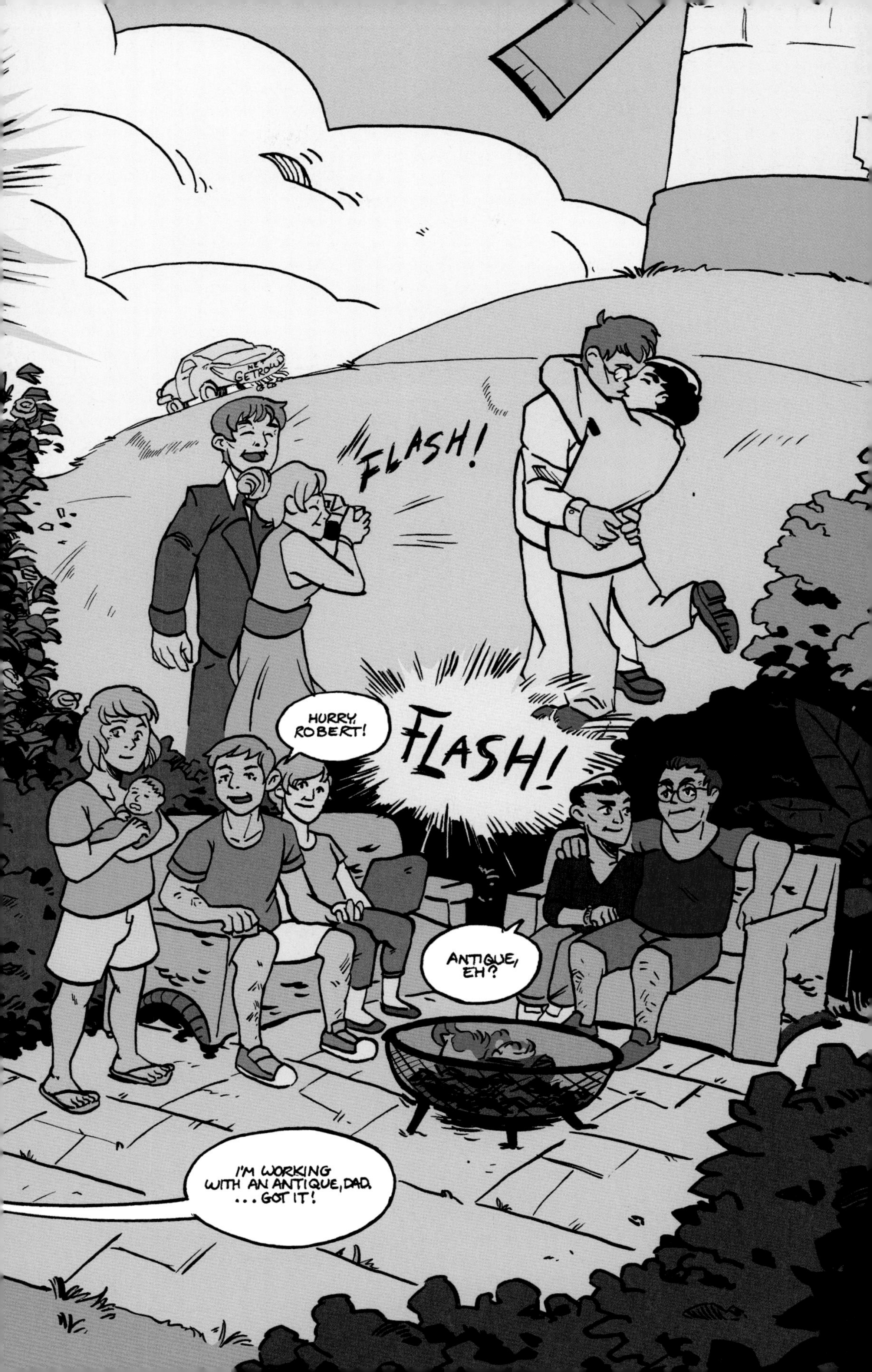
JUST MARRIED
FLASH!
HURRY, ROBERT!
FLASH!
ANTIQUE, EH?
I'M WORKING WITH AN ANTIQUE, DAD. ...GOT IT!

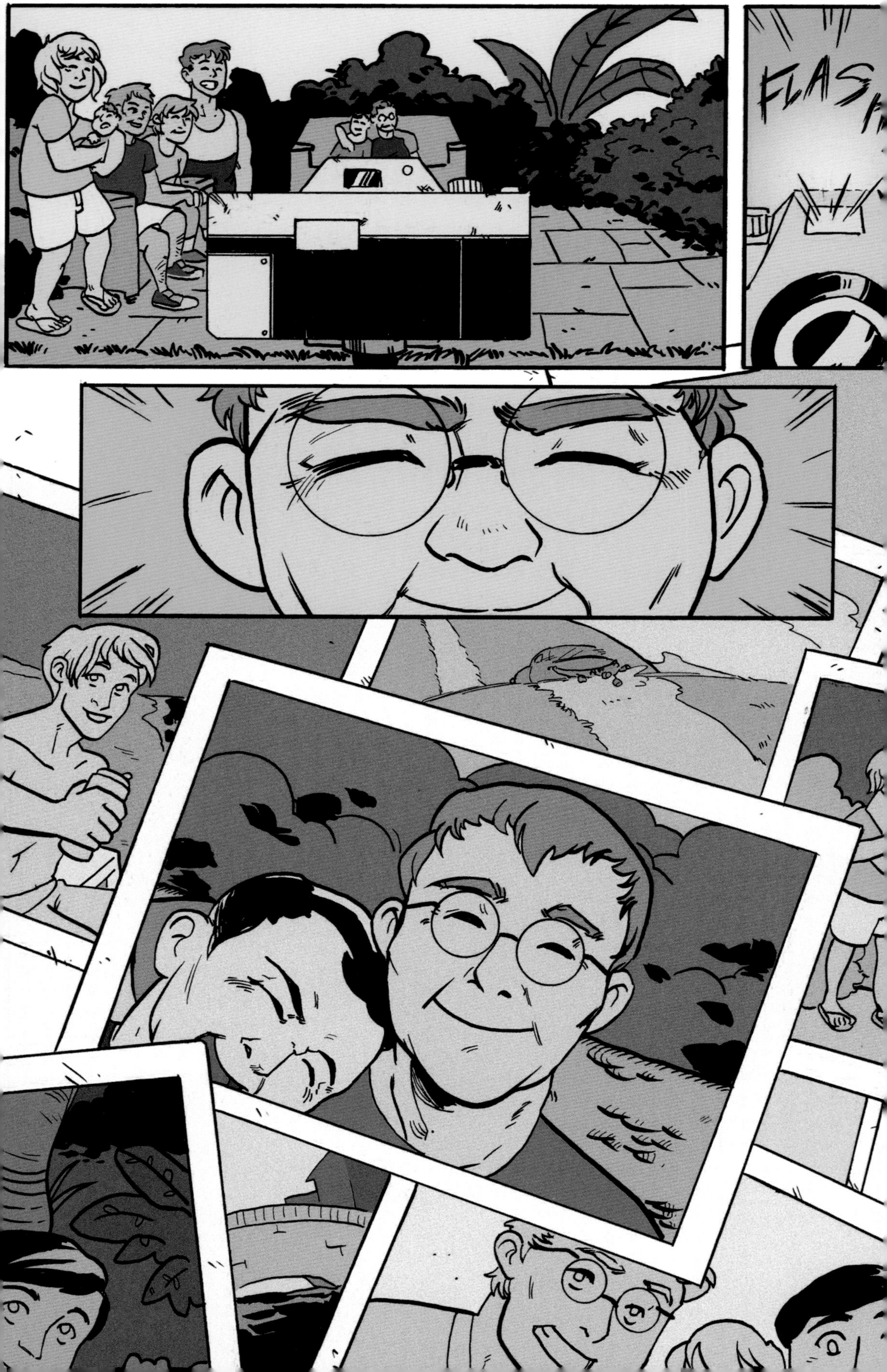
FLAS

ALWAYS

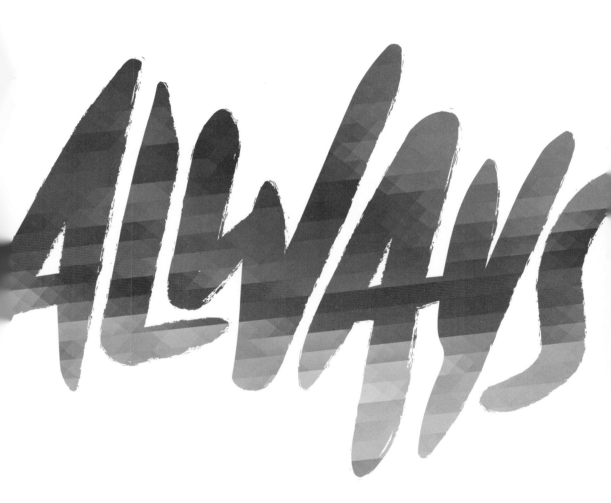

"LEAVES"

WRITER- CHRISTA HARADER • ARTIST-KATIE HICKS

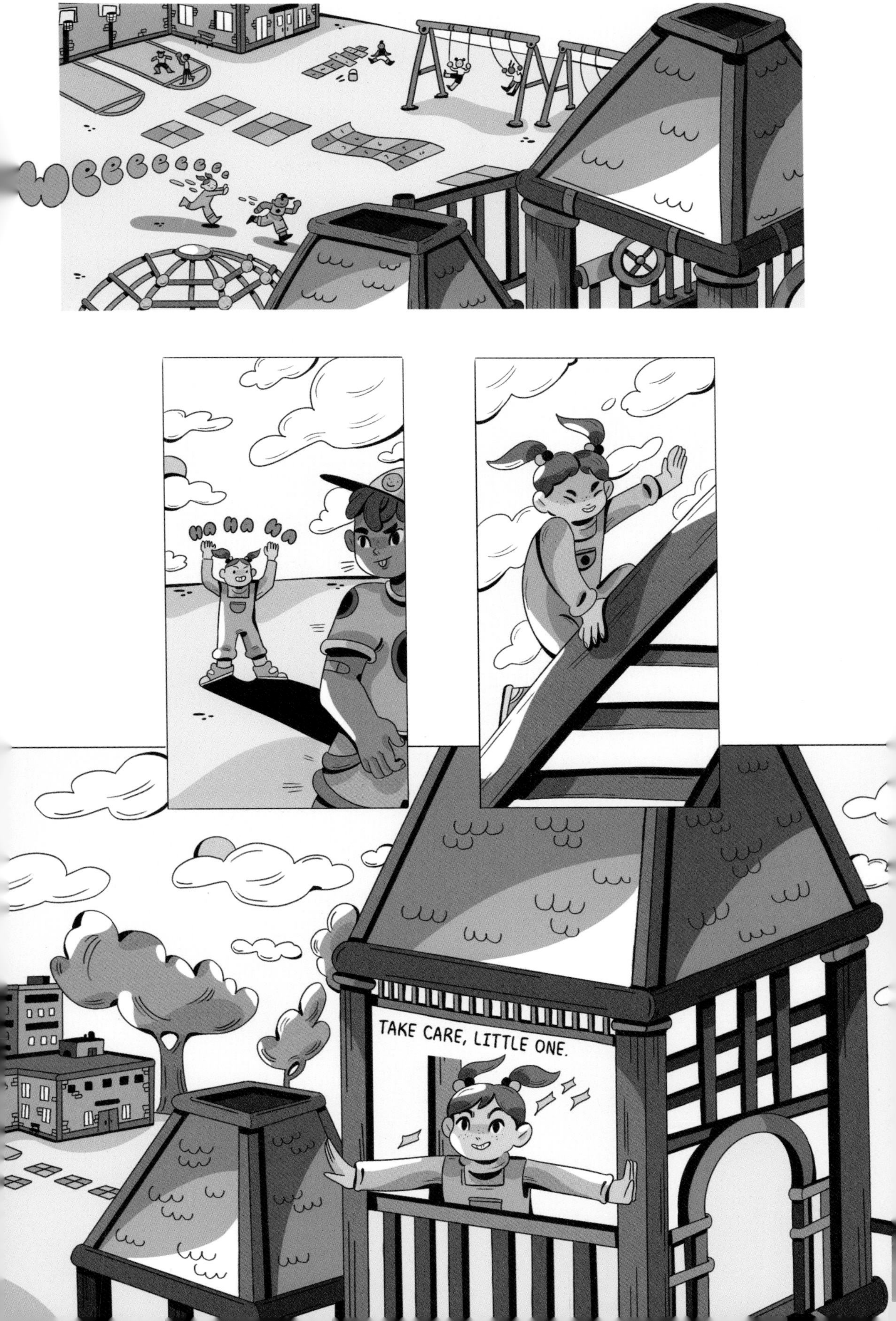
WEEEEEEEE
HA HA HA
TAKE CARE, LITTLE ONE.

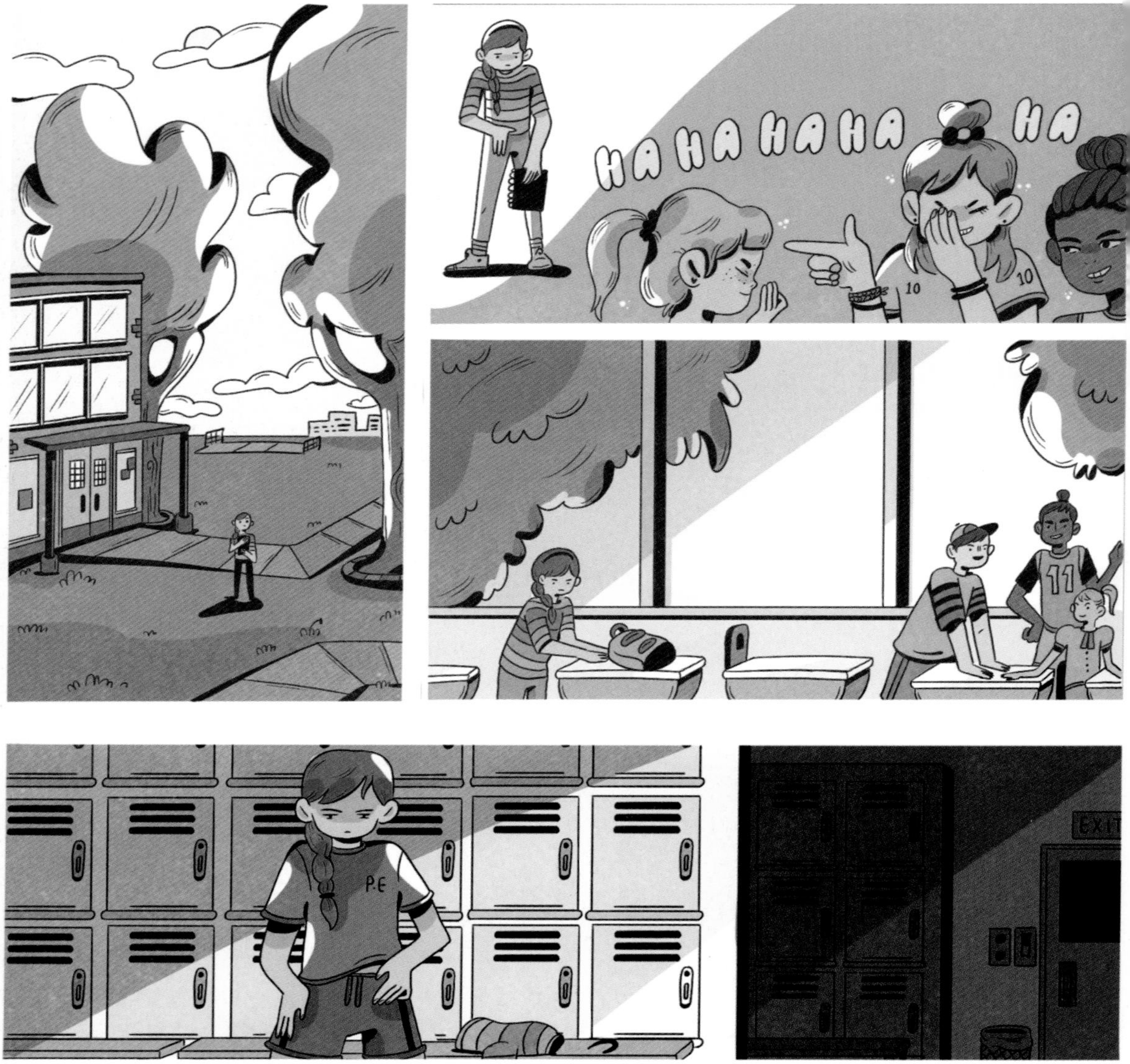
HA HA HA HA HA
10
10
10
11
P.E
EXIT

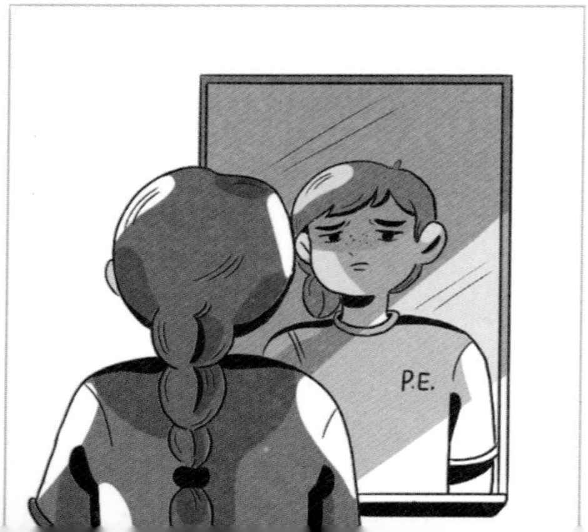
P.E.

IT DOESN'T ALWAYS GET BETTER.

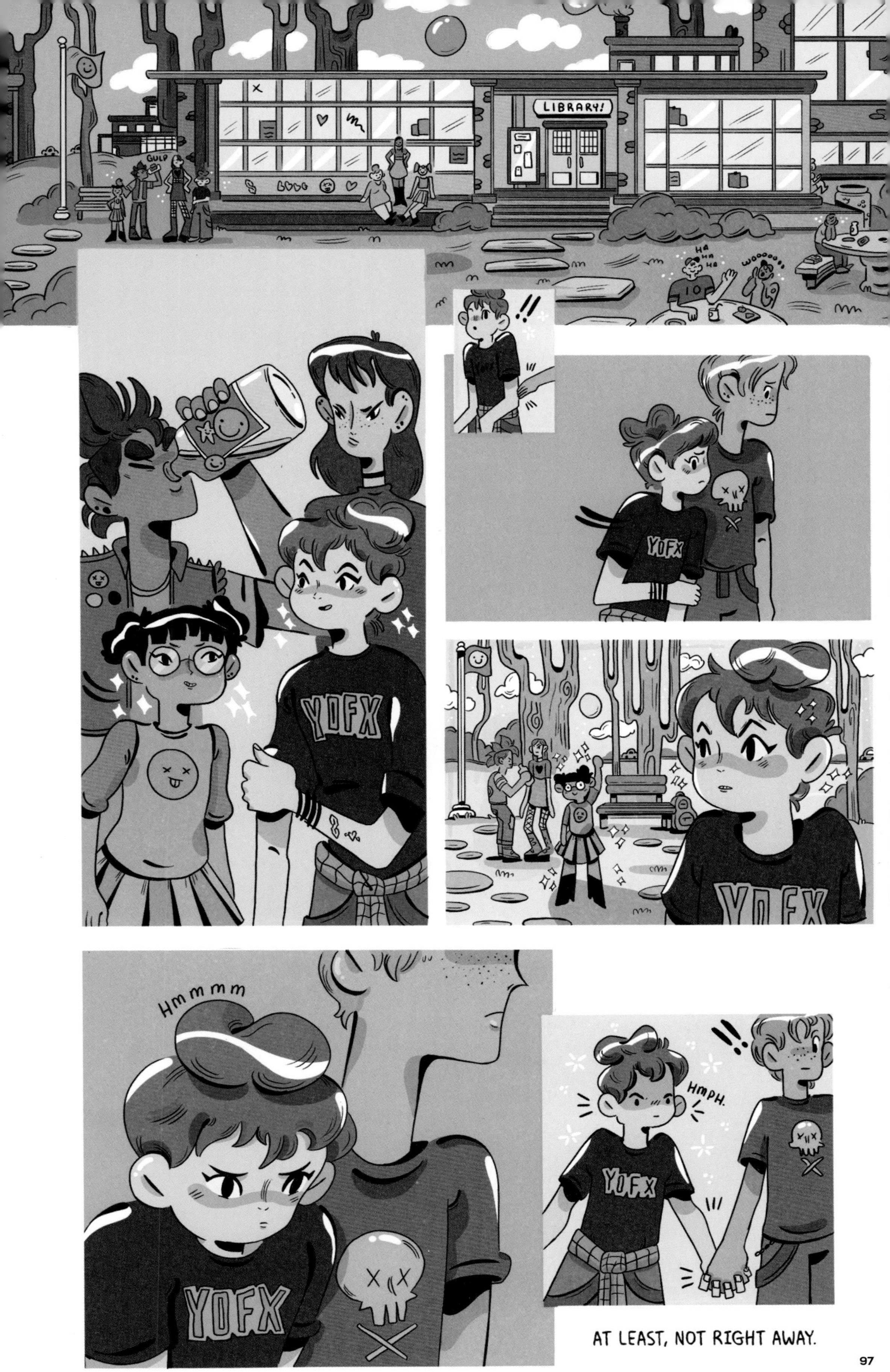
LIBRARY!
GULP
HA HA HA
WOOOOOO
HMMMM
HMPH.
AT LEAST, NOT RIGHT AWAY.

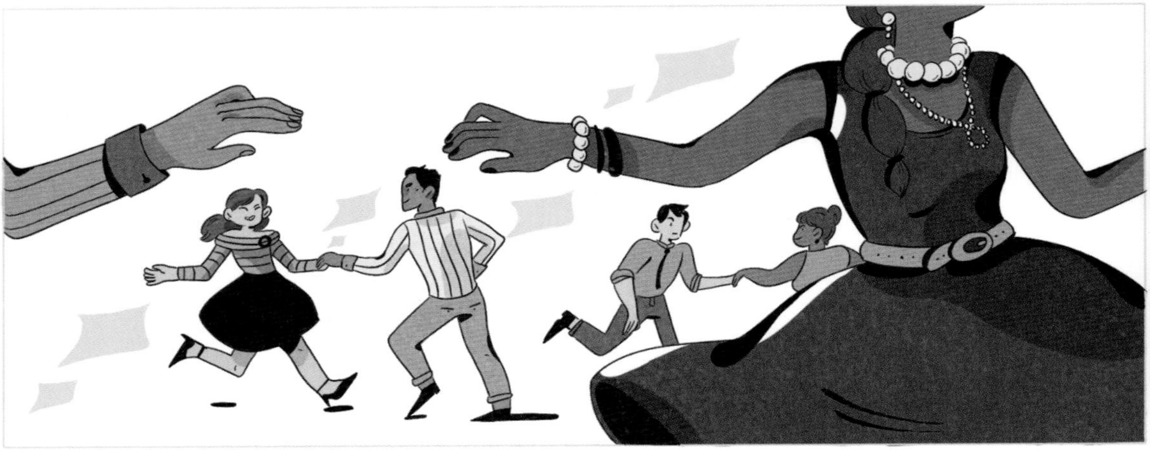

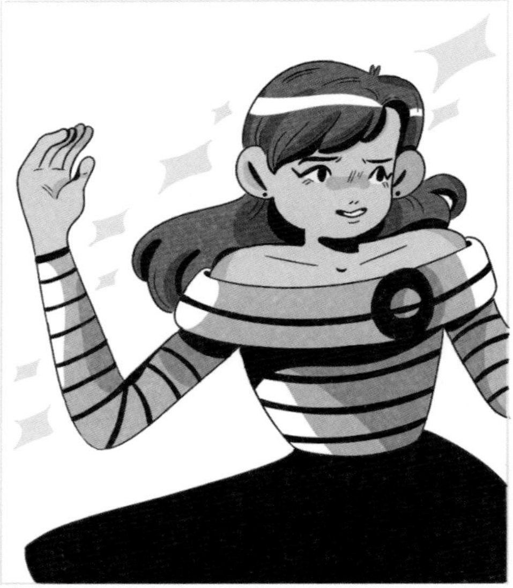

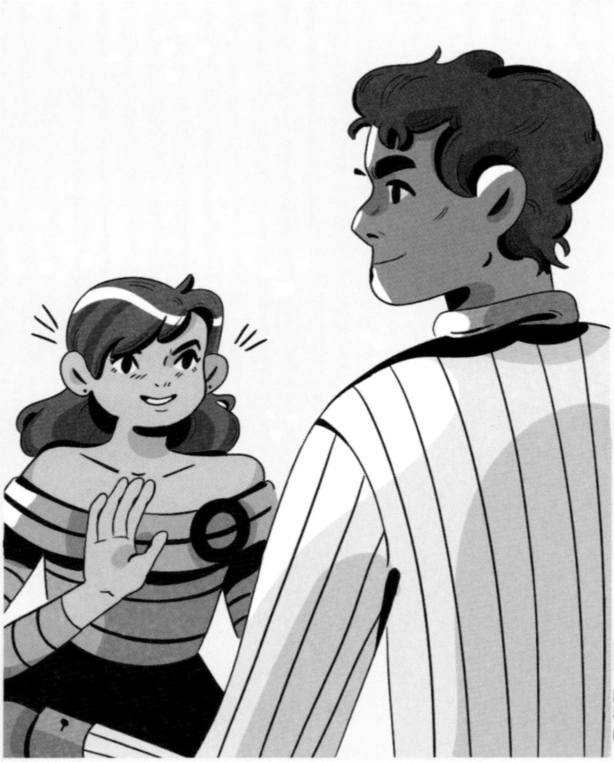

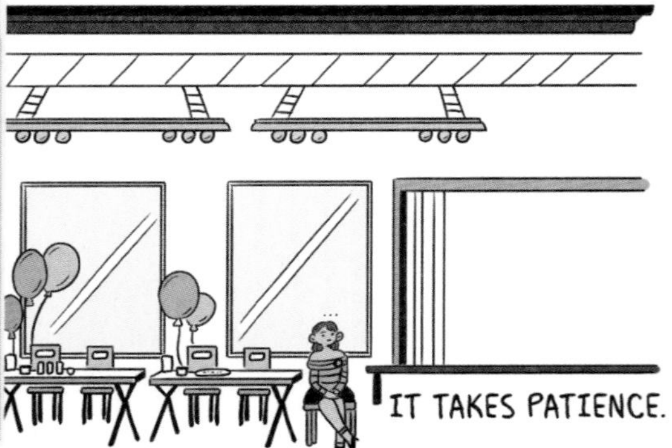
IT TAKES PATIENCE.

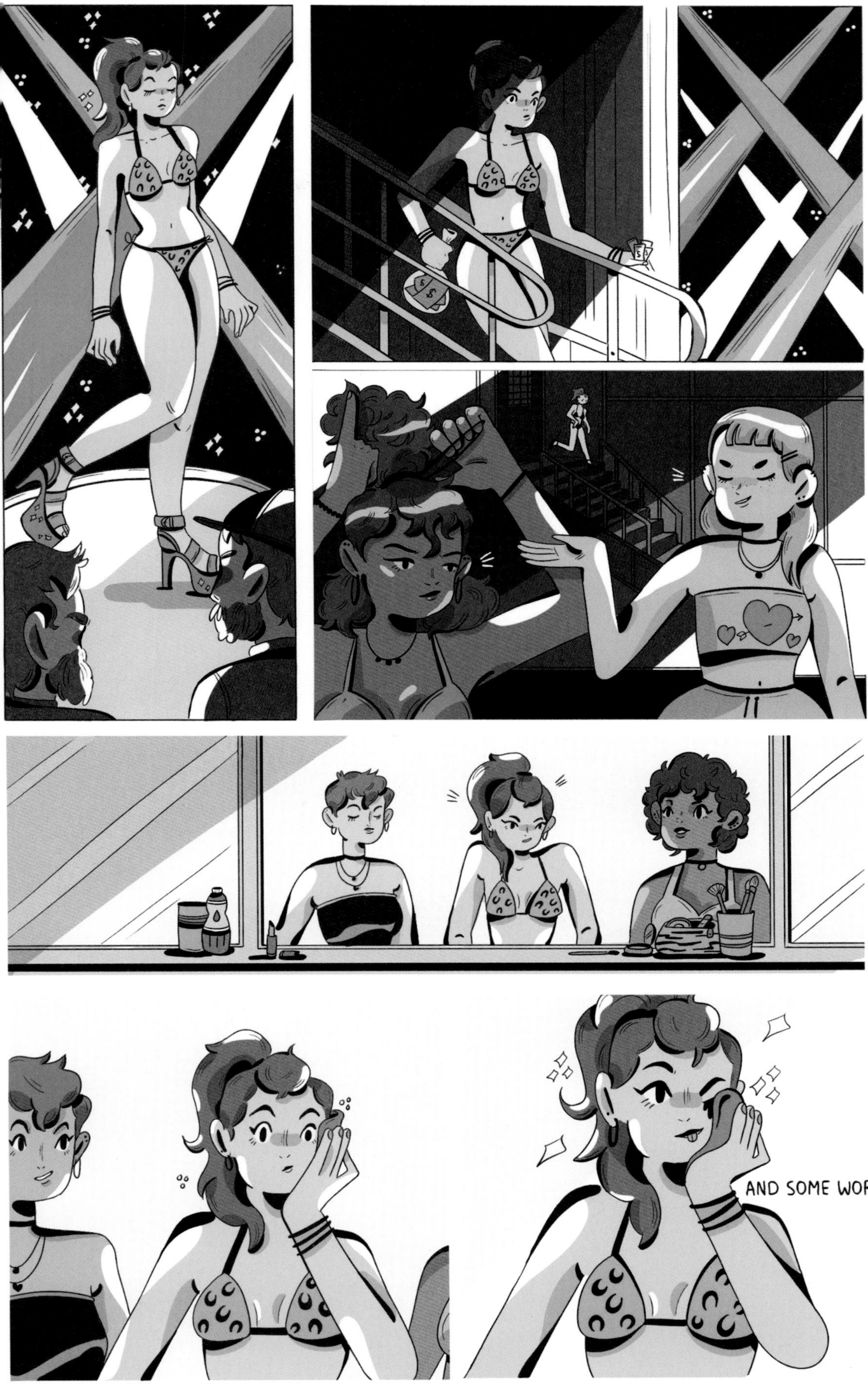
AND SOME WORK.

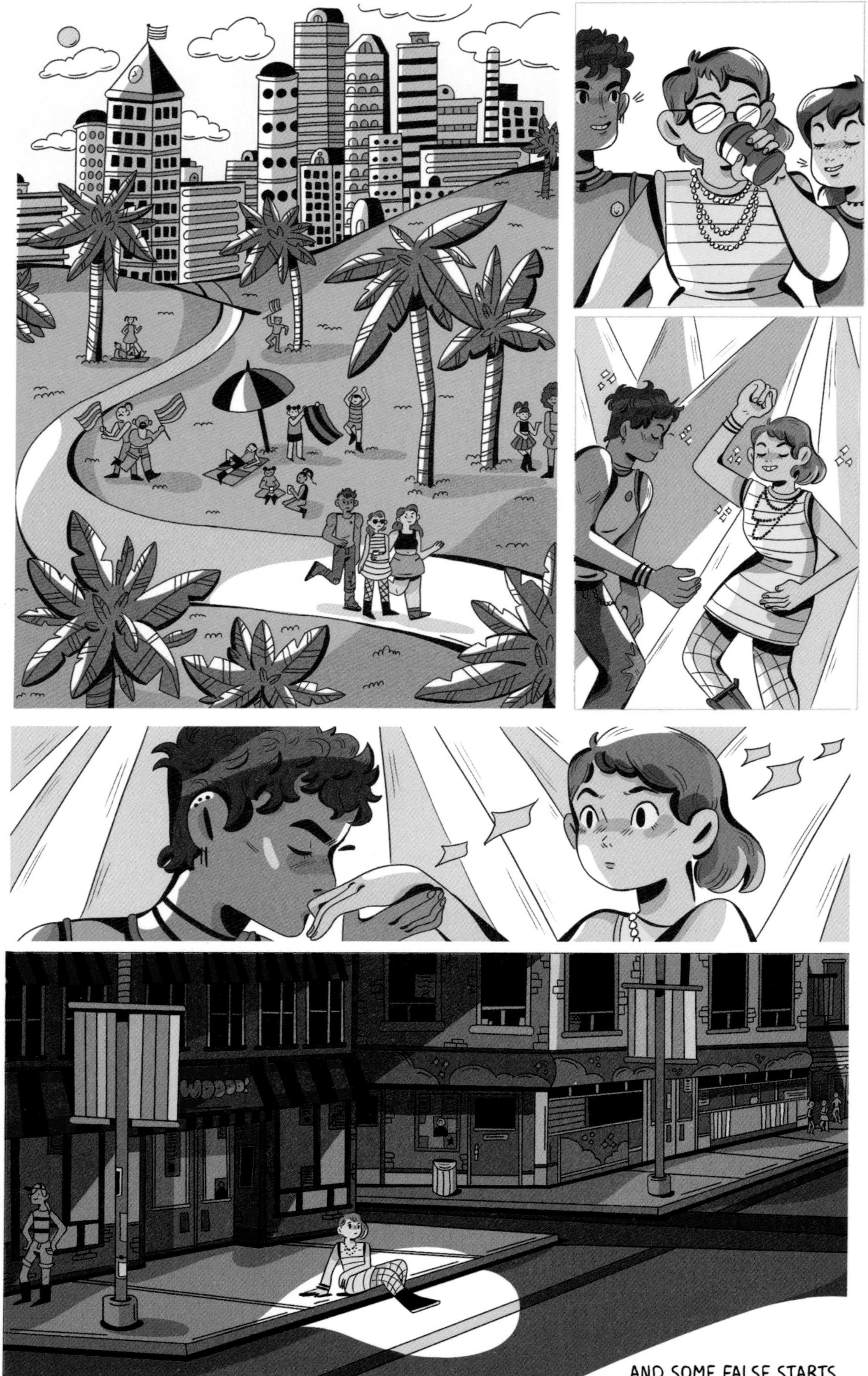
AND SOME FALSE STARTS.

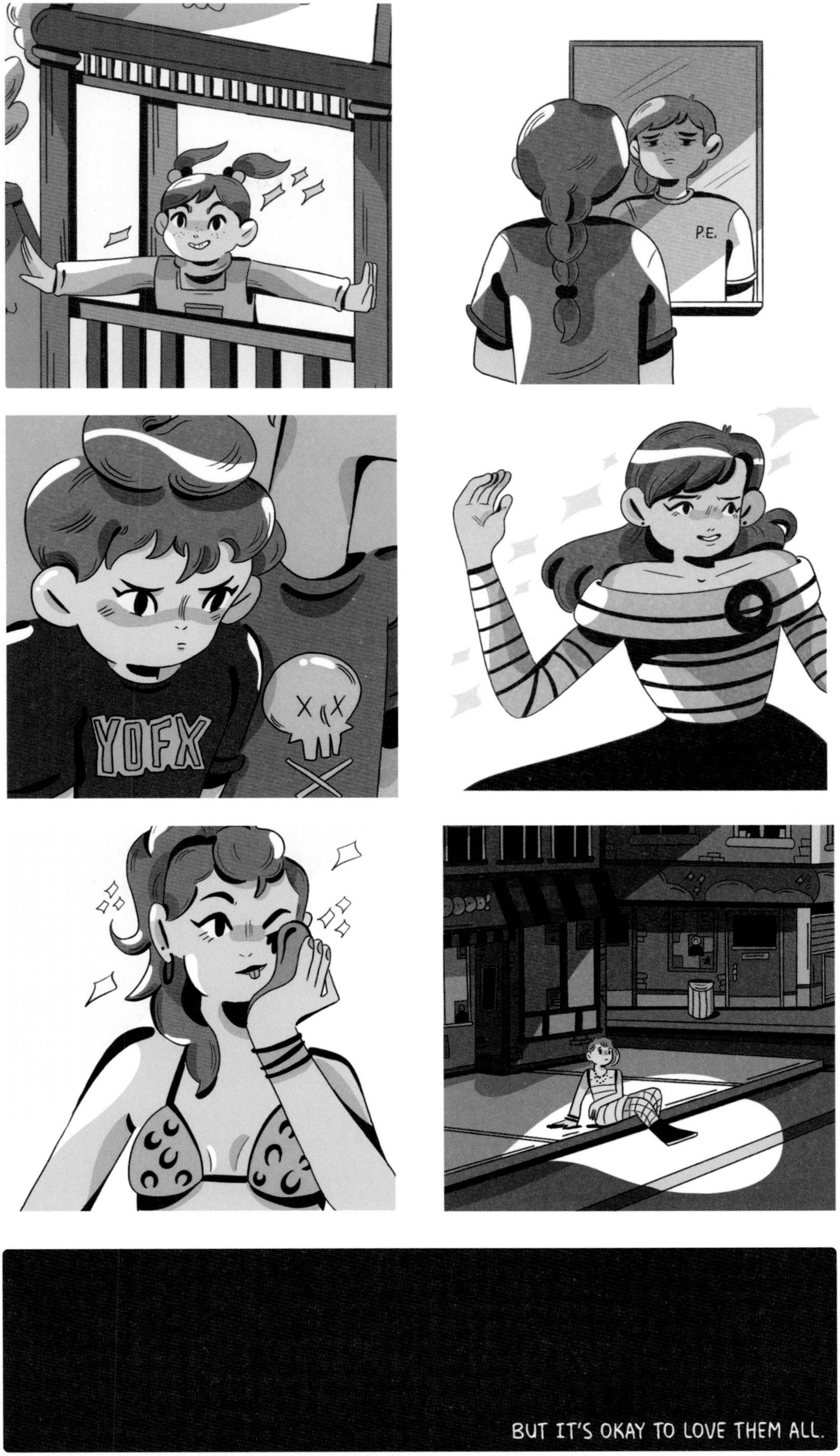
P.E.
YOFX
BUT IT'S OKAY TO LOVE THEM ALL.

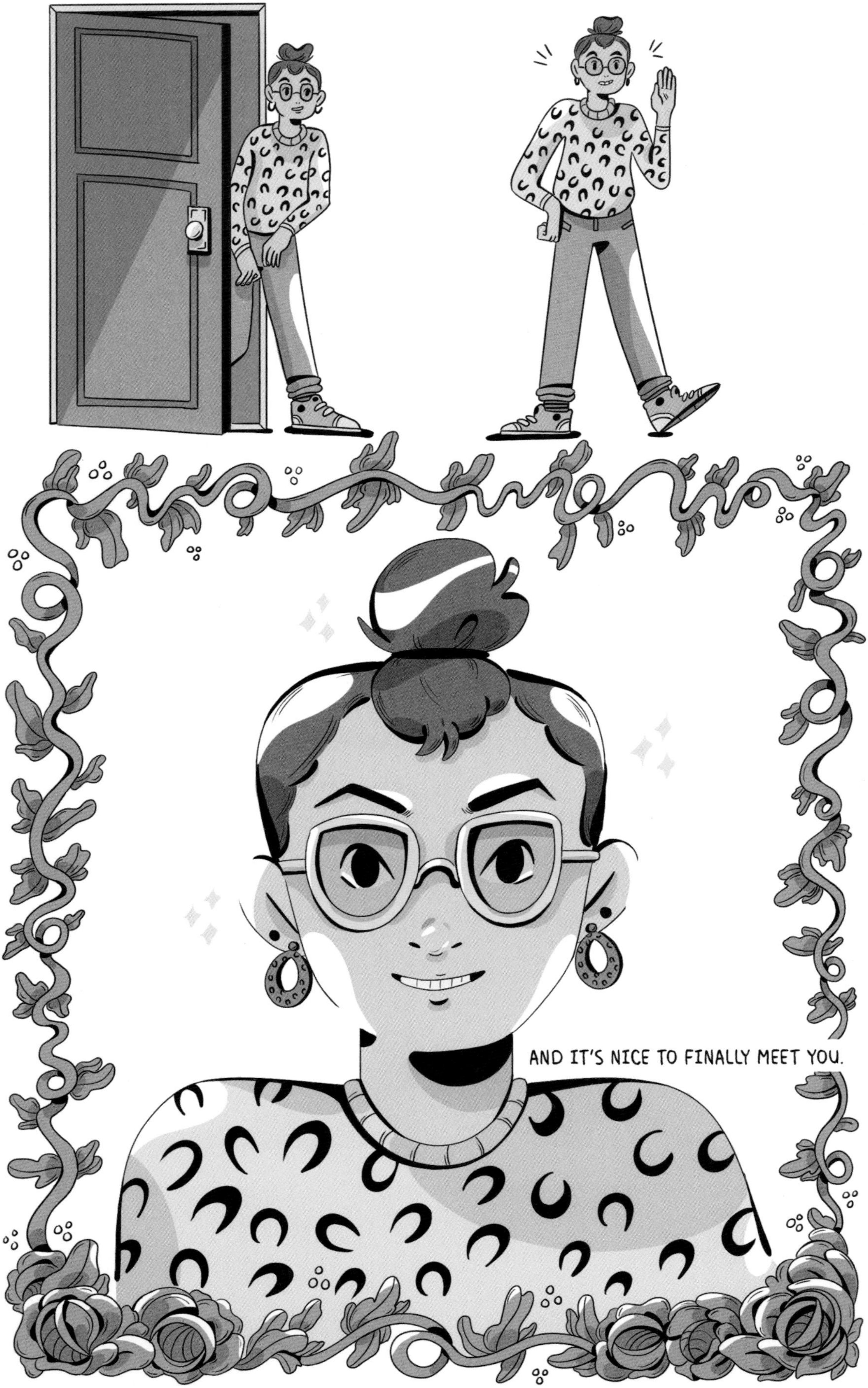
AND IT'S NICE TO FINALLY MEET YOU.

ALWAYS

"EVER MORE MYSELF"

WRITER AND ARTIST-KAJ E KUNSTMANN

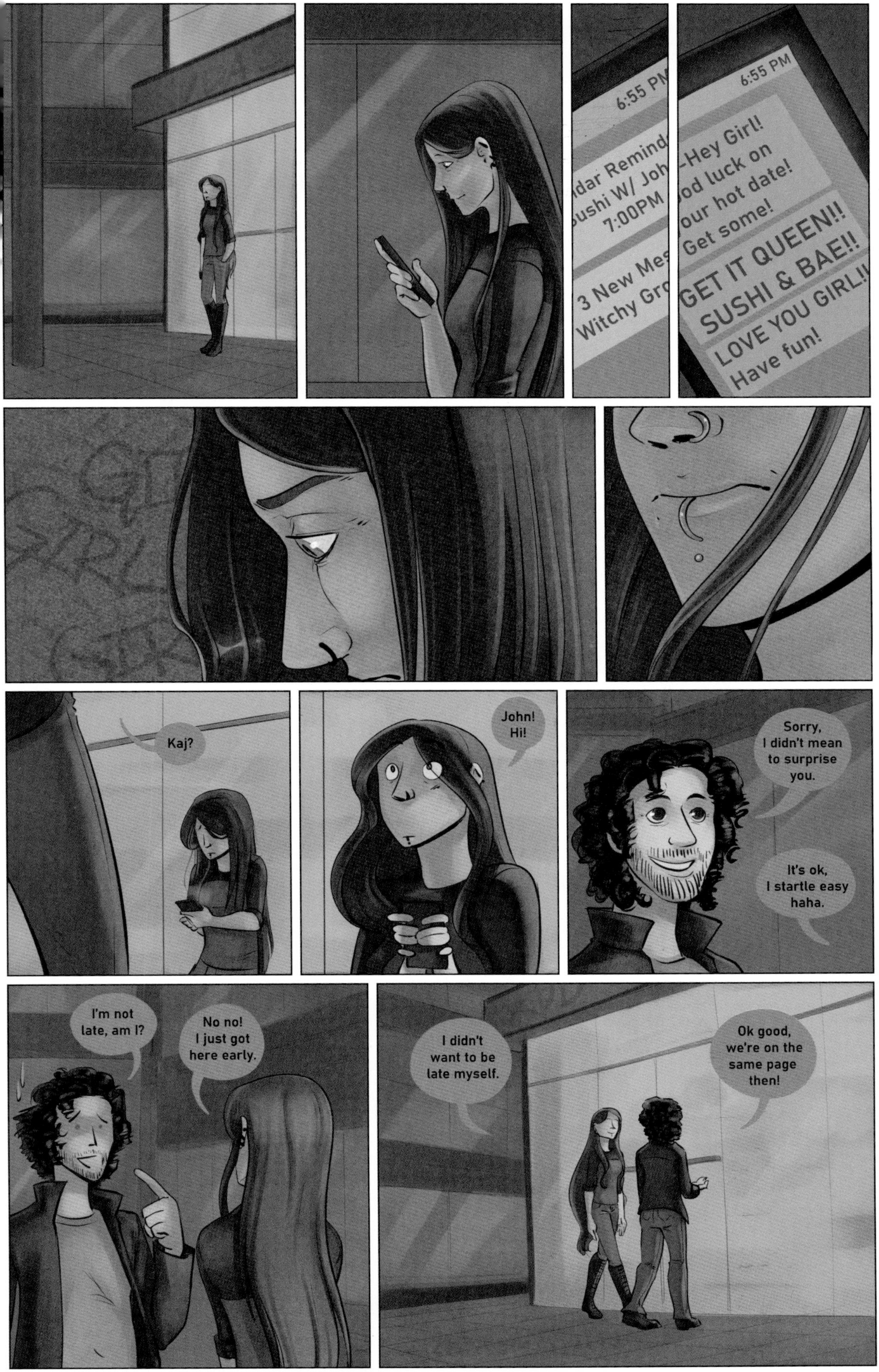

6:55 PM
6:55 PM
Hey Girl!
Get some!
GET IT QUEEN!!
SUSHI & BAE!!
LOVE YOU GIRL!!
Have fun!
Kaj?
John! Hi!
Sorry, I didn't mean to surprise you.
It's ok, I startle easy haha.
I'm not late, am I?
No no! I just got here early.
I didn't want to be late myself.
Ok good, we're on the same page then!

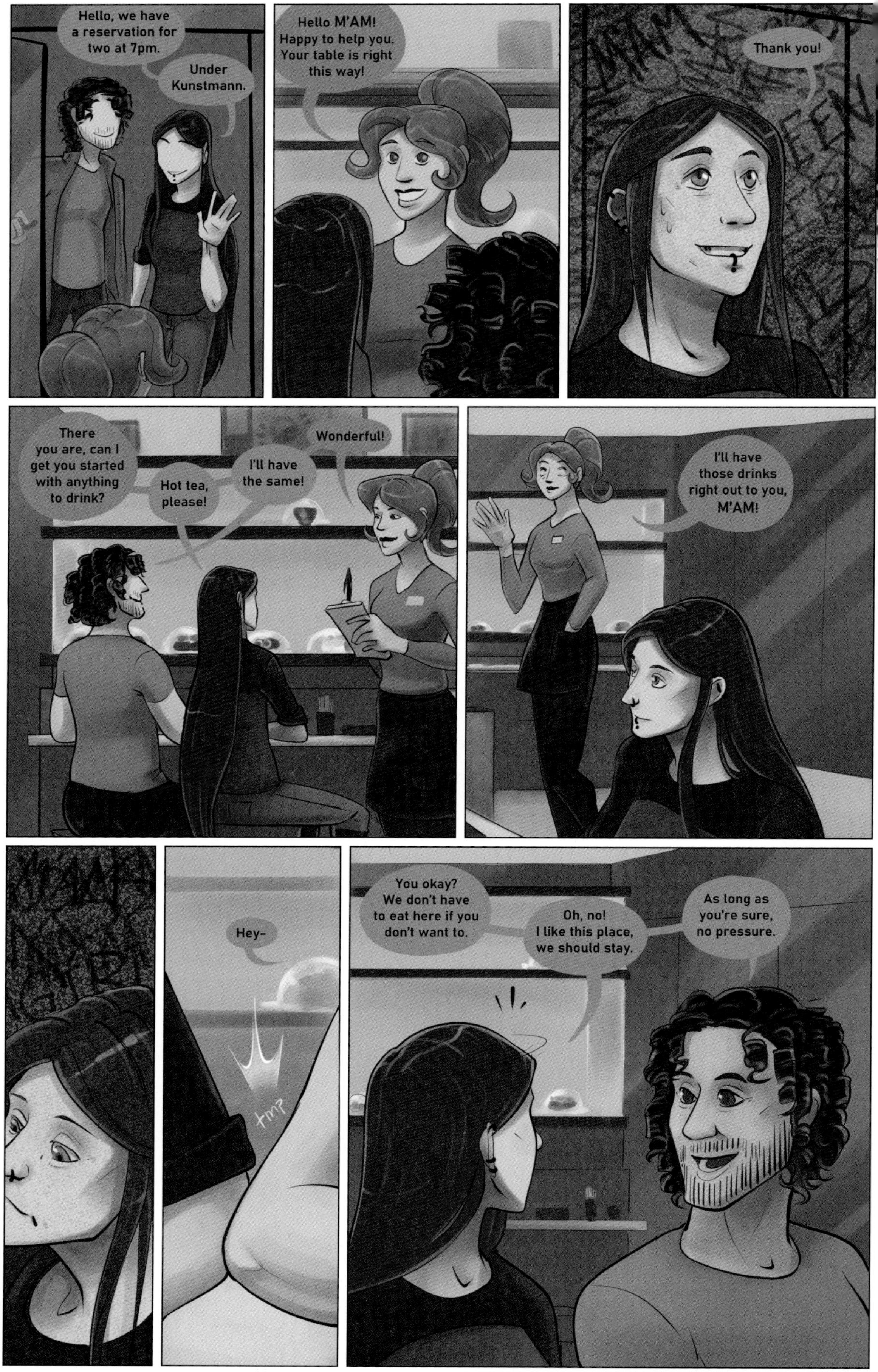
Hello, we have a reservation for two at 7pm.
Under Kunstmann.
Hello M'AM! Happy to help you. Your table is right this way!
Thank you!
There you are, can I get you started with anything to drink?
Hot tea, please!
I'll have the same!
Wonderful!
I'll have those drinks right out to you, M'AM!
Hey-
tmp
You okay? We don't have to eat here if you don't want to.
Oh, no! I like this place, we should stay.
As long as you're sure, no pressure.

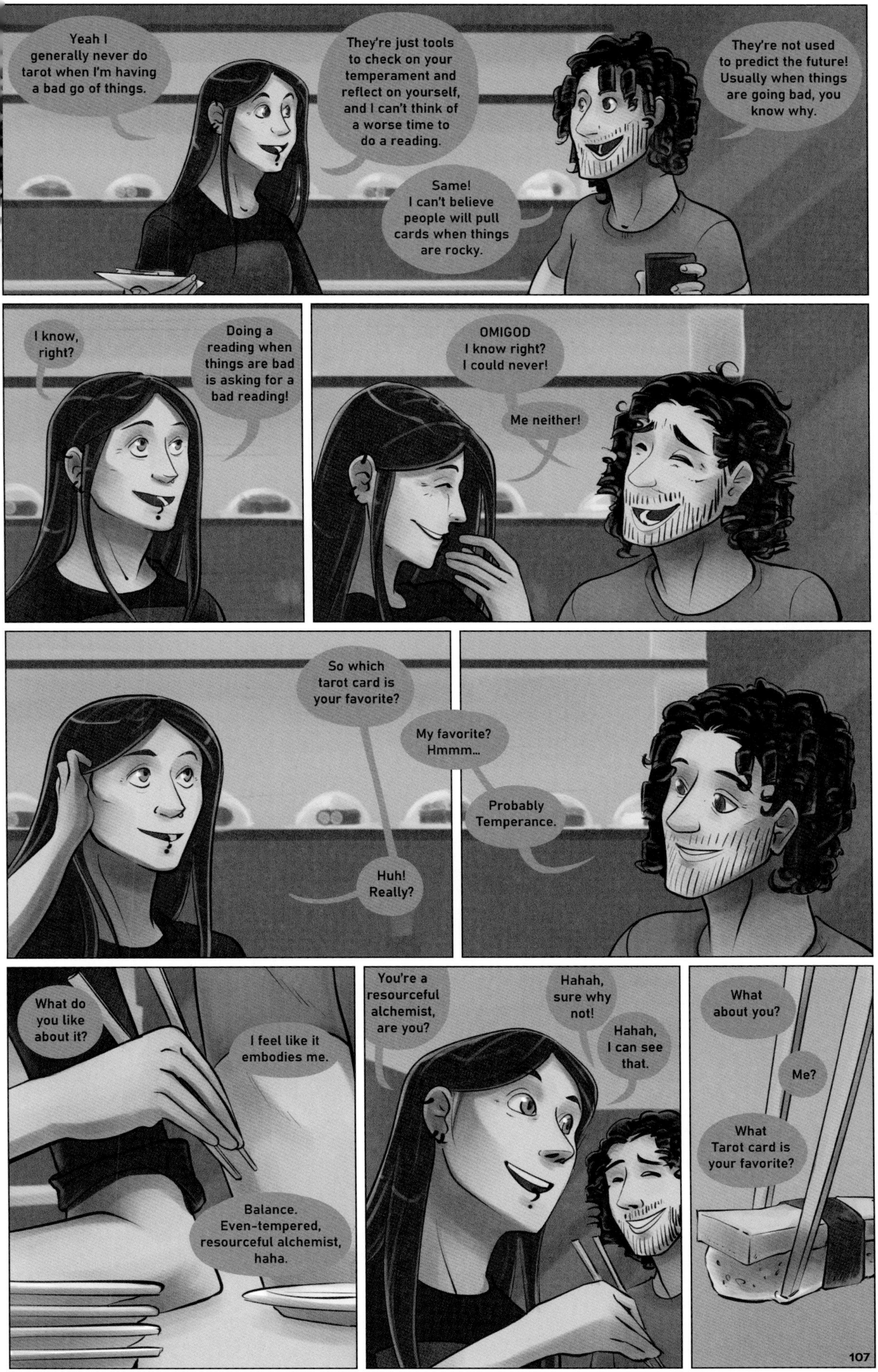
Yeah I generally never do tarot when I'm having a bad go of things.
They're just tools to check on your temperament and reflect on yourself, and I can't think of a worse time to do a reading.
They're not used to predict the future! Usually when things are going bad, you know why.
Same! I can't believe people will pull cards when things are rocky.
I know, right?
Doing a reading when things are bad is asking for a bad reading!
OMIGOD I know right? I could never!
Me neither!
So which tarot card is your favorite?
My favorite? Hmmm...
Probably Temperance.
Huh! Really?
What do you like about it?
I feel like it embodies me.
Balance. Even-tempered, resourceful alchemist, haha.
You're a resourceful alchemist, are you?
Hahah, sure why not!
Hahah, I can see that.
What about you?
Me?
What Tarot card is your favorite?

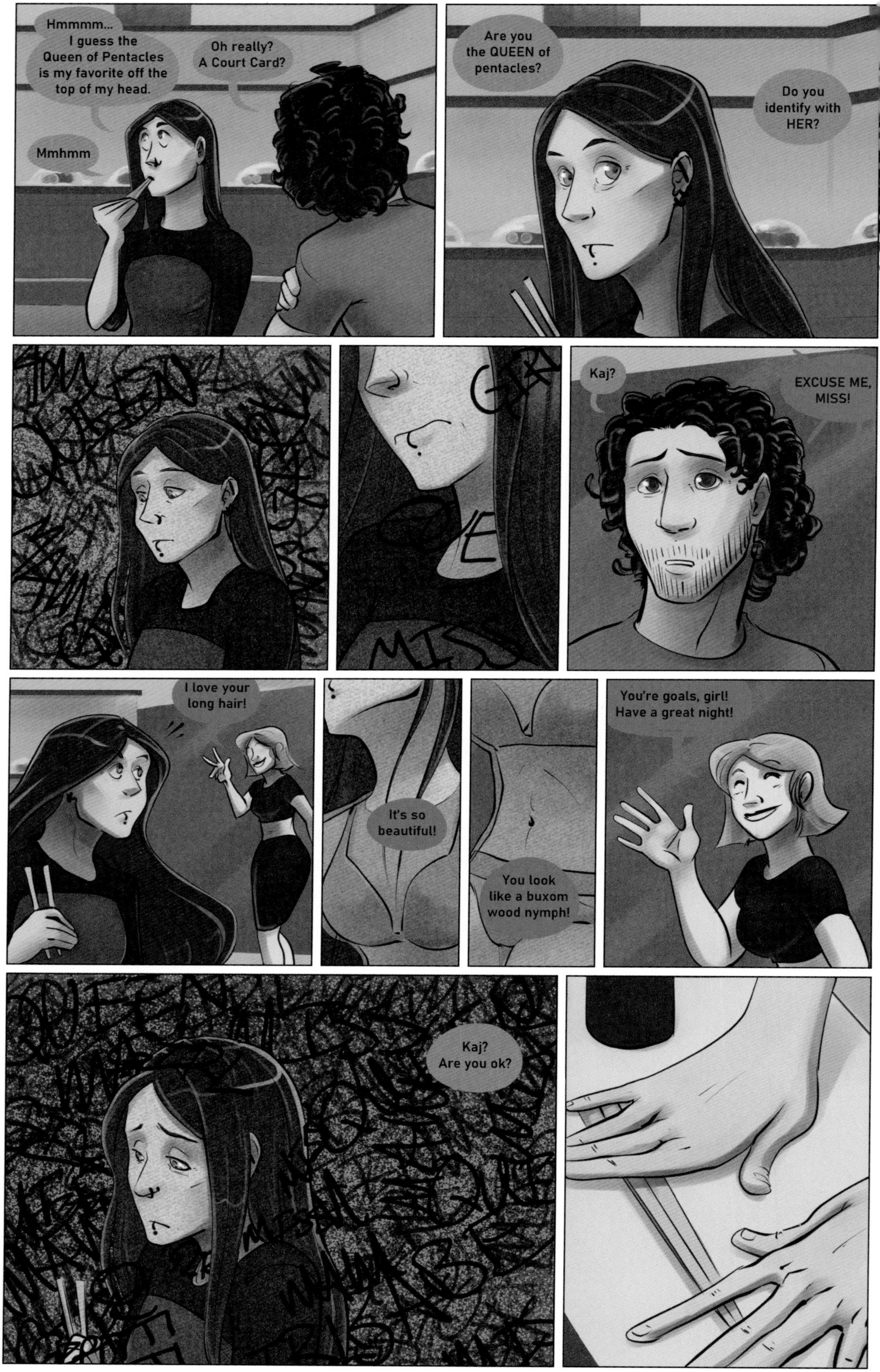
Hmmmm... I guess the Queen of Pentacles is my favorite off the top of my head.
Oh really? A Court Card?
Mmhmm
Are you the QUEEN of pentacles?
Do you identify with HER?
Kaj?
EXCUSE ME, MISS!
I love your long hair!
It's so beautiful!
You look like a buxom wood nymph!
You're goals, girl! Have a great night!
Kaj? Are you ok?

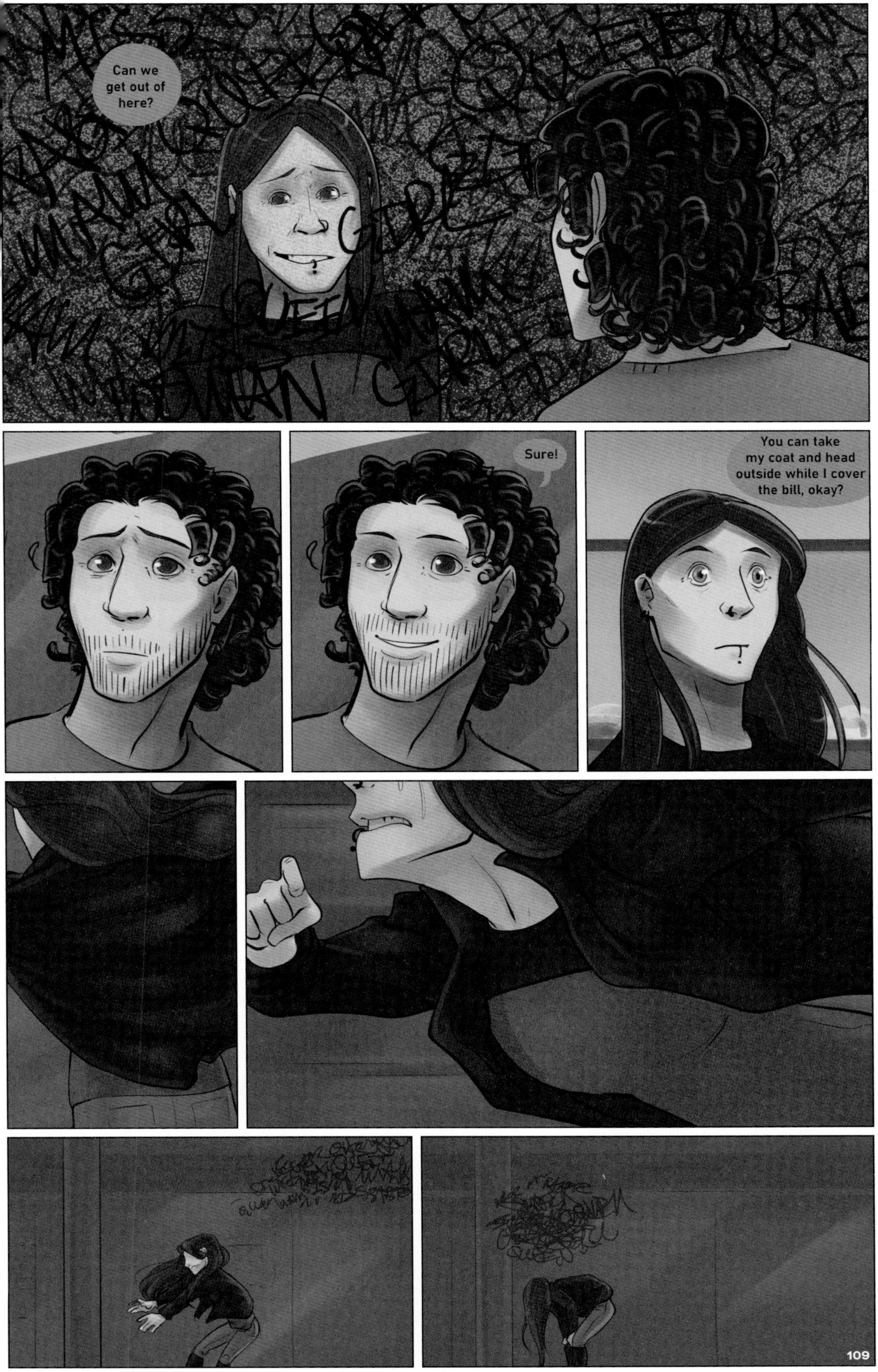

Can we get out of here?
Sure!
You can take my coat and head outside while I cover the bill, okay?

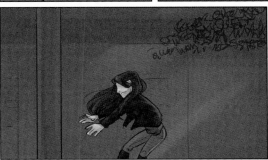

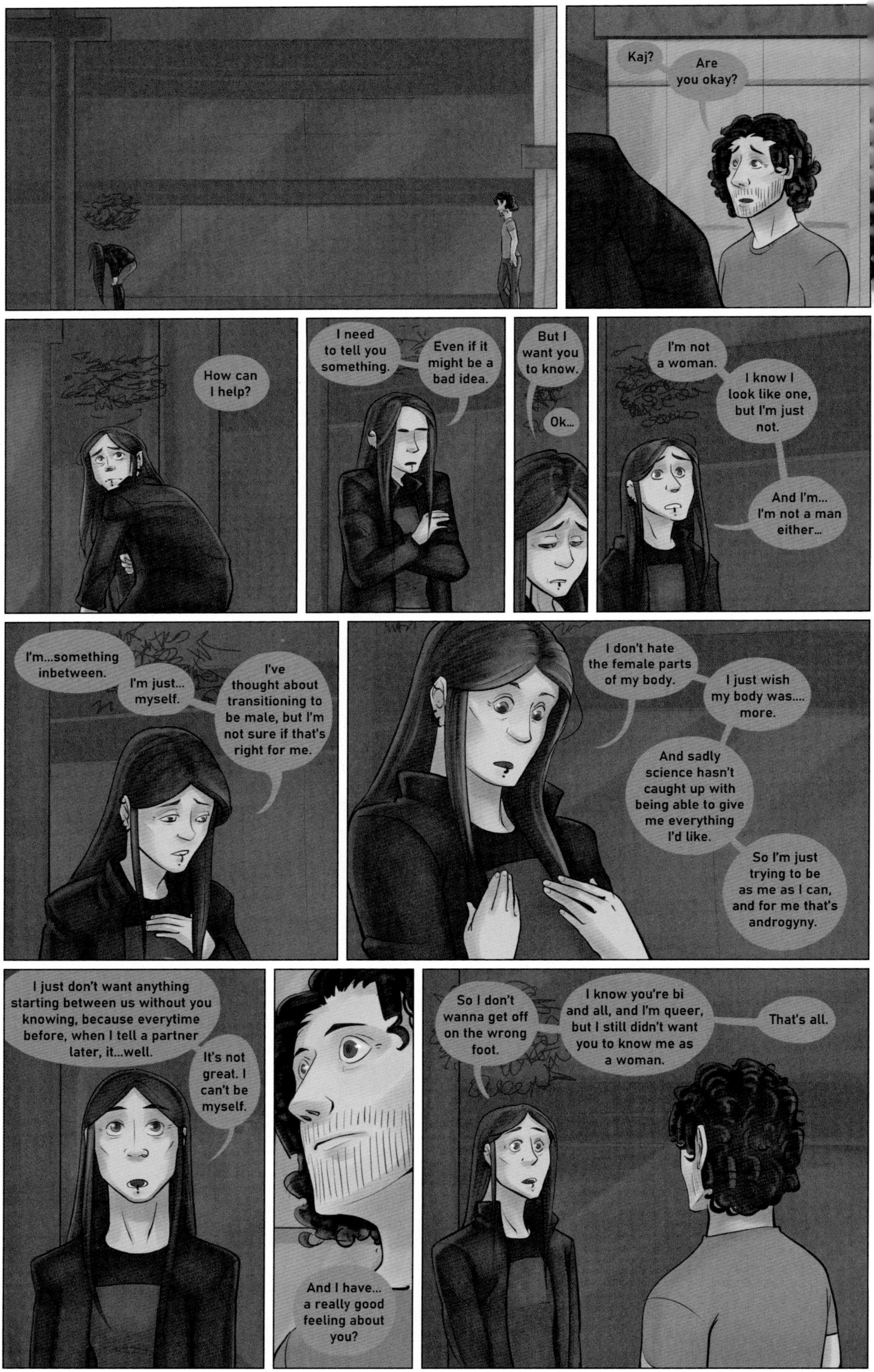

Kaj?
Are you okay?
How can I help?
I need to tell you something.
Even if it might be a bad idea.
But I want you to know.
Ok...
I'm not a woman.
I know I look like one, but I'm just not.
And I'm... I'm not a man either...
I'm...something inbetween.
I'm just... myself.
I've thought about transitioning to be male, but I'm not sure if that's right for me.
I don't hate the female parts of my body.
I just wish my body was.... more.
And sadly science hasn't caught up with being able to give me everything I'd like.
So I'm just trying to be as me as I can, and for me that's androgyny.
I just don't want anything starting between us without you knowing, because everytime before, when I tell a partner later, it...well.
It's not great. I can't be myself.
And I have... a really good feeling about you?
So I don't wanna get off on the wrong foot.
I know you're bi and all, and I'm queer, but I still didn't want you to know me as a woman.
That's all.

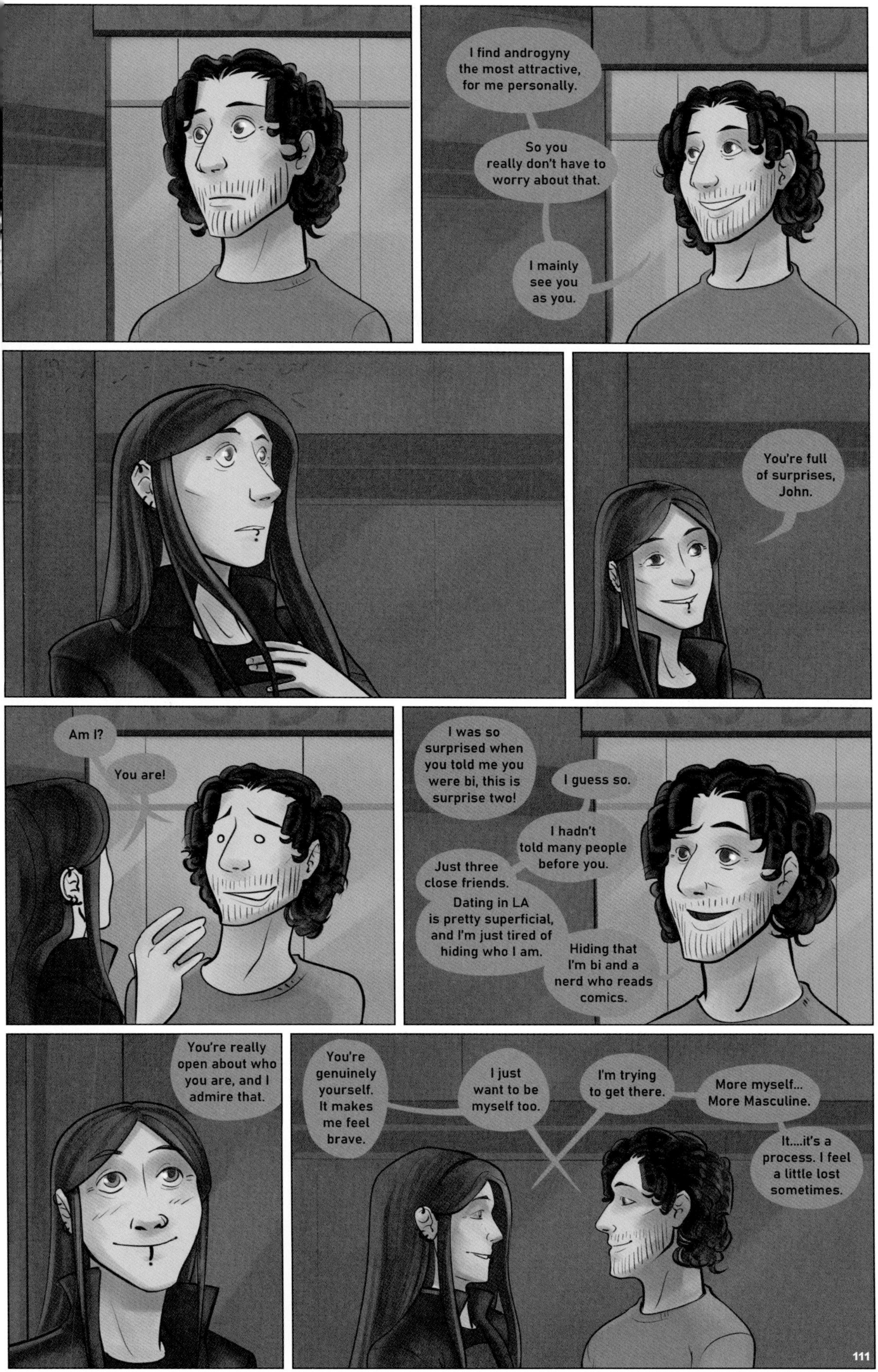
I find androgyny the most attractive, for me personally.
So you really don't have to worry about that.
I mainly see you as you.
You're full of surprises, John.
Am I?
You are!
I was so surprised when you told me you were bi, this is surprise two!
I guess so.
I hadn't told many people before you.
Just three close friends.
Dating in LA is pretty superficial, and I'm just tired of hiding who I am.
Hiding that I'm bi and a nerd who reads comics.
You're really open about who you are, and I admire that.
You're genuinely yourself. It makes me feel brave.
I just want to be myself too.
I'm trying to get there.
More myself... More Masculine.
It....it's a process. I feel a little lost sometimes.

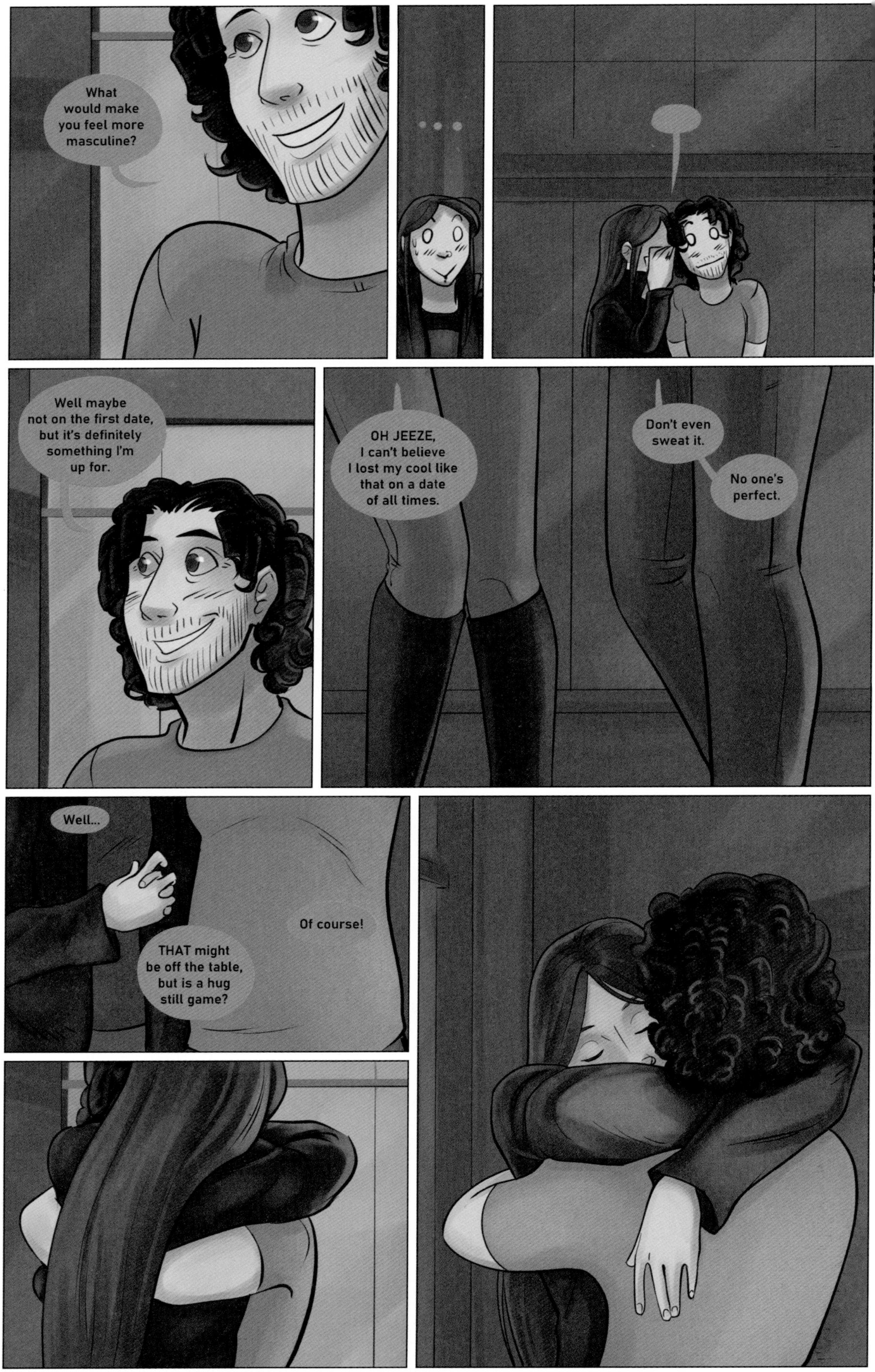
What would make you feel more masculine?
Well maybe not on the first date, but it's definitely something I'm up for.
OH JEEZE, I can't believe I lost my cool like that on a date of all times.
Don't even sweat it.
No one's perfect.
Well...
THAT might be off the table, but is a hug still game?
Of course!

So, how did that make you feel?

Great!

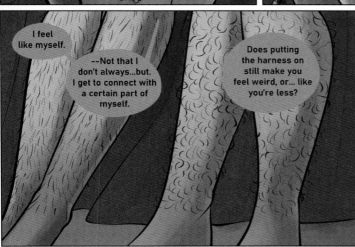

I feel like myself.

--Not that I don't always...but. I get to connect with a certain part of myself.

Does putting the harness on still make you feel weird, or... like you're less?

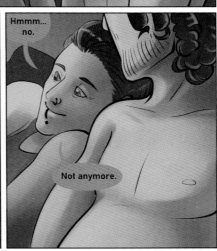

Hmmm... no.

Not anymore.

Now it's just part of the process.

It's sort of a reminder that I'm not a man or a woman, I'm something different.

Not that I wouldn't mind my own equipment.

I'm still not sure.

I'm not sure if I'll ever be sure.

There are so many aspects to it that might pan out in a way I'm not prepared for.

You know I support you going further.

HRT, Surgery...if you want to?

I think I'd like my friends to start using different pronouns, though.

Even if it'll be rough going.

But you make it less scary.

I'll help however I can.

You already do.

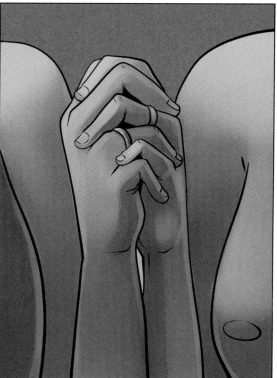

ALWAYS

"BOTH SIDES"

WRITER-BRITTANY "BRIGGSY" GONZALEZ · ARTIST-ELIZABETH MALETTE

I used to think you were incredible

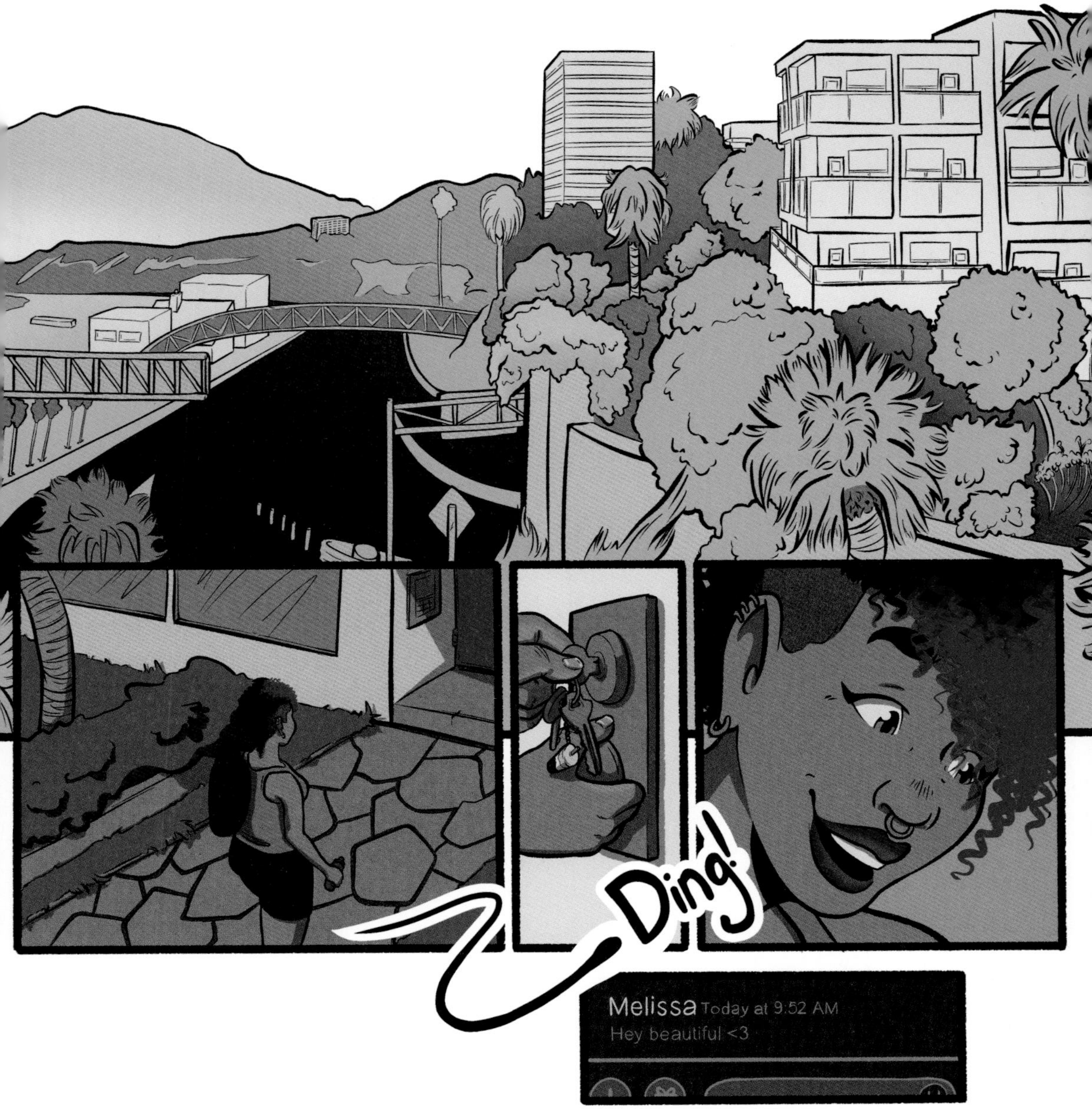

Ding!
Melissa Today at 9:52 AM
Hey beautiful <3

You were magical to me

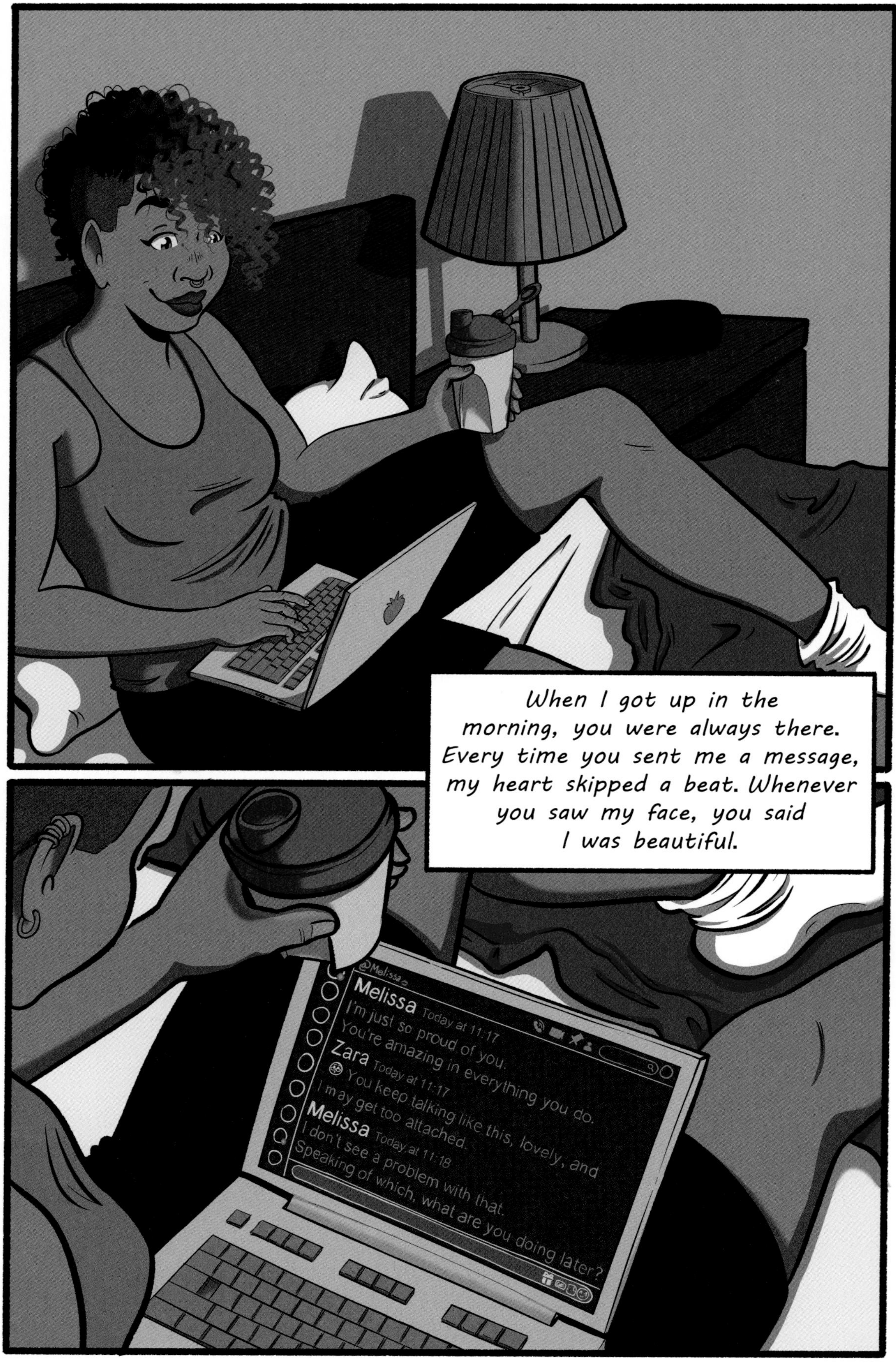
When I got up in the morning, you were always there. Every time you sent me a message, my heart skipped a beat. Whenever you saw my face, you said I was beautiful.
@Melissa
Melissa Today at 11:17
I'm just so proud of you.
You're amazing in everything you do.
Zara Today at 11:17
You keep talking like this, lovely, and
I may get too attached.
Melissa Today at 11:18
I don't see a problem with that.
Speaking of which, what are you doing later?

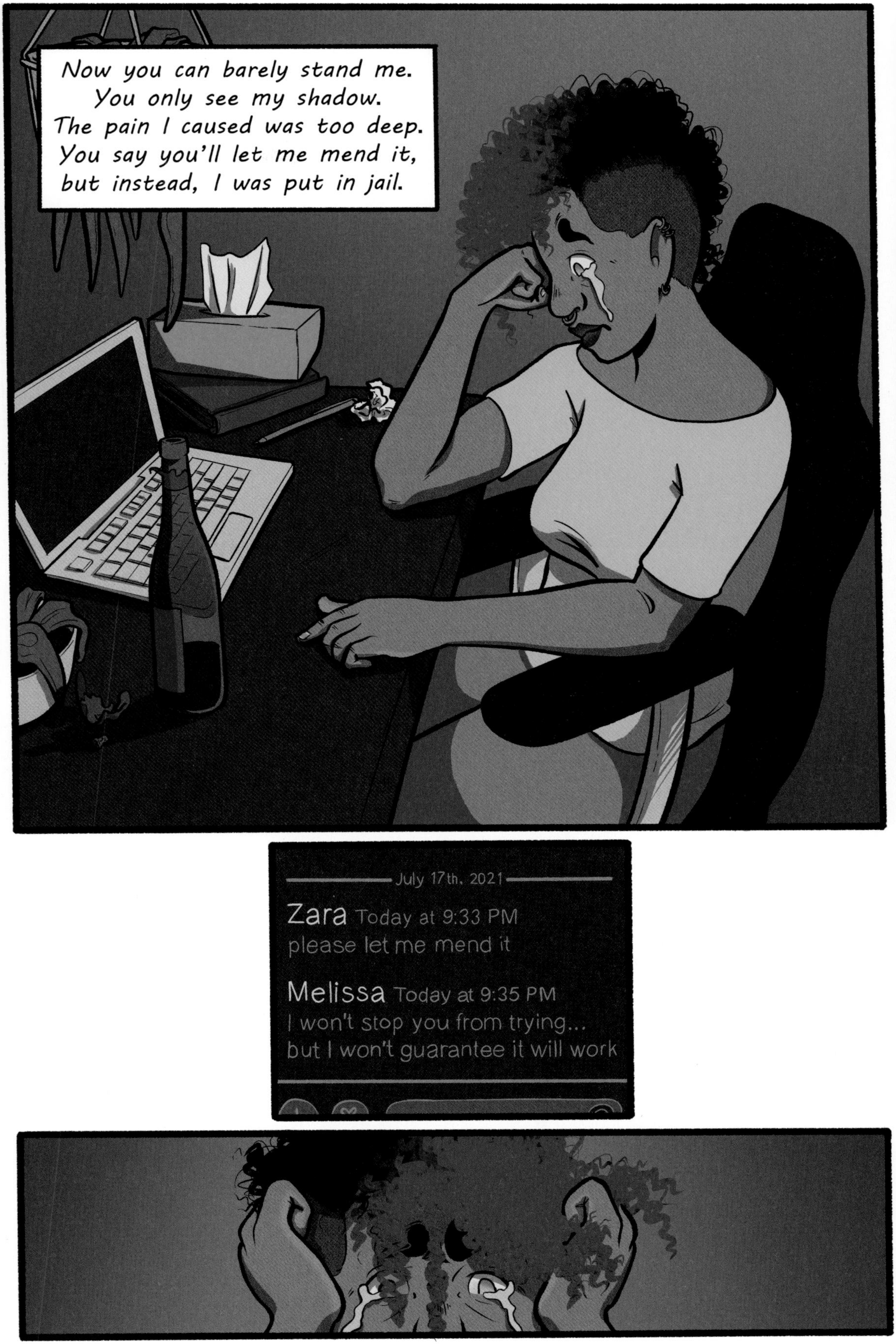
Now you can barely stand me.
You only see my shadow.
The pain I caused was too deep.
You say you'll let me mend it,
but instead, I was put in jail.
July 17th, 2021
Zara Today at 9:33 PM
please let me mend it
Melissa Today at 9:35 PM
I won't stop you from trying...
but I won't guarantee it will work

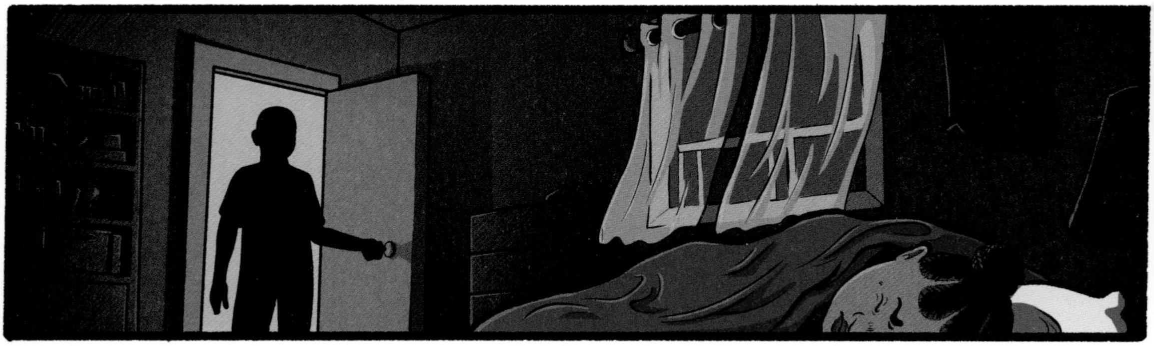

I wish I could make you understand

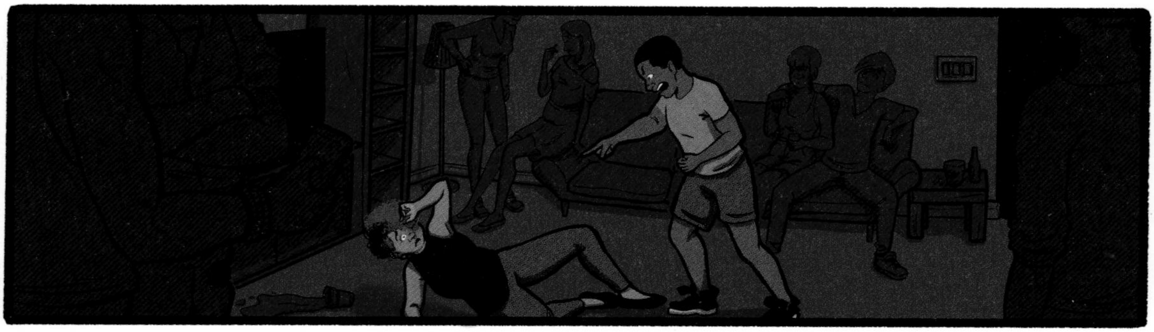

How I spent my whole life protecting myself

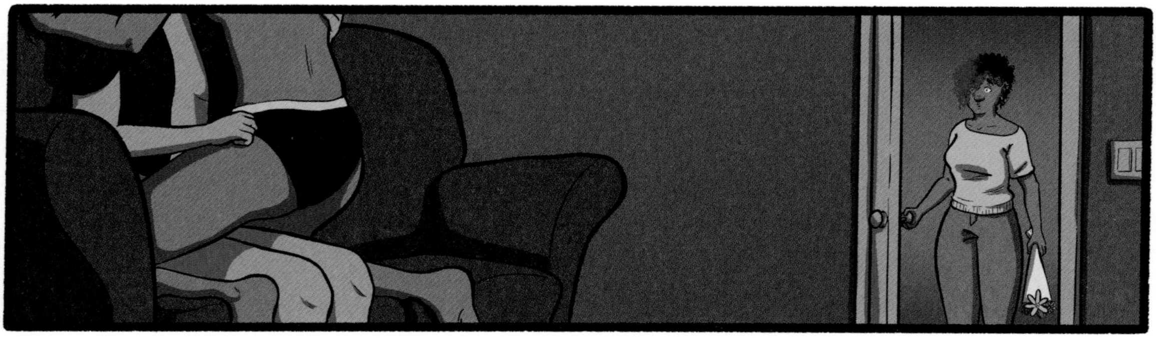

How I had never encountered unconditional love from anyone

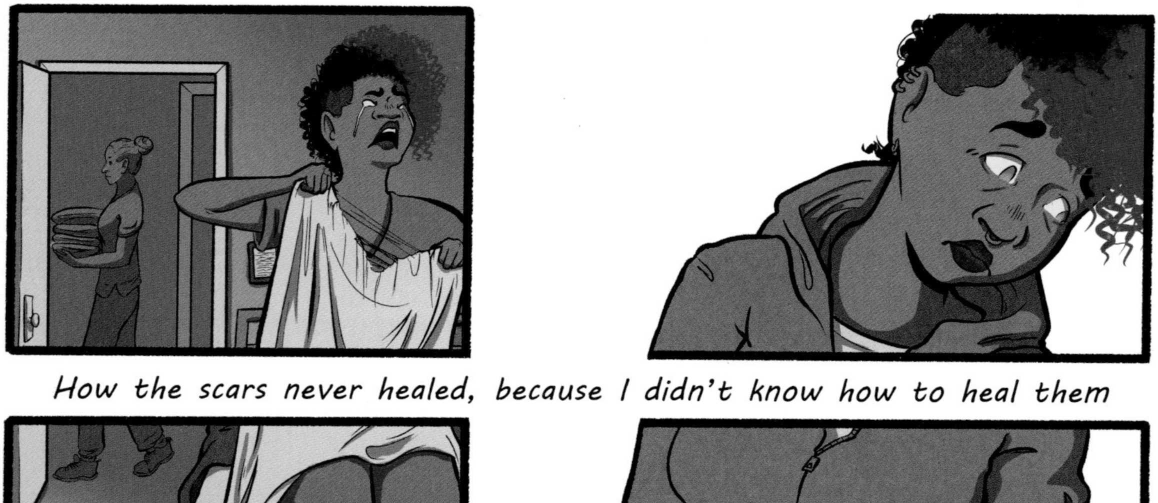

How the scars never healed, because I didn't know how to heal them

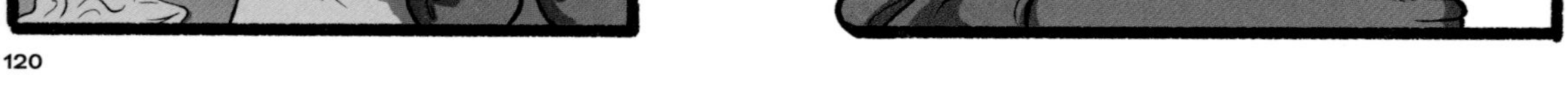

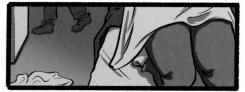

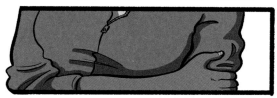

And you hurt me too. Your tongue was sharper than any needles on my skin. Your trauma was deeper than even you anticipated.

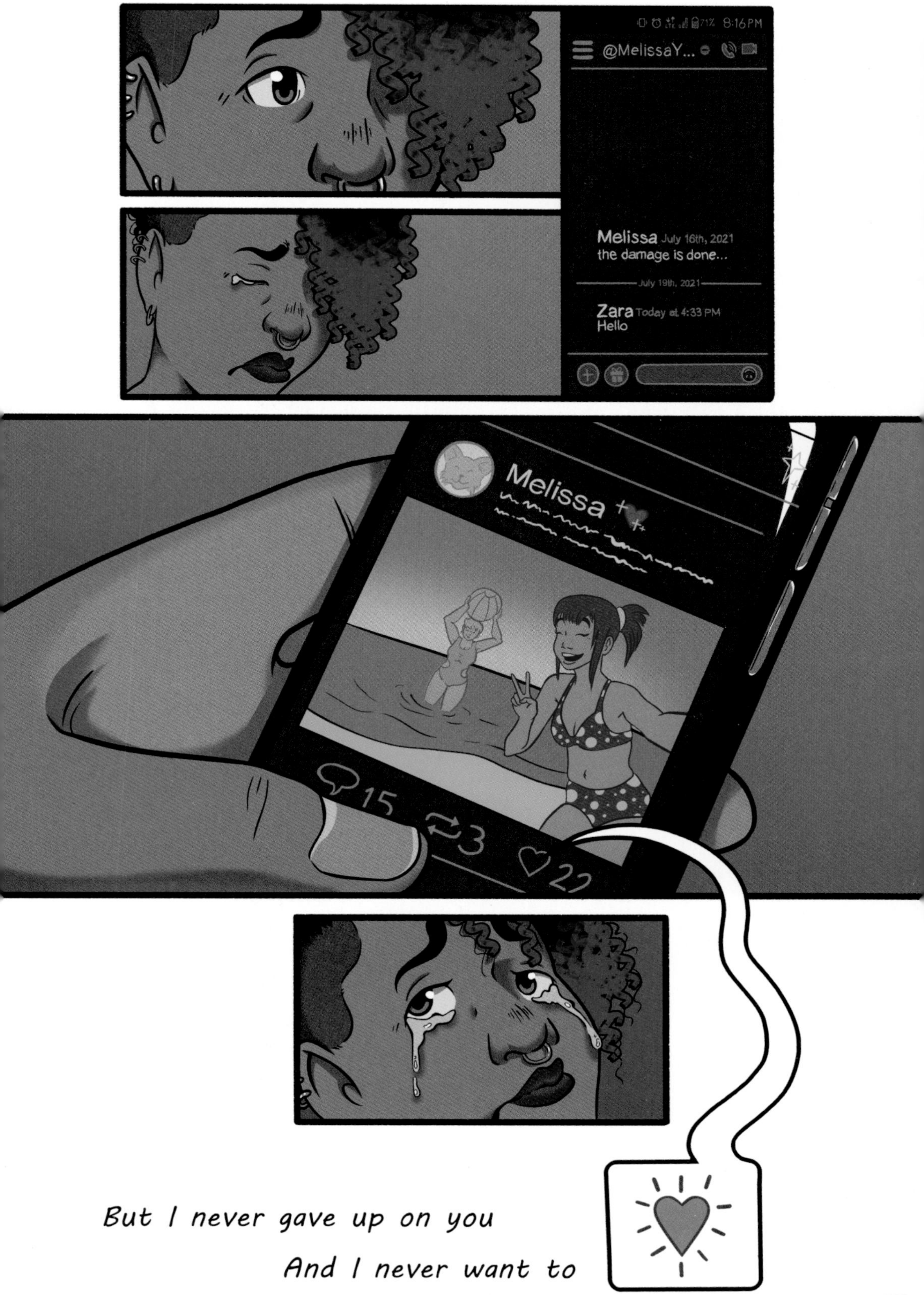
71% 8:16PM
@MelissaY...
Melissa July 16th, 2021
the damage is done...
July 19th, 2021
Zara Today at 4:33 PM
Hello
Melissa
15
3
22

But I never gave up on you

And I never want to

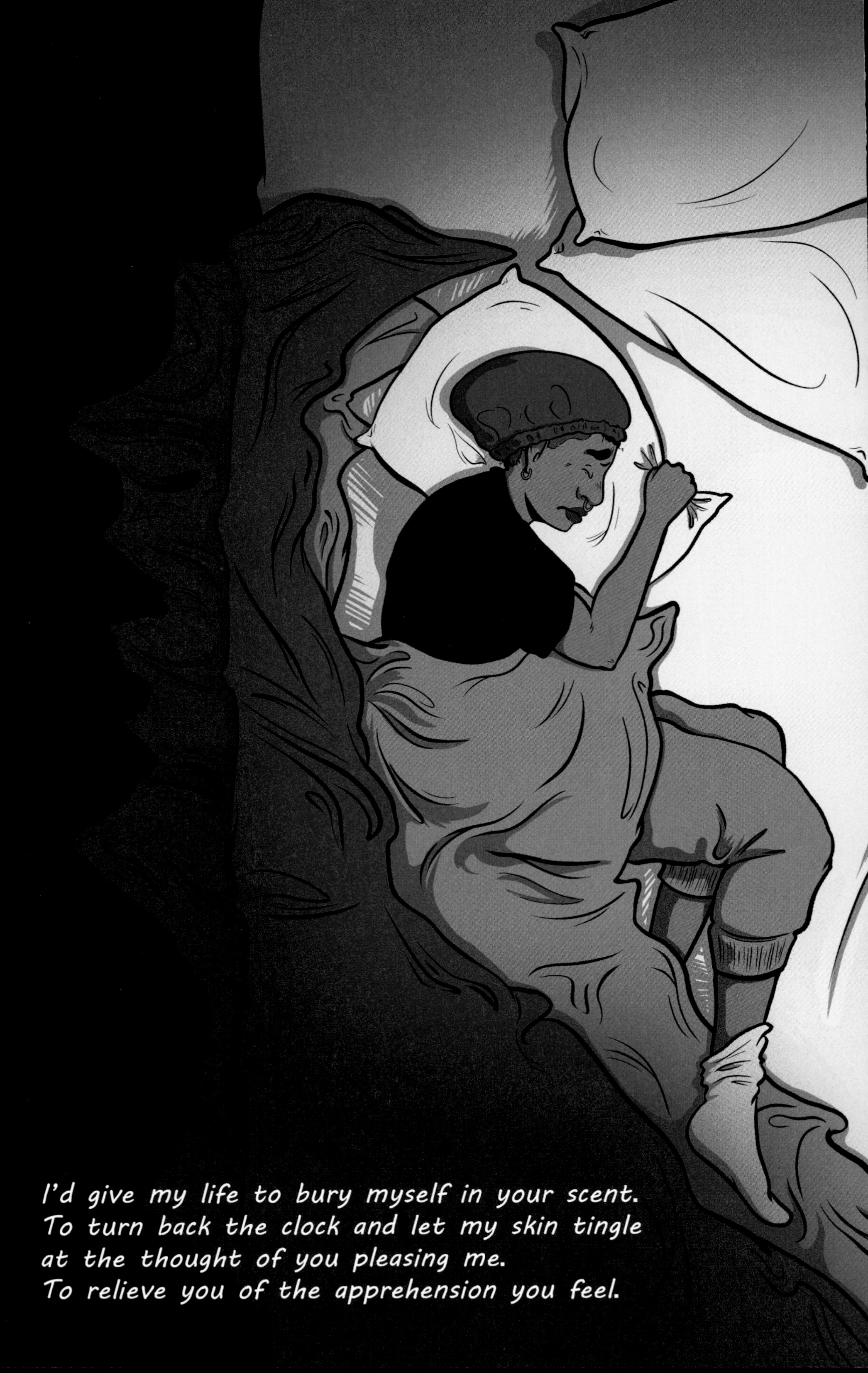
I'd give my life to bury myself in your scent.
To turn back the clock and let my skin tingle
at the thought of you pleasing me.
To relieve you of the apprehension you feel.

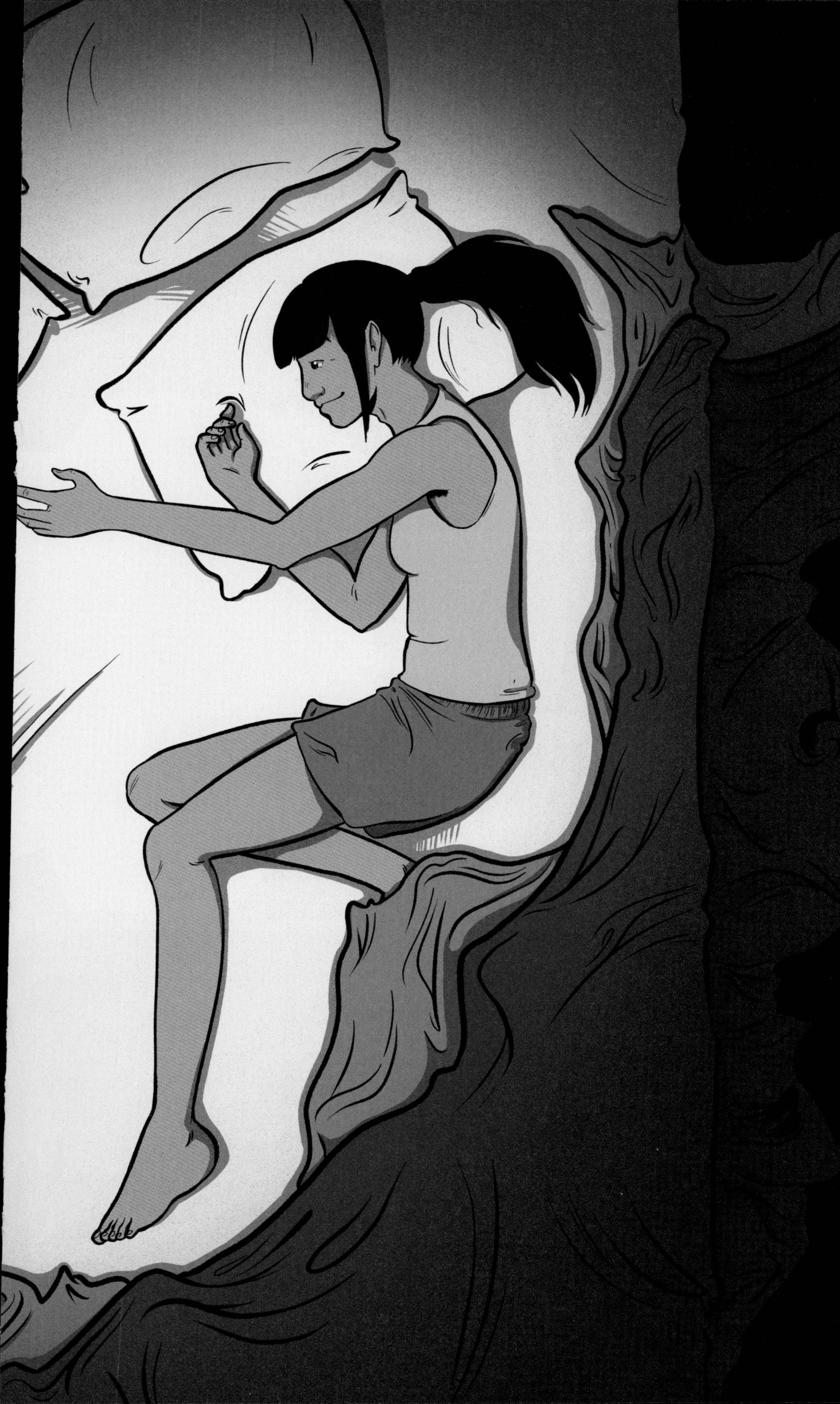

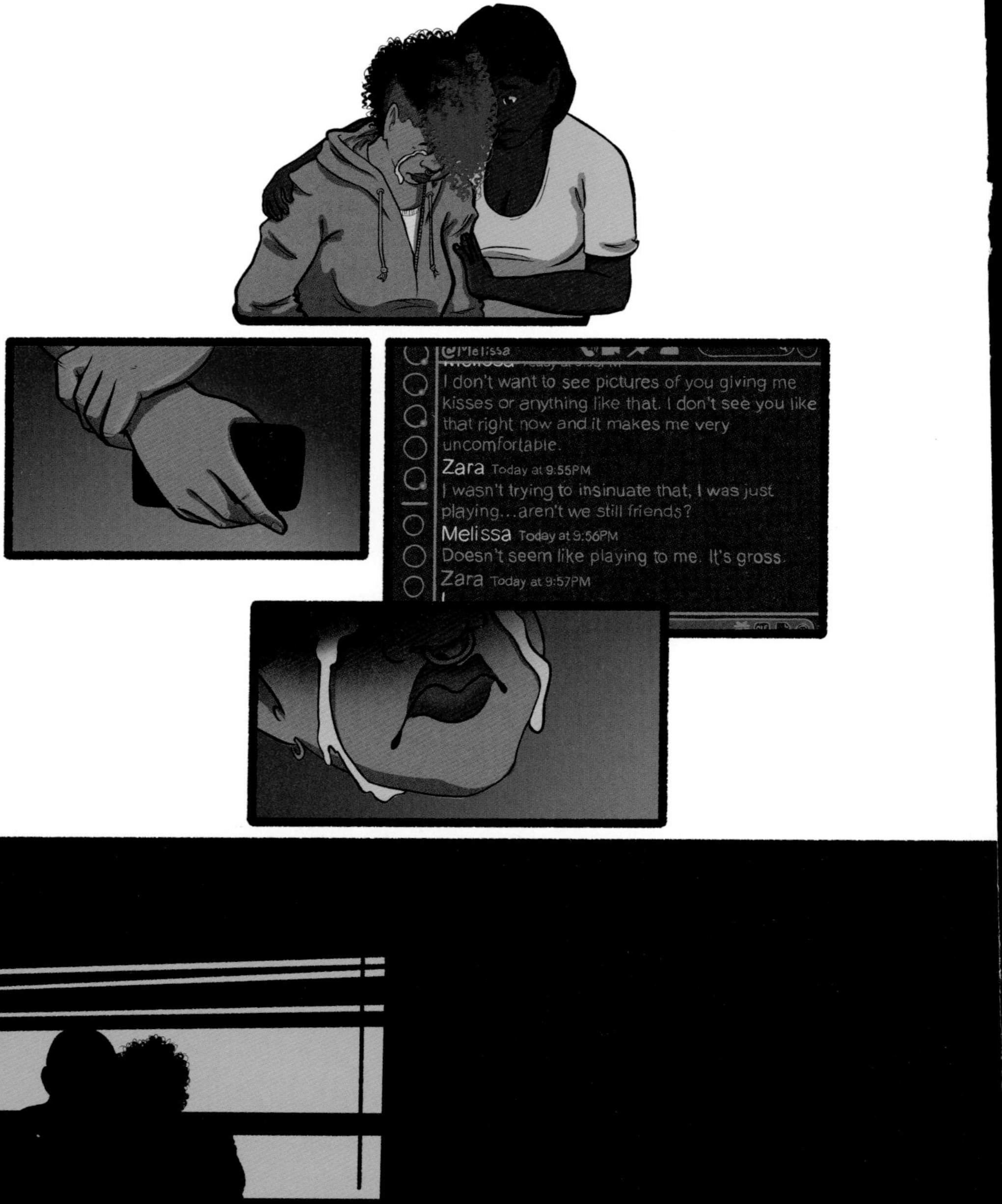

@Melissa
I don't want to see pictures of you giving me kisses or anything like that. I don't see you like that right now and it makes me very uncomfortable.
Zara Today at 9:55PM
I wasn't trying to insinuate that, I was just playing…aren't we still friends?
Melissa Today at 9:56PM
Doesn't seem like playing to me. It's gross.
Zara Today at 9:57PM

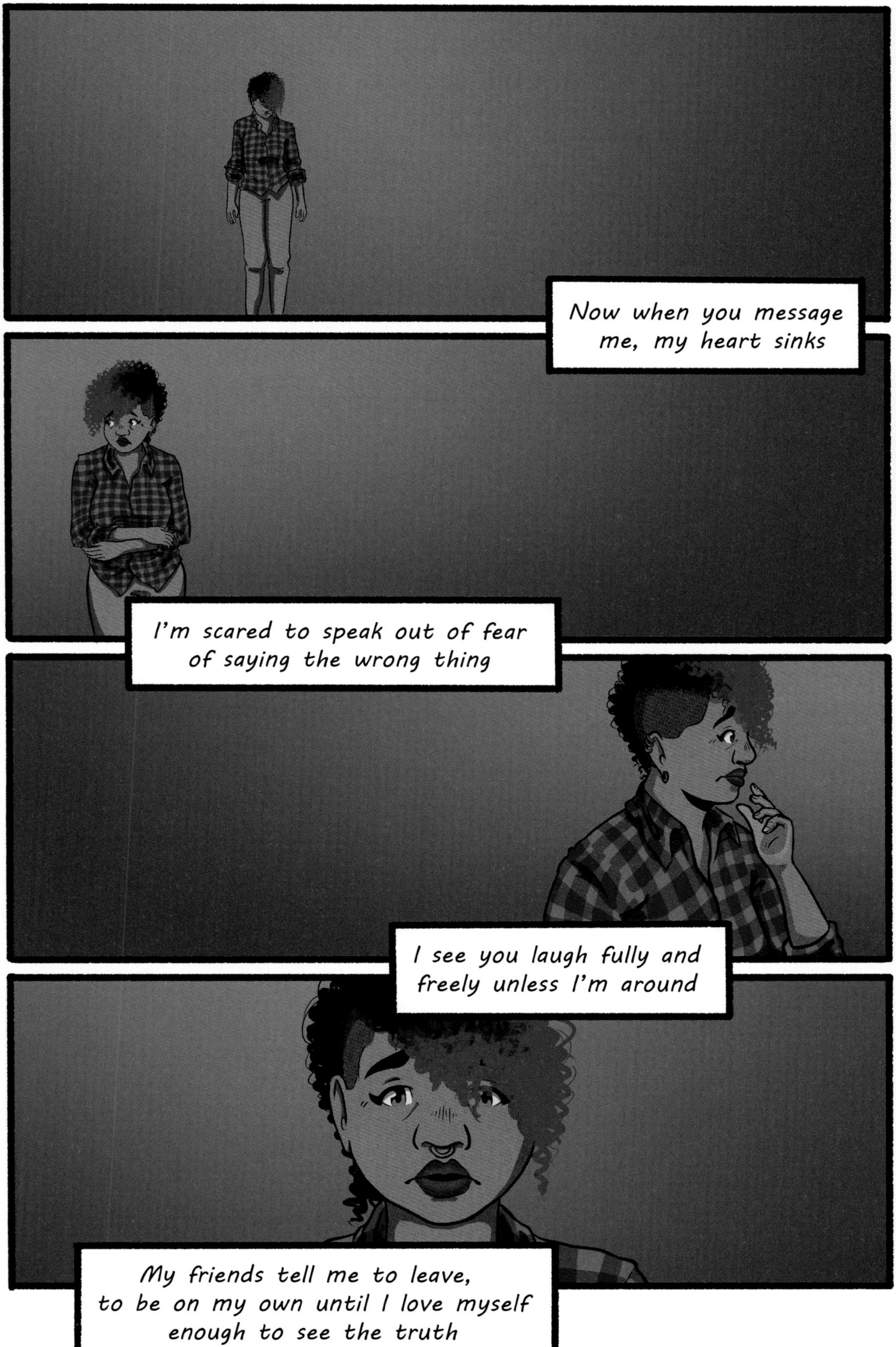

Now when you message me, my heart sinks
I'm scared to speak out of fear of saying the wrong thing
I see you laugh fully and freely unless I'm around
My friends tell me to leave, to be on my own until I love myself enough to see the truth

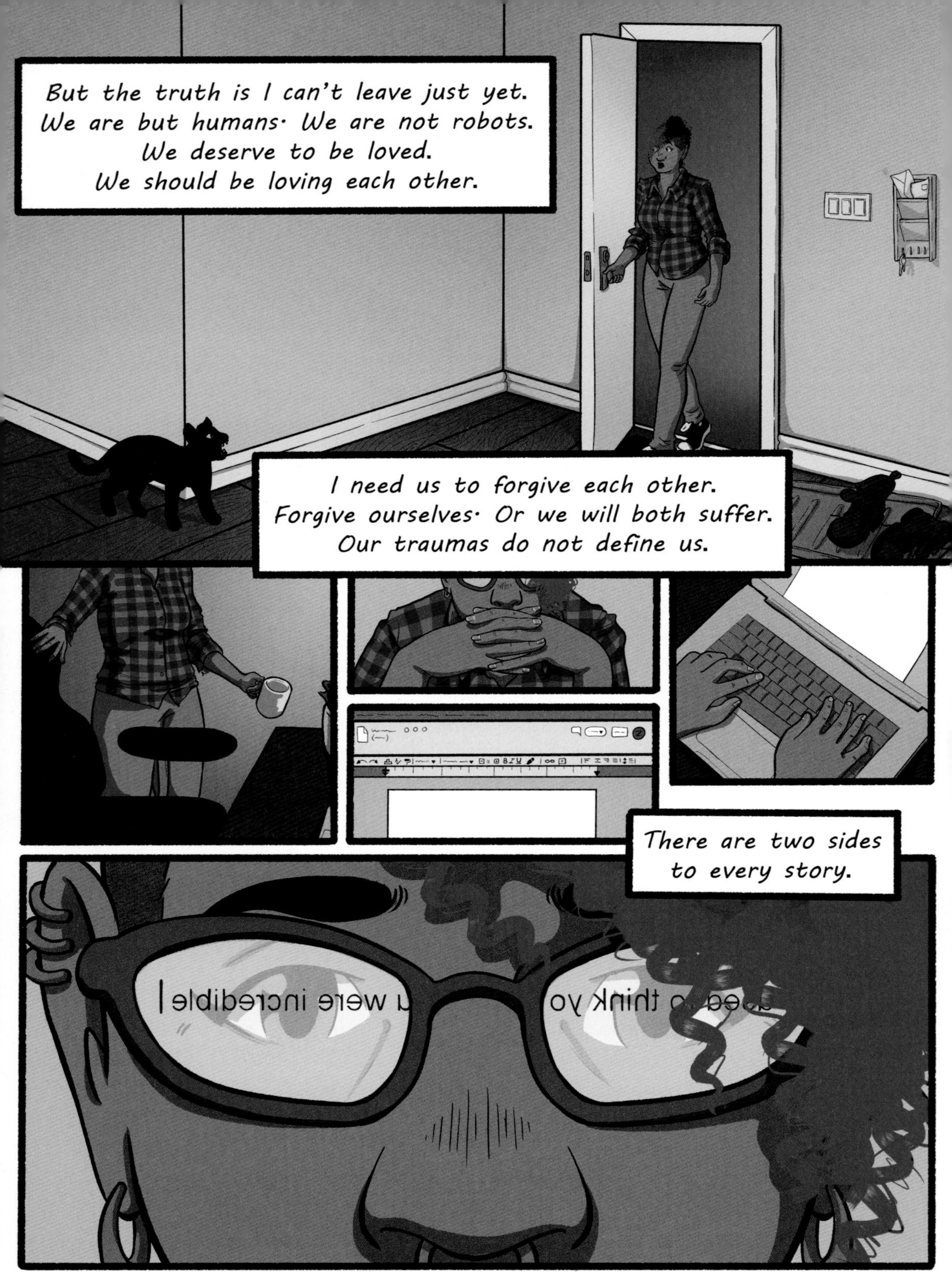
But the truth is I can't leave just yet. We are but humans. We are not robots. We deserve to be loved. We should be loving each other.
I need us to forgive each other. Forgive ourselves. Or we will both suffer. Our traumas do not define us.
There are two sides to every story.

I'll always be here for you until you're ready to tell yours

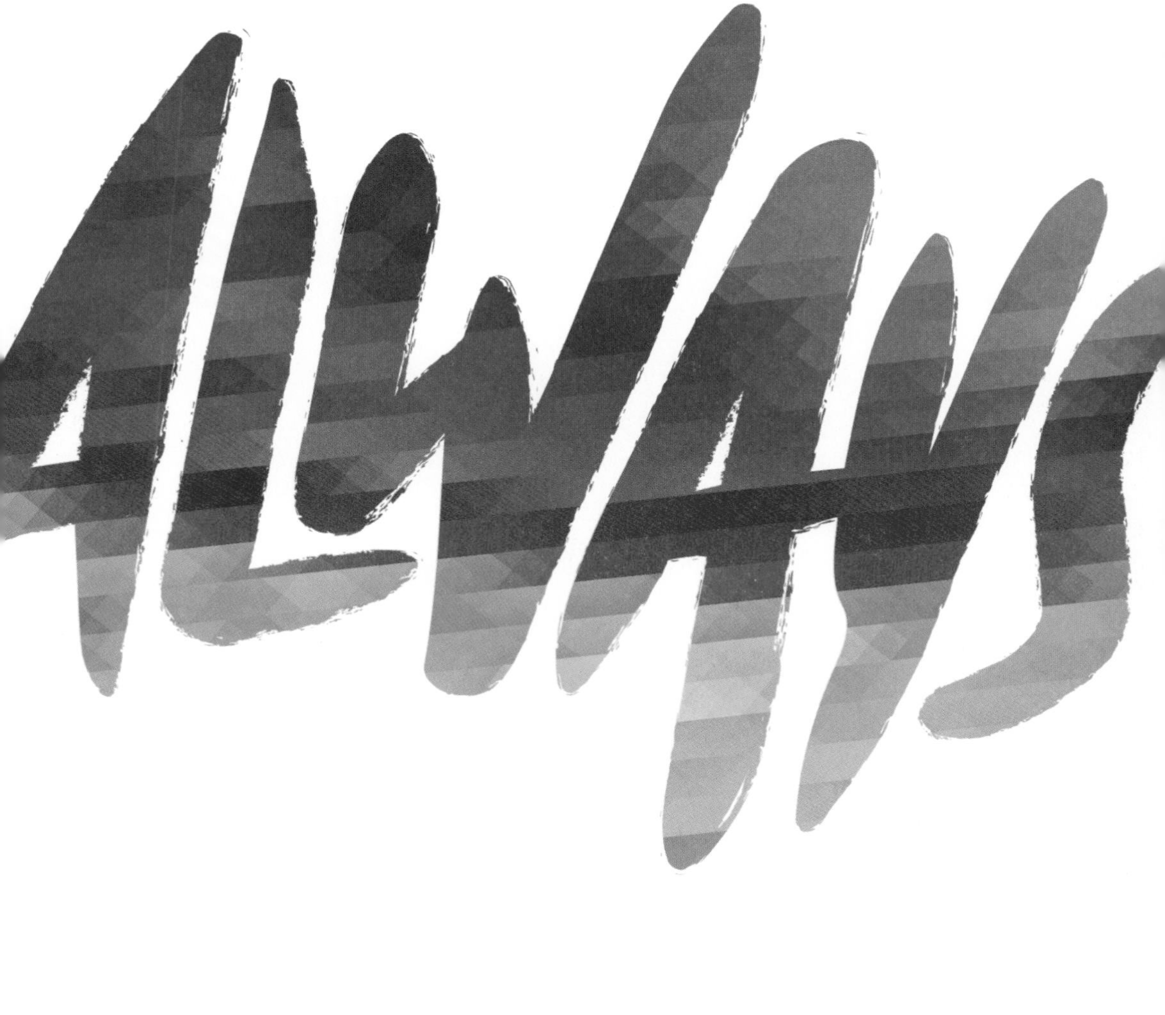
ALWAYS

"DRAWING LINES || POSTING SIGNS"

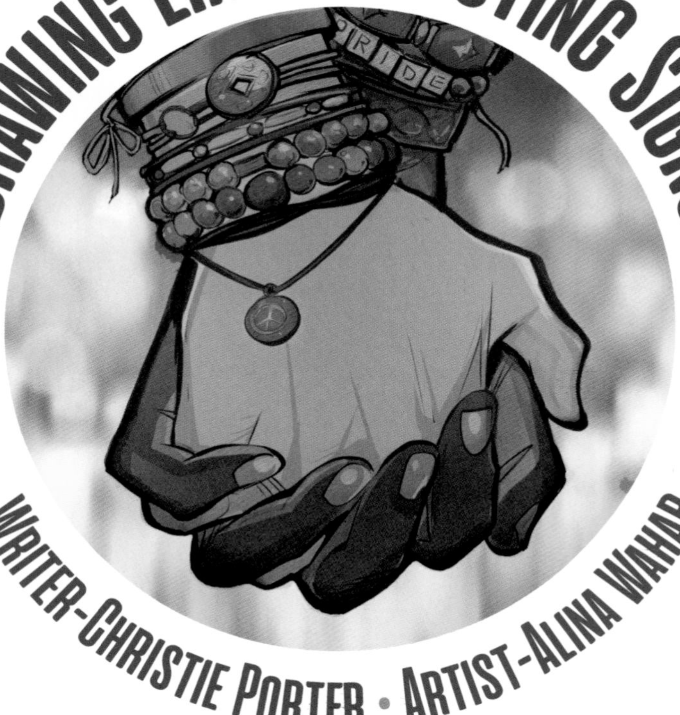
RIDE

WRITER-CHRISTIE PORTER • ARTIST-ALINA WAHAB

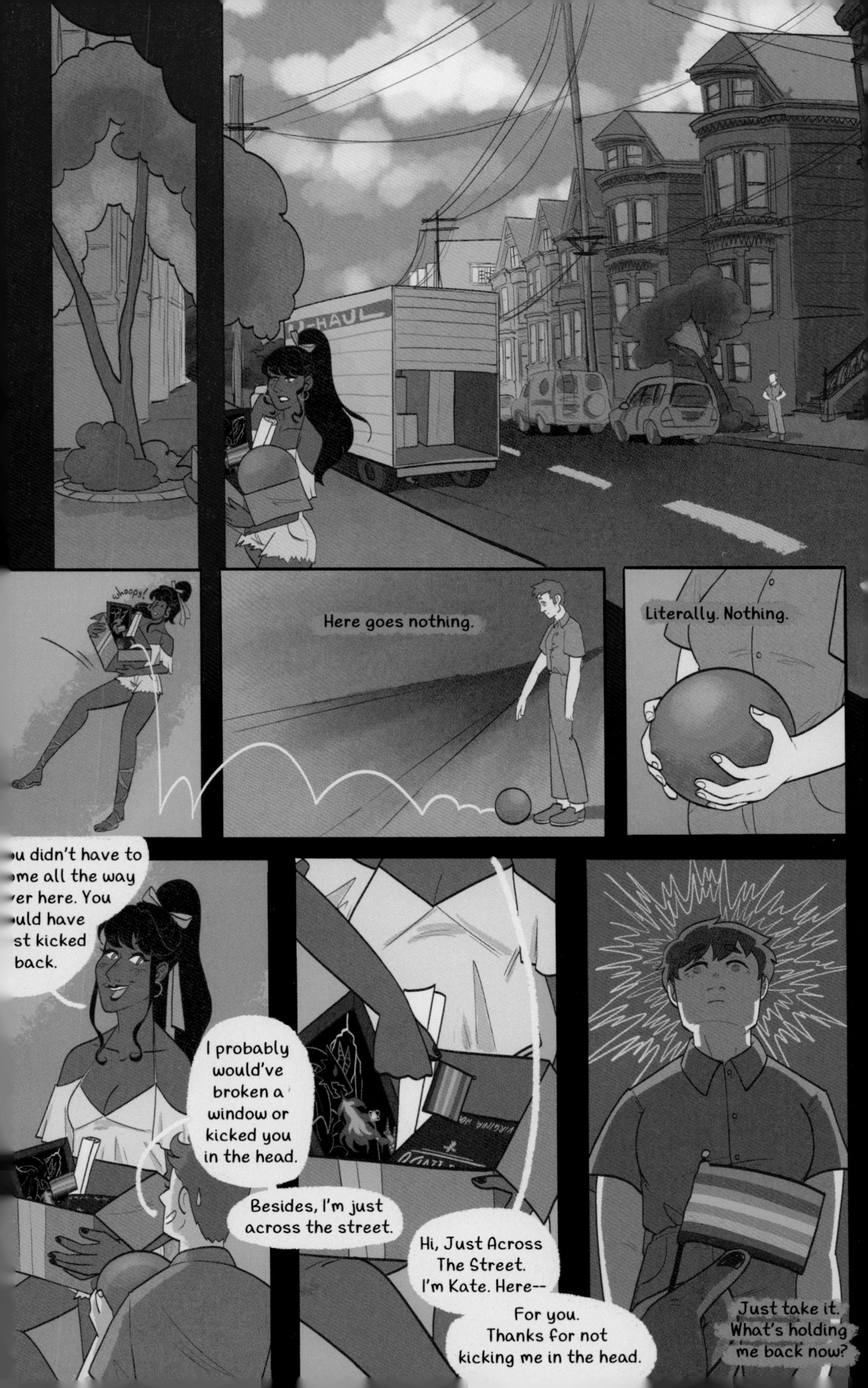
U-HAUL
whoops!
Here goes nothing.
Literally. Nothing.
...u didn't have to ...me all the way ...er here. You ...uld have ...st kicked ... back.
I probably would've broken a window or kicked you in the head.
Besides, I'm just across the street.
Hi, Just Across The Street. I'm Kate. Here--
For you. Thanks for not kicking me in the head.
Just take it. What's holding me back now?

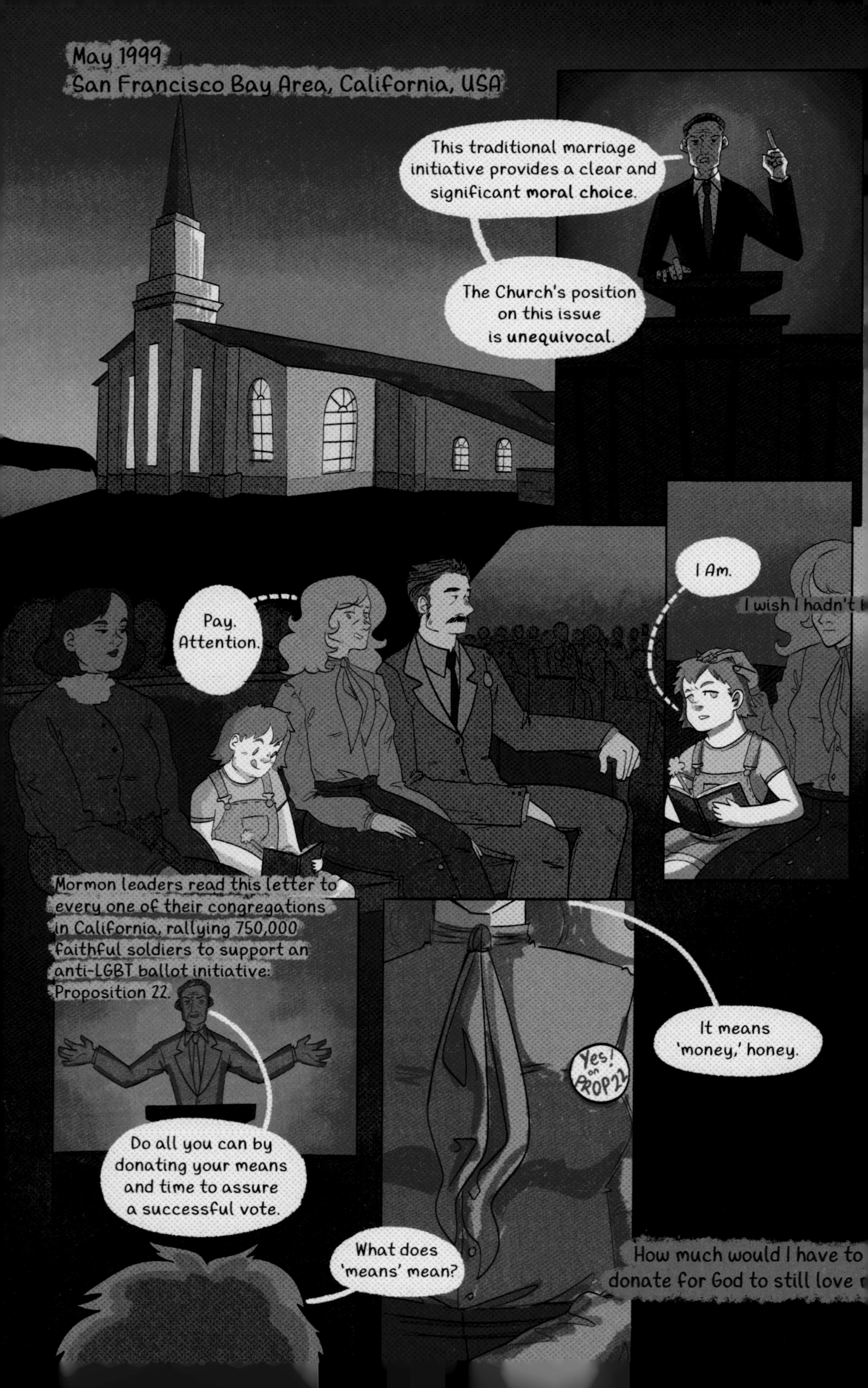
May 1999
San Francisco Bay Area, California, USA
This traditional marriage initiative provides a clear and significant moral choice.
The Church's position on this issue is unequivocal.
Pay. Attention.
I Am.
I wish I hadn't
Mormon leaders read this letter to every one of their congregations in California, rallying 750,000 faithful soldiers to support an anti-LGBT ballot initiative: Proposition 22.
Do all you can by donating your means and time to assure a successful vote.
What does 'means' mean?
It means 'money,' honey.
Yes! on PROP 22
How much would I have to
donate for God to still love

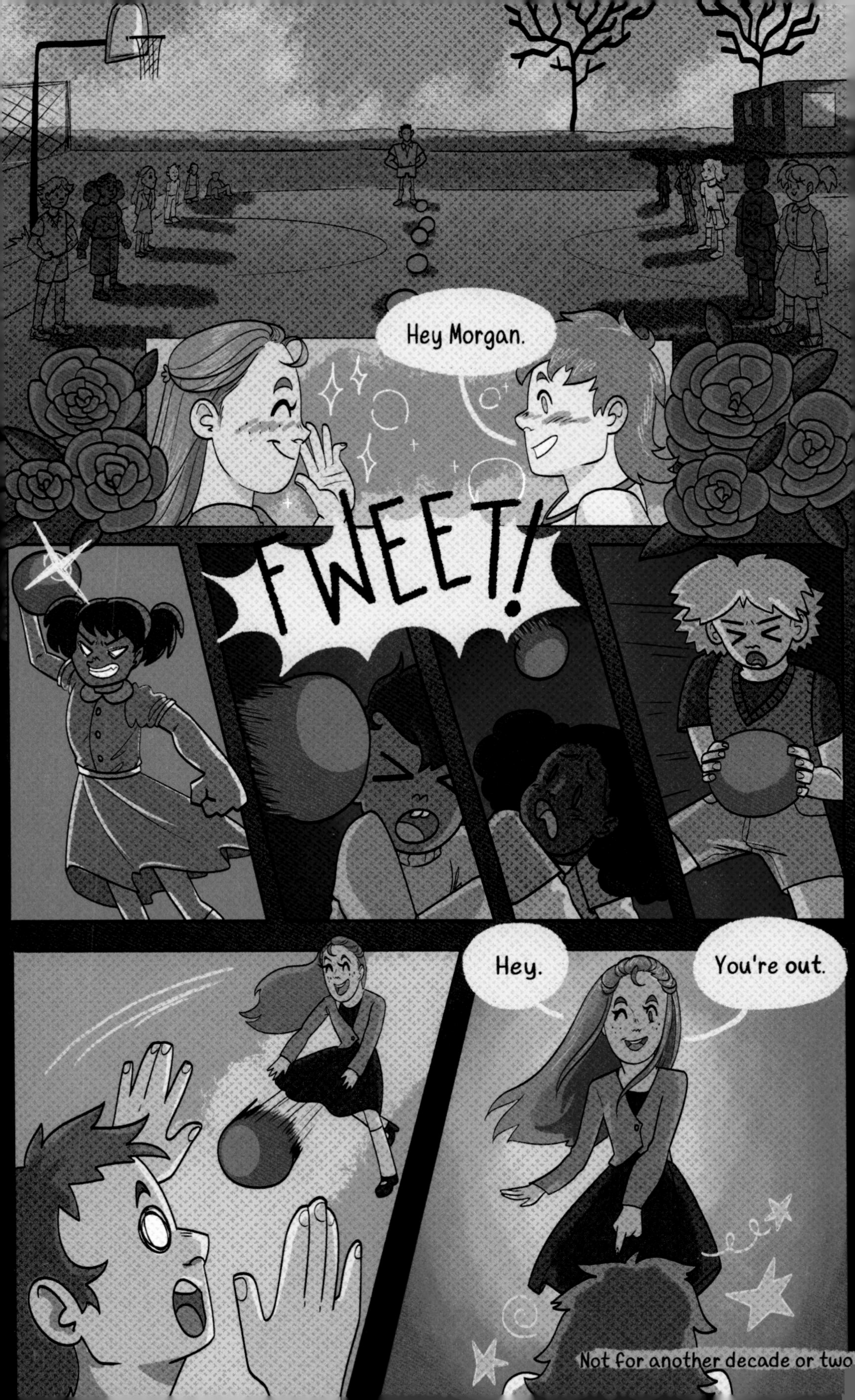
Hey Morgan.
FWEET!
Hey.
You're out.
Not for another decade or two

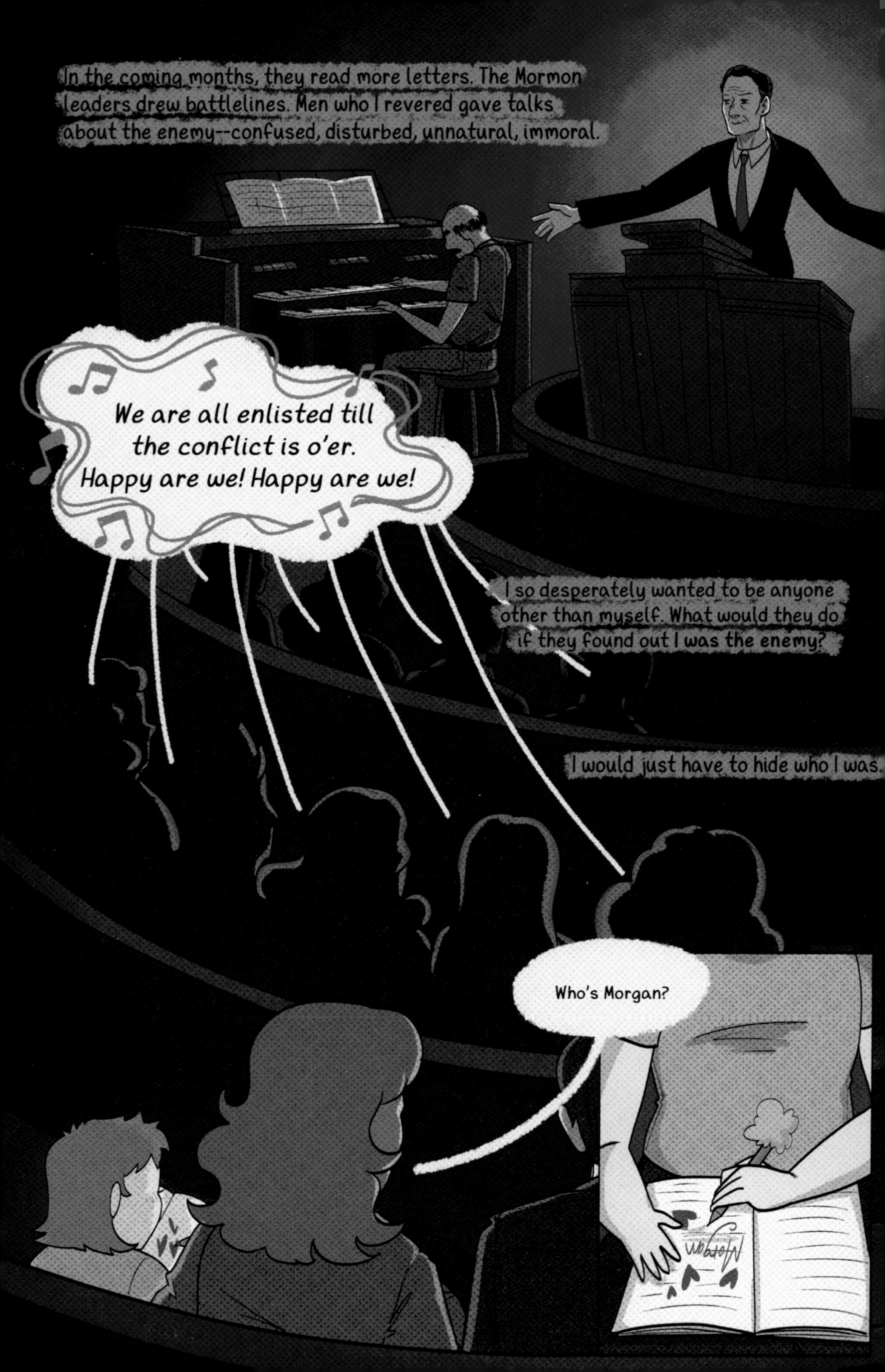
In the coming months, they read more letters. The Mormon leaders drew battlelines. Men who I revered gave talks about the enemy--confused, disturbed, unnatural, immoral.
We are all enlisted till the conflict is o'er. Happy are we! Happy are we!
I so desperately wanted to be anyone other than myself. What would they do if they found out I was the enemy?
I would just have to hide who I was.
Who's Morgan?
Morgan

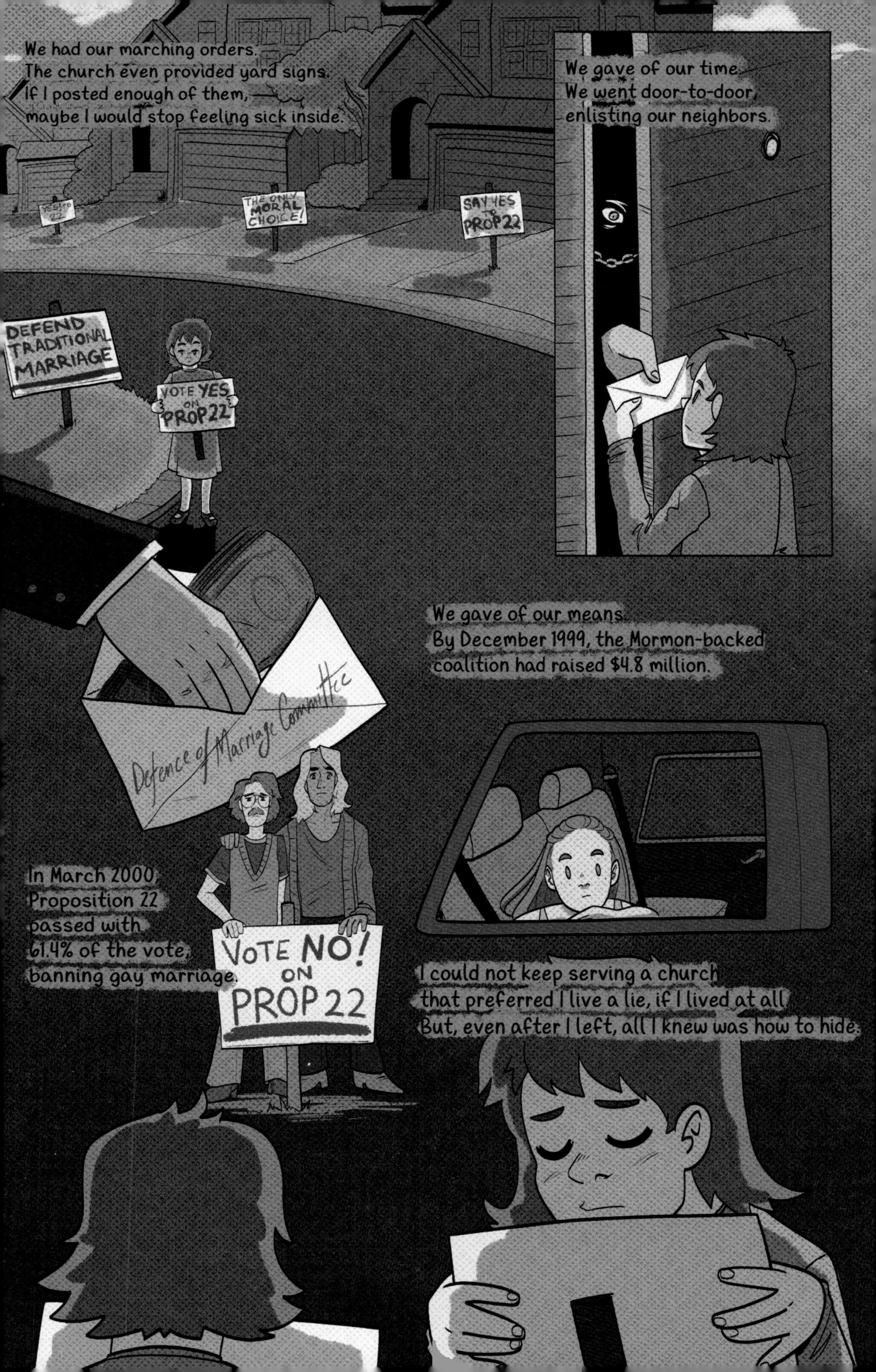

We had our marching orders.
The church even provided yard signs.
If I posted enough of them,
maybe I would stop feeling sick inside.
THE ONLY MORAL CHOICE!
SAY YES TO PROP 22
We gave of our time.
We went door-to-door,
enlisting our neighbors.
DEFEND TRADITIONAL MARRIAGE
VOTE YES ON PROP22
We gave of our means.
By December 1999, the Mormon-backed
coalition had raised $4.8 million.
Defence of Marriage Committee
In March 2000,
Proposition 22
passed with
61.4% of the vote,
banning gay marriage.
VOTE NO! ON PROP 22
I could not keep serving a church
that preferred I live a lie, if I lived at all.
But, even after I left, all I knew was how to hide.

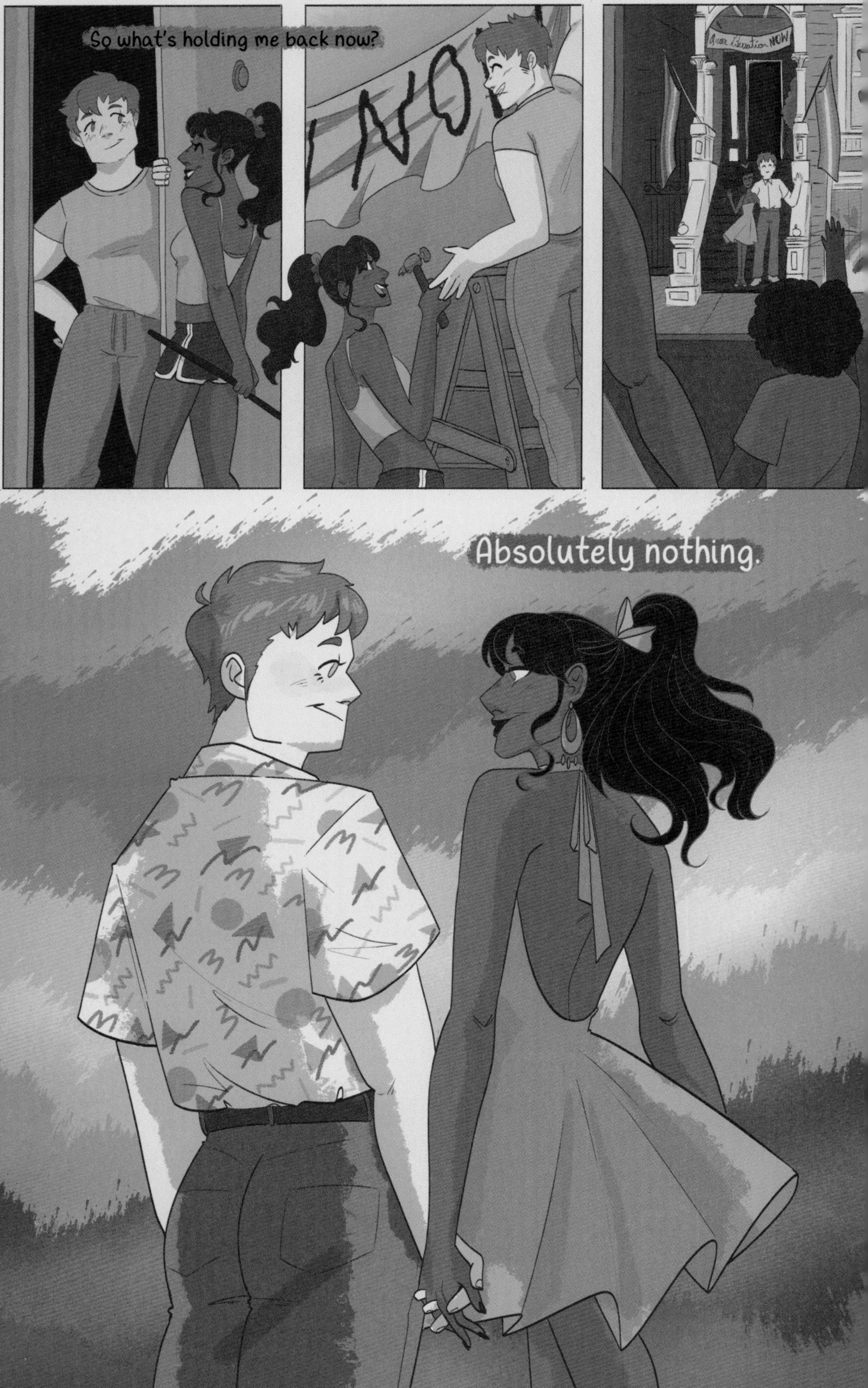
So what's holding me back now?
Absolutely nothing.

ALWAYS

"An Open Love Letter"

Writer-Jazzlyn Stone • Artist-Liana Kangas • Colors-Gab Contreras • Letters-Joamette Gil

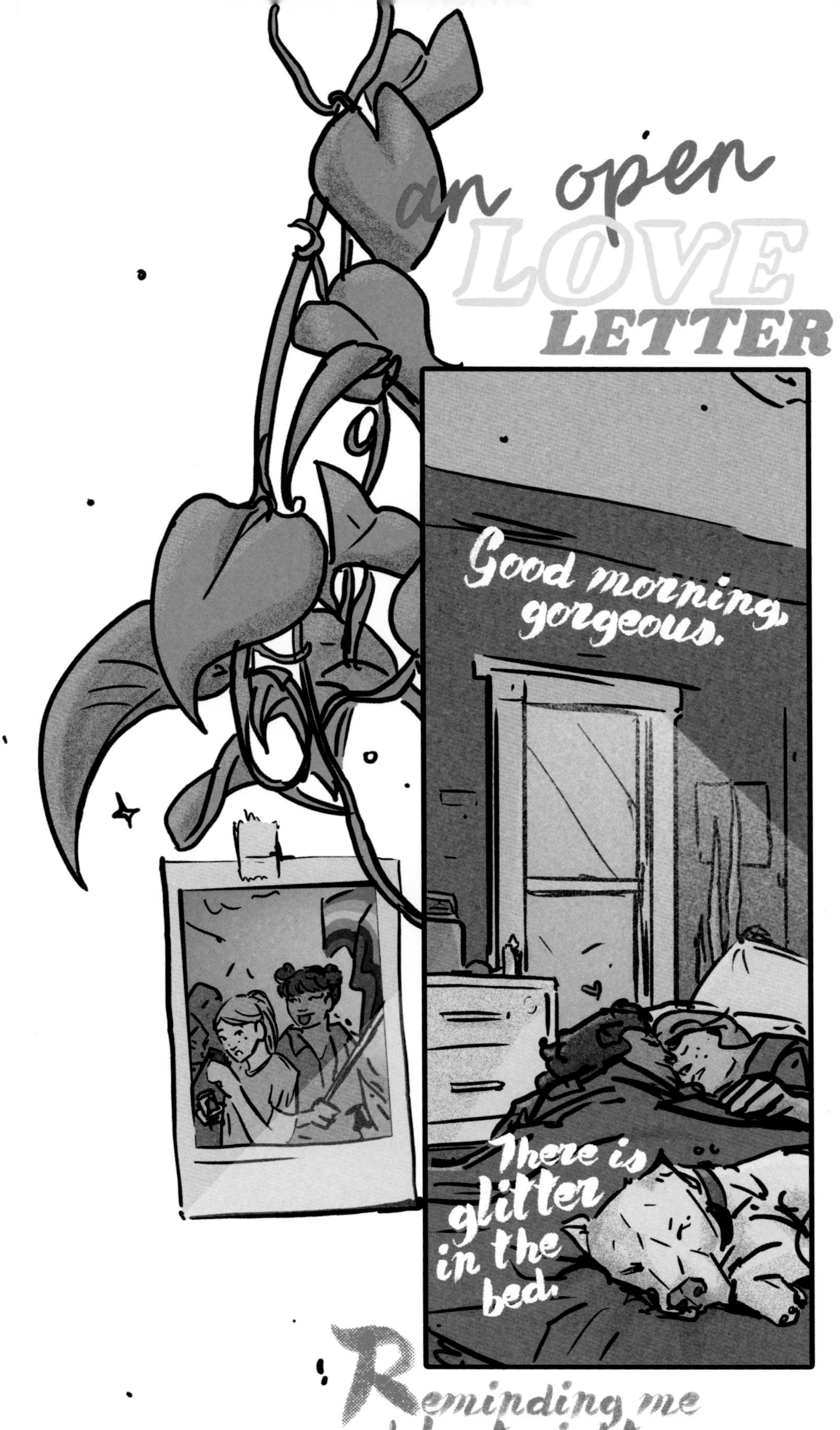
an open
LOVE
LETTER
Good morning, gorgeous.
There is glitter in the bed.
Reminding me of last night.

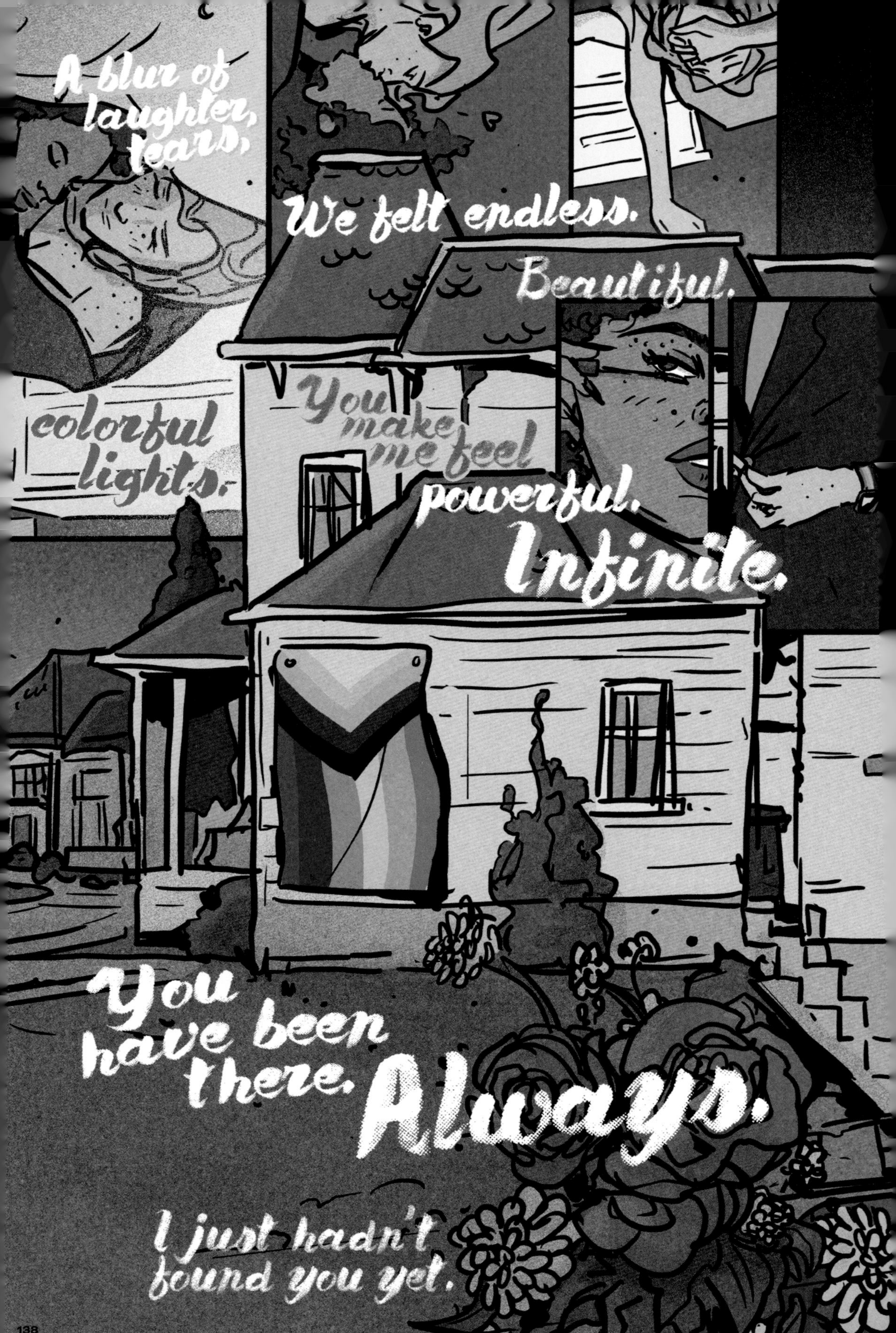
A blur of laughter, tears,
colorful lights.
We felt endless.
Beautiful.
You make me feel
powerful.
Infinite.
You have been there.
Always.
I just hadn't found you yet.

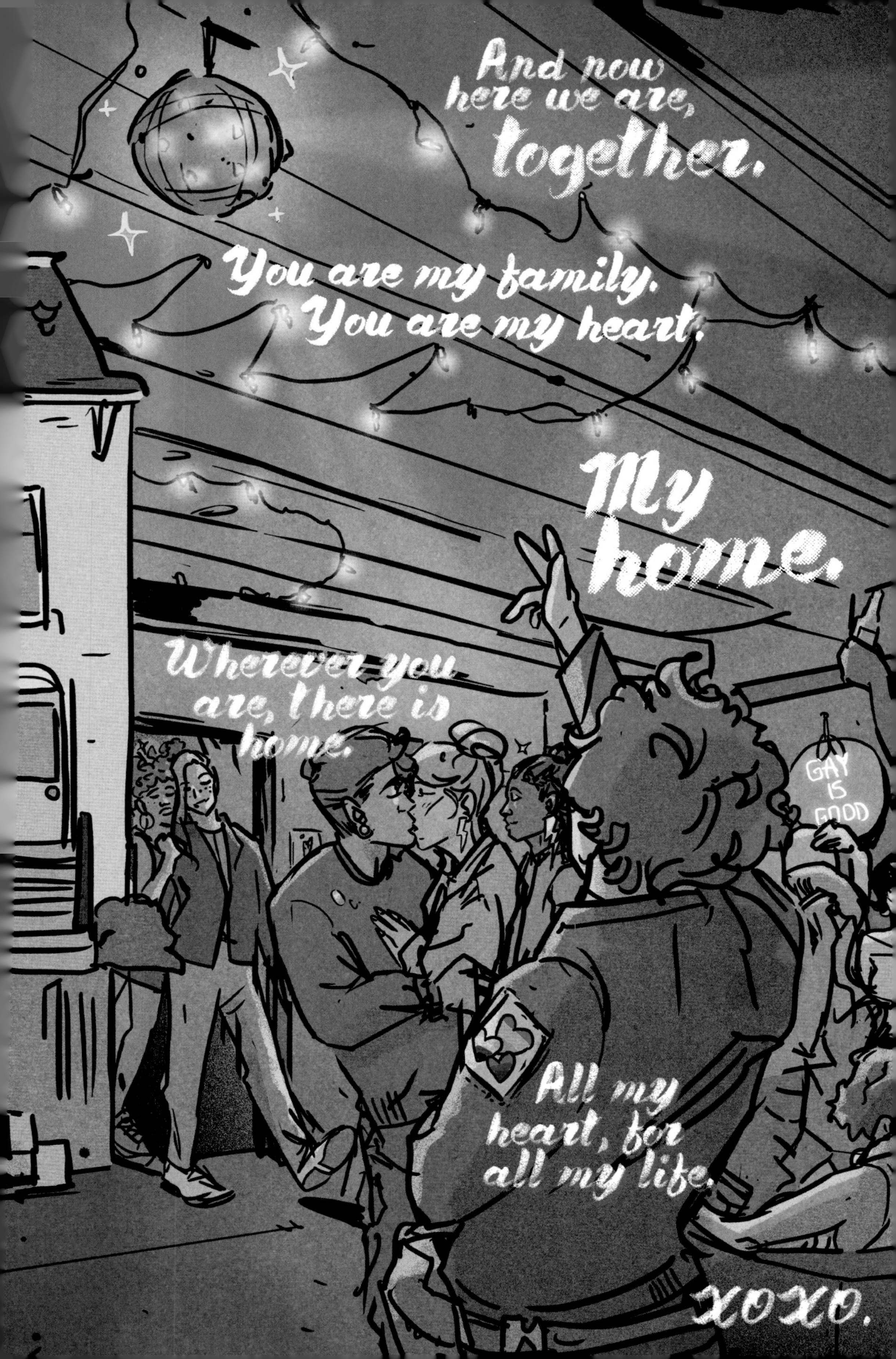
And now here we are, together.
You are my family. You are my heart.
My home.
Wherever you are, there is home.
GAY IS GOOD
All my heart, for all my life.
xoxo.

FOR GAIL, FOR SHARING WISDOM.
FOR LIANA, FOR OFFERING COMMUNITY.
FOR FELL, FOR GIVING ME A CHANCE.
FOR MICHELE, FOR BELIEVING IN ME.
...AND FOR MAGAN, WHO LOVES ME.

BRENT

ALONE IN MY ROOM
SAT ON MY BED WITH MY THOUGHTS
I SPLIT IN TWO

I'M SEATED TO MY LEFT
WE SHAKE HANDS
AND I STARE
INTO THE BLANK MIRRORED EYES
OF MY MINDS CREATION

MY HAND ON HER FACE, MY FACE
I LONG FOR SOME COLOR THERE
A SPECKLE OF LIFE
ON MY PALE SKIN

LOOKING OVER AT MYSELF
LOOKING AT EACH OTHER
WE PAUSE, WE EMBRACE

FROM MY LEFT
SHE FELL INTO ME
AND NOW I ONLY IMAGINE
THAT I AM NOT ALONE.

- MICHELE ABOUNADER [AGE 18]
FOR ME BACK THEN, FOR ME NOW.
AND THE NEVER-ENDING FIGHT FOR SELF ACCEPTANCE AND LOVE.

MICHELE

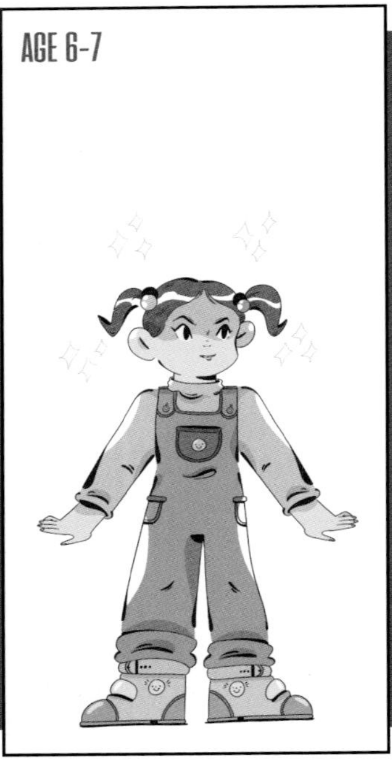
AGE 6-7

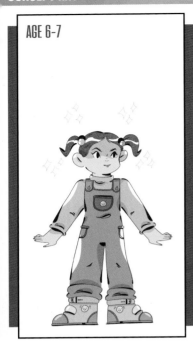

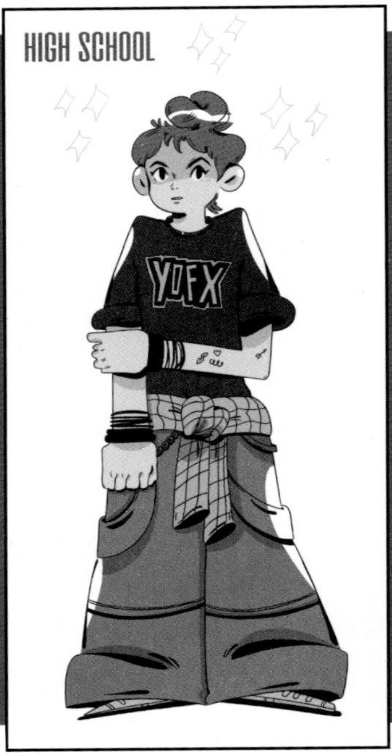
HIGH SCHOOL
YOFX

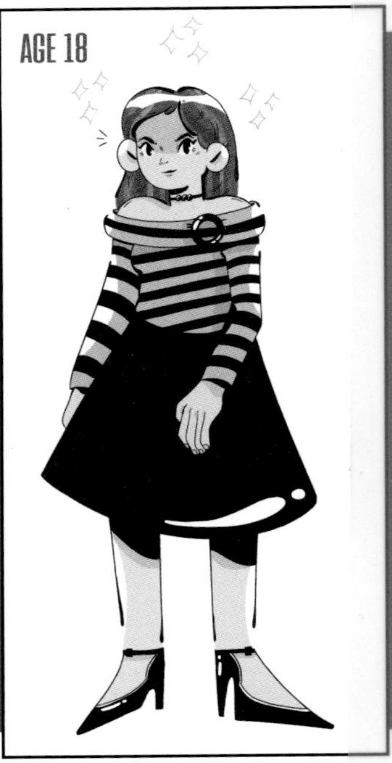
AGE 18

ABOVE:
CONCEPT ARTWORK FOR **"LEAVES"**
WRITER: **CHRISTA HARADER.**
ARTIST: **KATIE HICKS.**
PAGE 94.

RIGHT AND BELOW:
CONCEPT ARTWORK FOR **"SEA CHANGE"**
WRITER: **LILLIAN HOCHWENDER.**
ARTIST: **GABE MARTINI.**
PAGE 28.

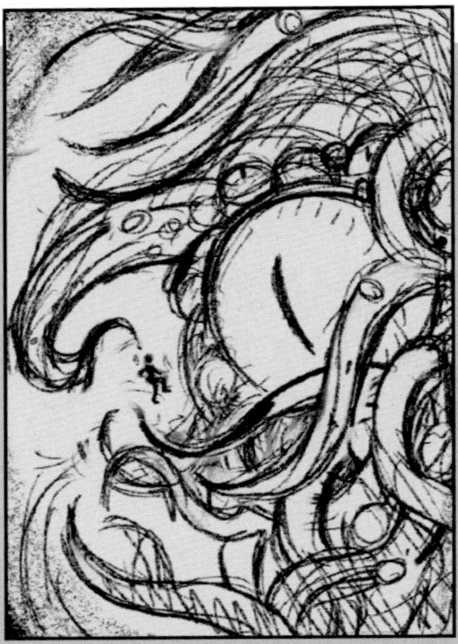

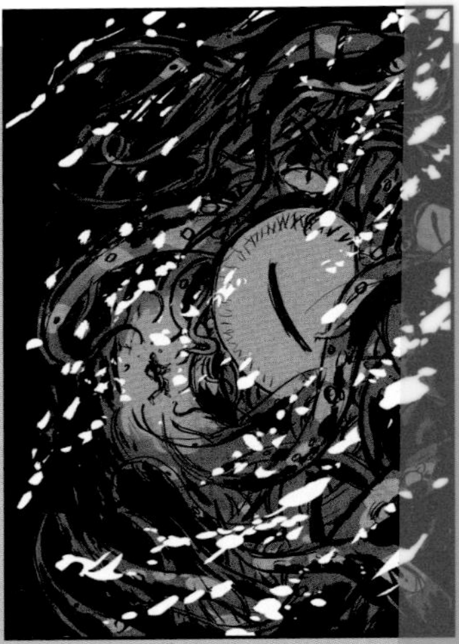

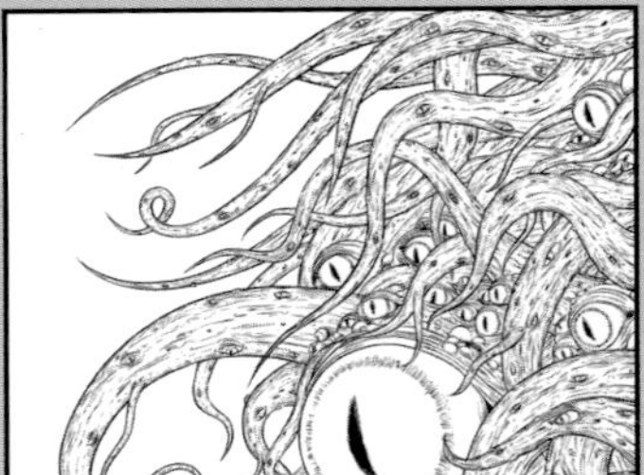

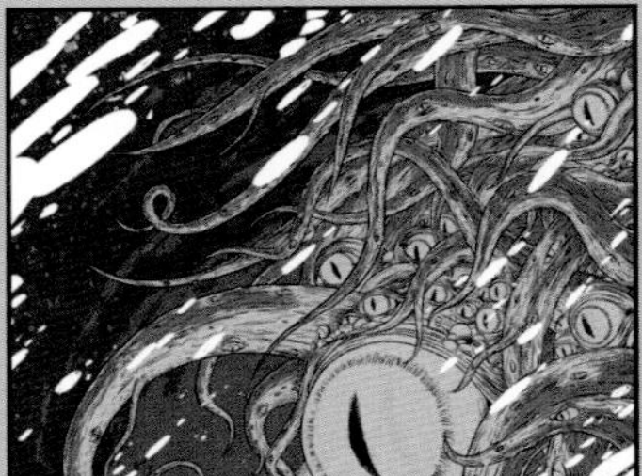

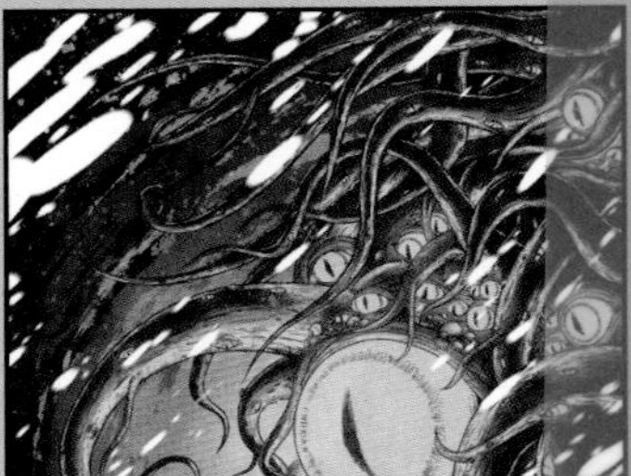

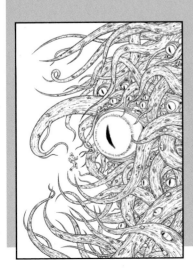

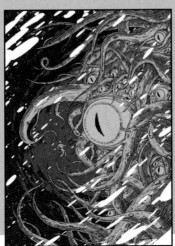

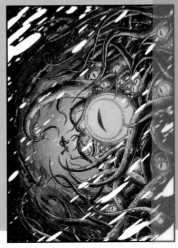

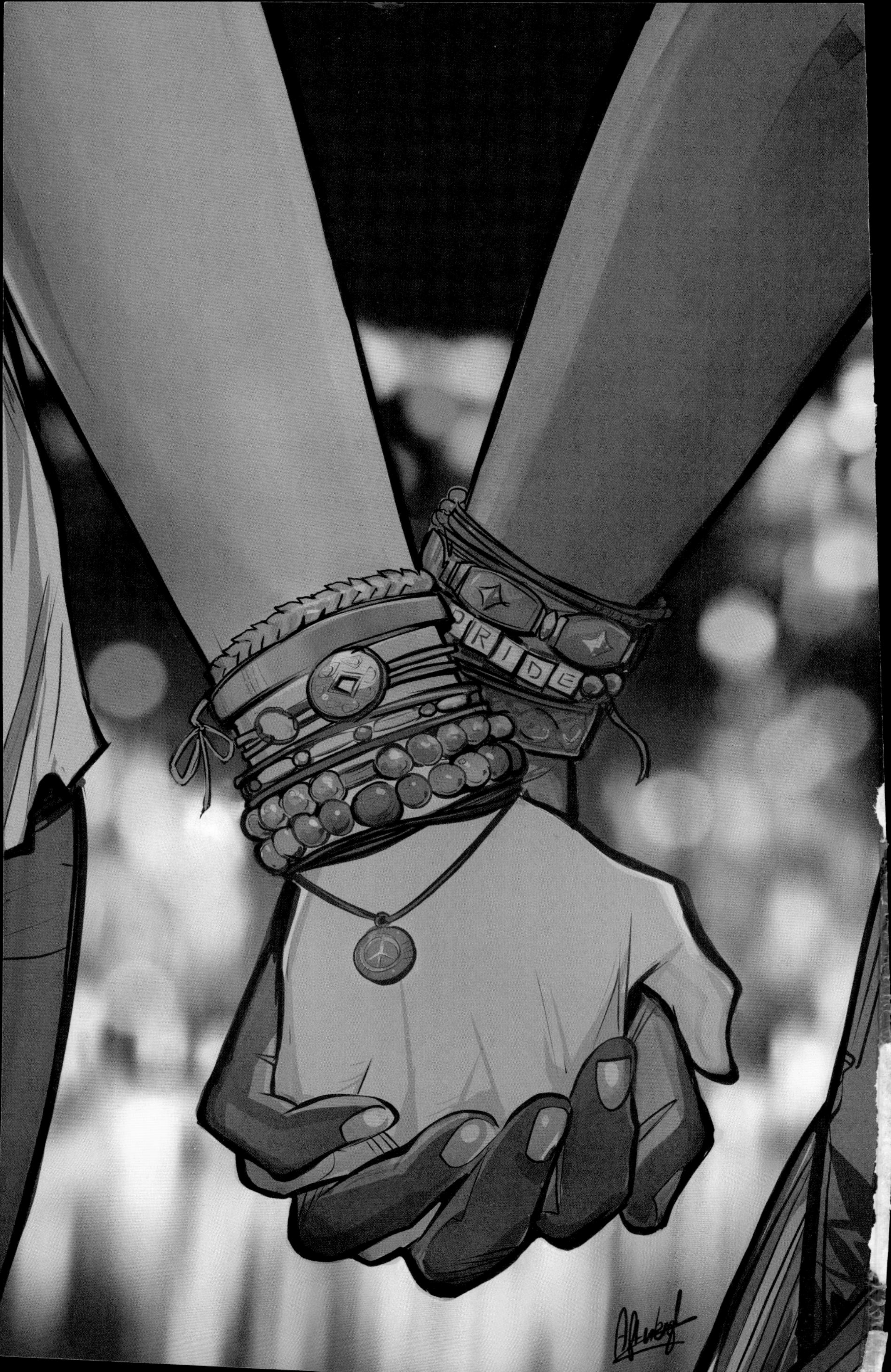
PRIDE

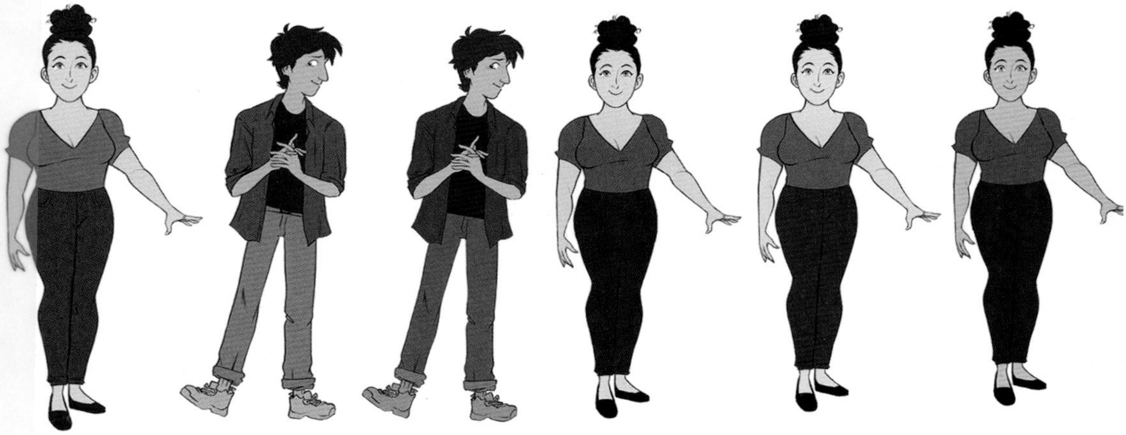

ABOVE: CONCEPT ARTWORK FOR **"CLADDAGH"**
WRITER: **JULIA PAIEWONSKY**. ARTIST: **ALEX PUTPRUSH**. PAGE 10.

CONCEPT ARTWORK FOR "ALL THAT GLITTERS"
WRITER: **MICHELE ABOUNADER.**
ARTIST: **TENCH [ALEKSANDRA OREKHOVA].**
PAGE 58.

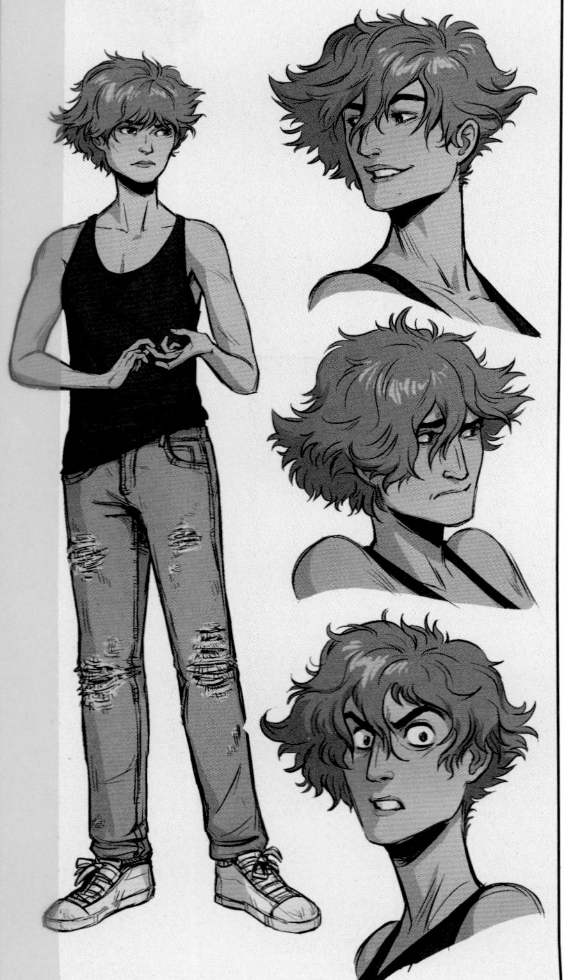

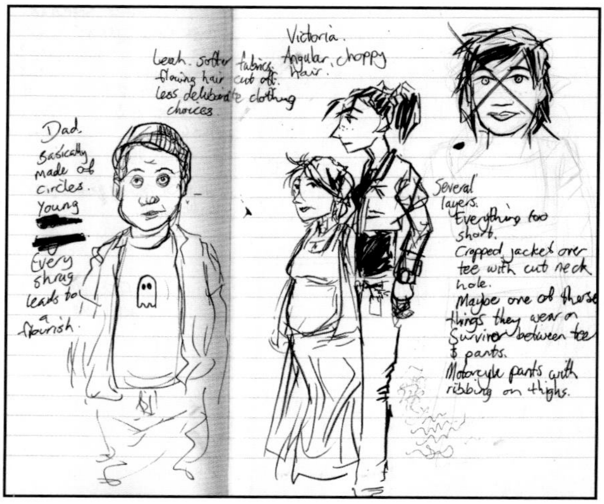
Victoria. Angular, choppy hair.
Leah. softer fabrics. flowing hair cut off. less deliberate clothing choices
Dad. Basically made of circles. Young
Every shrug leads to a flourish.
Several layers. Everything too short. Cropped jacket over tee with cut neck hole. Maybe one of these things they wear on Survivor between tee & pants. Motorcycle pants with ribbing on thighs.

ABOVE: CONCEPT ARTWORK FOR **"LONG AWAY"**
WRITERS: **TILLY BRIDGES / SUSAN BRIDGES.**
ARTIST: **RICHARD FAIRGRAY**. PAGE 48.

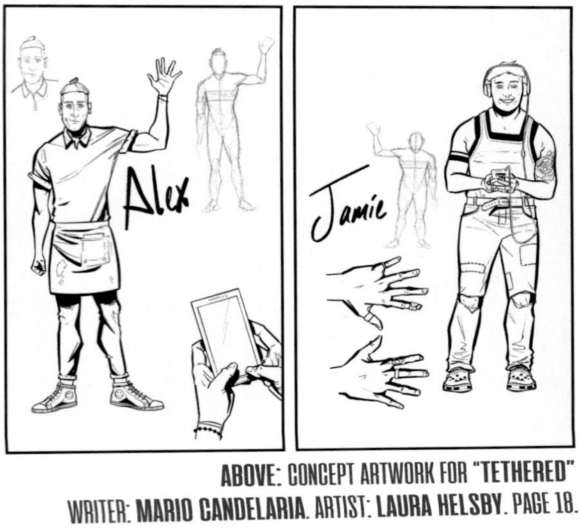
Alex
Jamie

ABOVE: CONCEPT ARTWORK FOR **"TETHERED"**
WRITER: **MARIO CANDELARIA**. ARTIST: **LAURA HELSBY**. PAGE 18.